In this engaging, cleverly organized book, Jenn expands on the content that has captivated millions of devoted followers. Unlike a typical cookbook, this comprehensive handbook offers strategies, tools, tips, meal plans, and more than 125 delicious recipes. Jenn includes a wide range of adaptable dishes that suit any vibe, budget, or dietary need, from breakfast and lunch to appetizers, dinner, drinks, snacks, and desserts, including:

- **Goat Cheese and Kale Egg Muffins,** a quick, satisfying reheatable breakfast
- **Barbecue Chicken Chopped Salad,** more filling and budget-friendly than the one from your favorite food chain
- **Street-Corn-Inspired Shrimp Skillet,** a high-protein dinner done in 30 minutes
- **Sheet Pan Butternut Squash Mac and "Cheese,"** a delicious, plant-powered wonder
- **Fudgy Sweet Potato Brownies,** so good you'll forget about the box mix

Don't Think About Dinner is designed to streamline the way you cook and think about your meals. With a fully stocked kitchen and a plan in place, you'll be amazed at how much easier it is to create healthy, budget-conscious, standout meals.

DON'T THINK ABOUT DINNER

Save time and money with 125+ easy, nourishing, delicious recipes for every meal

Jenn Lueke

wm
WILLIAM MORROW
An Imprint of HarperCollins*Publishers*

To my family—my first taste testers, biggest supporters, and favorite people to cook for

PART ONE:
HOW TO MAKE IT ALL HAPPEN

Introduction ix
About the Book xiii

WHY PLAN & PREP? 2

MY SUSTAINABLE STRATEGIES 3

ABOUT THE RECIPES 6

LET'S GET TO IT! 8

POP QUIZ: WHAT STYLE OF PLANNER ARE YOU? 9

HOW TO GET IT DONE 10

PLAN IT 11
My Weekly Plan 12
What You Need to Know: Dinner Plans & Grocery Lists 15
  The Anatomy of a Grocery List 16

STOCK IT 19
In the Pantry 19
Countertop Produce 23
In the Fridge & Freezer 24
Swap or Sub It 26

SHOP IT 27
Rules to Shop By 28
Quick Money-Saving Tips 28
Swap & Save 29

PREP IT 30
Food Safety Guidelines 30
The Best Way to Reheat Food 31
Where to Start: Breakfast & Lunch Meal Prep 32
Tips to Make Meal Prep Easier 33

STORE IT 34
Meal-Prep Storage Equipment 34
Meal Storage, Freezing & Reheating Guide 35

KEEP AT IT 36
Roadblocks to Your Routine: The What-If? 36

GET COOKING! 38
Basic Knife Skills 39
Equipment Essentials 40

12 WEEKS OF DINNER PLANS & GROCERY LISTS 42

Better-Than-Takeout Week 44
Dairy-Free Favorites Week 45
Comfort Classics Week 46
Budget-Friendly Week 47
Winter Vibes Week 48
Spring Vibes Week 49
Summer Vibes Week 50
Autumn Vibes Week 51
Perfectly Plant-Based Week 52
10 Ingredients (or Less) Week 53
Vacay Mode Week 54
Jenn's Top Hits Week 55

PART TWO:
THE RECIPES

BREAKFAST BLUEPRINT 58

QUICK LUNCHES, UPGRADED 90

NOURISHING SNACKS & DIPS 120

ONE-POT WONDERS 134

DONE IN 30 160

HIGH-PROTEIN HITS 184

PLANT-POWERED 220

A LITTLE FANCIER 248

STANDOUT SIDES & BASICS 278

EVERYDAY ELEVATED SAUCES 292

FUNCTIONAL SIPS 304

SWEET TREATS 316

Every Ingredient You'll Need 336

Seasonal Produce List 338

Substitution Guides 339

Acknowledgments 342

Universal Conversion Chart 344

Index 345

INTRODUCTION

Frustrated trying to figure out how to make healthy, delicious dishes each day? Tired of the repetition? Overwhelmed by the idea of planning and prepping meals in advance? Annoyed by having to run to the grocery store multiple nights a week and even more annoyed how much you spend each time you go? **Well, then, you're like me. Or at least how I used to be.**

In 2019, I was a college student grappling with various health issues, including an autoimmune condition, joint problems, gastrointestinal issues, acid reflux, and disordered eating. Until that point, I felt helpless regarding my health, struggling in a culture that prioritized being thin over being well. Raised on a random mix of fresh and processed foods, I never learned the connection between nutrition and health or, more importantly, how to successfully plan and follow a healthier diet. I wanted to understand how to change my eating habits to improve, maybe even cure, my ailments.

I was having trouble connecting with my doctor's advice, and the internet was trying to sell me on a new quick-fix fad diet every week, each one contradicting the others. I had no idea what a correct, healthy choice was anymore. One week, I was told that fruit was off-limits, the next that meat caused cancer or that oats spiked blood sugar, dairy was inflammatory, soy was overprocessed, leafy greens were full of oxalates, and seafood was basically poison. I didn't know which way was up. **And so many "healthy" recipes I found online pushed fad diet ingredients I'd never heard of and couldn't find or afford—products that would probably spoil in my pantry after just one use.** It all left me feeling overwhelmed and frustrated, and far from reaching my health goals.

The only thing I knew I could trust was my love of cooking. Growing up, I practically lived in our family's kitchen, shadowing my mom, begging her to let me help out and learn how she made our favorites, like chili, chicken Parmesan, and spaghetti and meatballs, whenever she had some extra time to make something special. But more often, my busy working parents didn't plan meals ahead of time (who can blame them?), so the dreaded "What's for dinner?" question would come up each weeknight as we peered into our half-empty fridge, sending us in search of the quickest and easiest thing to grab. So we ate a lot of take-out, frozen dinners, meals from the drive-thru, and stuff that came out of a box (cereal for dinner was common). Instead of going into the week with any meal plan in mind, we were more of a play-it-by-ear kind of family, leading to fast but less healthy options or stressful, last-minute, expensive grocery runs.

As a teenager, I became the family cook, which I loved! I happily prepared meals for my parents and two siblings. However, my health began to worsen, and I knew I had to change not only the *types* of ingredients I was using but also *how* I was using them. I didn't want to give up my favorite dishes; I just wanted to make them healthier and add more intentionality to the process while keeping them delicious. When I became a college student and had to cook for myself, making sure the recipes were quick, easy, and affordable became a priority as well. **In the process of figuring this out, I unknowingly took the first step toward changing my life.**

On a random Sunday in 2019, I gathered the knowledge I had picked up from a few podcasts and books—mainly that eating whole foods was the best and simplest course of action. I got out a pen and paper and wrote out a grocery list for the week ahead, and starting small, I came up with five simple recipes that fit my meager student budget. I focused on real, whole foods that I could prepare easily in my tiny, poorly outfitted apartment kitchen. **The recipes were simple, prioritizing single-ingredient foods, leaving out the ultraprocessed stuff, and making a point to have fresh food—mostly plants—dominating every plate.** With the recipes in hand and a pantry inventory taken, I ventured to the grocery store and started week one of what is now my weekly shopping routine.

Making a game plan to set myself up for success by planning each meal, shopping with a grocery list, and putting aside time to prepare nutrient-dense dishes changed my life. Mentally, I no longer stressed about my meals for the week, and physically, everything changed due to my healthier choices. I lost more than seventy pounds, ditched my GI meds, healed my joint pain, and freed myself from disordered thoughts around food. Nothing was off-limits, and I found myself reaching for a

variety of plants and proteins over my previous fixes because I found a way to make healthy meals fun and absolutely delicious.

These recipes, plans, lists, and trips to the store became the framework of a healthy, happy life and have actually become fun and inspiring on their own. My meal-planning system is the part of my life that makes the rest of it possible, and I don't even think of it as a chore. And now I've even gotten my husband, Brian, in on the act. He's right there with me and getting almost as into it as I am!

I was so excited that I wanted to share what I'd learned, so the next part of my journey was spreading the word about how I changed my lifestyle. The recipes got me there, and I built an amazing community with the @jenneatsgoood social account. This community has enriched my entire world and led to this book. **My hope is that what I'm sharing here will help you enrich yours.**

ABOUT THE BOOK

Unlike a typical cookbook or meal-prep book, *Don't Think About Dinner* is a comprehensive handbook that offers strategies, tools, tips, and meal plans, *plus* more than 125 delicious and foolproof recipes for a healthier lifestyle. Because it's my book, there's an emphasis on meal planning and prepping—and it's designed to work with the way you *already* cook and think of your meals. Follow the grocery lists and plans I put together for you or just flip through the recipes to choose your own; it's completely up to you. And *of course* you'll find lots of hacks and tips to help you build skills that will improve your kitchen time, well-being, and confidence for easy, healthy, and flavor-packed meals.

Figuring out what's for dinner doesn't need to be stressful, and grocery shopping doesn't have to be a dreaded time suck. Meal planning and meal prep—if they're things you want to do—don't need to be complicated. You can use this book from front to back if you're ready to dive full-on into all the tools I've compiled, or just skim it to glean what you need and skip to the recipes so you can get cooking.

HEALTHY COOKING DOESN'T HAVE TO BE:
X Overwhelming   X Bland   X Expensive   X Time-consuming

Part One of this book is all about what you can do in advance to get and keep that healthy lifestyle when you're busy but still want to eat well at home. You'll find the best and simplest ways to succeed at meal planning and prepping, with information on how to build your pantry, stock your fridge and freezer, store your food, create grocery lists, and shop efficiently and economically. Plus, I'll share favorite breakfast and lunch meal-prep ideas and essential kitchen gear, and on page 42 you'll find twelve weekly themed dinner plans with corresponding grocery lists, including Budget-Friendly Week, Dairy-Free Favorites Week, seasonal vibes weeks, and more.

PART ONE:
HOW TO MAKE IT ALL HAPPEN

WHY PLAN & PREP?

I get this question a lot, and the answer is simple: A little planning and prepping will give you the power to take control of your time, reduce mealtime decision fatigue, save money, and ensure that a nourishing option makes it to your plate. I love a plan, and devised this easy-to-follow approach for your weekly routine.

When your kitchen is fully stocked with everything you need each week and you have a plan in place, you'll be shocked at how much more appealing it will be to make healthy meals and avoid expensive, questionable takeout, knowing all the drudge work is done and a great nourishing meal is only a few simple steps away.

30 minutes to plan your meals and create a grocery list to reduce time spent shopping

90 minutes of meal prepping at least one breakfast and lunch option to save energy

0 minutes spent anguishing about what to have for dinner—by having preplanned weeknight dinners!

MY SUSTAINABLE STRATEGIES

My goal is to help you learn the strategies for building a sustainable, healthy lifestyle—without sacrificing flavor, of course. When you focus on plants and protein as the stars of your meals, you'll create a strong foundation for a realistic, less stressful, and delicious approach to eating well. And it's simpler than you think. It's all about leveraging familiar ingredients in creative, no-fuss ways to bring out bold tastes, vibrant textures, and endless variety. Cooking with intention is about embracing the experience and exploring recipes that inspire you, turning simple ingredients into dishes that energize and satisfy you. Let flavor lead the way!

Learning to plan and prep has kept me on track, and a key to success is knowing that this isn't meant to be restrictive and doesn't need to be overly regimented. Things happen, and your day can change. These are tools to help you, not limit you. Remember, when it comes to cooking, I can tell you my tricks and recipes, but ultimately, it's not about me. So always remember who you're cooking for, and you do *you*!

Speaking of you, are you vegan? Dairy-free? Gluten-free? Vegetarian? Nut-free? All or some of the above? Or maybe you're an omnivore! The great news is that you don't have to buy a special cookbook to match your dietary preferences. You can find meals in all these categories. I offer swaps and substitutions to make almost any recipe in this book work for you, however you eat, both in the recipes and in charts (see page 339).

But remember that if you start to feel overwhelmed by picking out your meals in advance and making a list, don't be afraid to go back to basics. There's nothing wrong with eating the same meal multiple days in a row (you'll probably want to do that, anyway, after you find some favorites in the book). I've created this book to offer a wide range of simple recipes that can be made on repeat for any eater!

JENN'S KEYS TO SUCCESS

1. **Plan it out:** Set aside 30 minutes each week. Get out your pen and paper (or notes app!) and figure out your meals, **always leaving a little room for flexibility when you get to the store**.

2. **Keep it simple:** Creating **a workable pantry** and **go-to list of favorite recipes** goes hand in hand with meal planning. And there is absolutely nothing wrong with basic! **Using repeat ingredients** that you're familiar with enables you to **shop efficiently**, **prep faster**, and **save money on groceries**.

3. **Take inventory:** Look to see what you have in your pantry, fridge, and freezer, and **make your grocery list accordingly.** Trust me, this weekly ritual will transform your week, and you'll get the time back when you stop standing in front of the refrigerator with decision fatigue.

4. **Prioritize plants and protein:** When in doubt, focusing on plants and protein can guide your choices. **Why?** Eating **lots of fruits and vegetables**, fresh or frozen, gets you important vitamins, minerals, antioxidants, and fiber that support your health. **Protein**, the most satisfying macronutrient, keeps you full, increases muscle mass, repairs your cells, and builds new ones. This is why choosing **whole foods**—like fruit, vegetables, whole grains, nuts, beans, unprocessed meat, fish, and eggs—is key.

5. **Be efficient: Protecting your time and money is a priority** with my strategy. Meal planning, shopping, prepping, and cooking take time, I'm not denying that. But I'm all about making the process as efficient as possible. It all goes back to **being intentional with your time** and **avoiding wasting resources**. And over time, you'll become more and more efficient.

6. **Have fun:** Let's face it, we all have to figure out what we're going to eat each week. Why not make it as enjoyable as possible? Reframing your perspective becomes easier as you **build a routine** and **gain confidence in the kitchen**. Identify what sparks joy: Is it exploring new flavors? Getting creative with the ingredients you already have? Involving your family in the process? Once you **allow yourself to have fun** with this healthy habit, your potential expands.

7. **Build a sustainable lifestyle:** Make your plan a realistic one and keep at it. At the end of the day, sustainable habits are the ones that tend to stick. **Don't feel pressured to go from 0 to 100 in one week.** Experiment with the tools to see what works for you and **add on one habit at a time**. Small changes lead to big results.

8. **Be flexible:** Once you establish a planning, shopping, prepping, and cooking routine, **allow flexibility**. Not every week will look the same—life would get boring if it did—**making adjustments or taking shortcuts is okay**. Finding that balance is the most essential part of a healthy lifestyle.

ABOUT THE RECIPES

Every chapter is tailored to your day, offering recipes that balance bold flavors, ease, and versatility. From pre-prepped breakfasts to lunches that fuel your afternoon, snacks that hit the spot, and sips to elevate your mood, there's something for every moment. Dinners range from hearty one-pot meals to vibrant plant-based dishes and effortlessly chic mains, and you'll want to save room for dessert! With globally inspired flavors and easy-to-find ingredients, the recipes are specifically designed to keep things exciting and achievable, and each chapter starts with a list of recipes, for easy choosing.

Breakfast Blueprint (p. 58) is designed to help you get out of bed in the morning. These protein-packed breakfasts can often be prepped and be in your fridge or freezer for you to heat and eat, leaving you satisfied until lunchtime.

Quick Lunches, Upgraded (p. 90) is packed with stress-free, plant-forward lunches to be prepped in advance or made in the moment. Think loaded salads, wraps, and bowls that go beyond basic and bring excitement.

Nourishing Snacks & Dips (p. 120) are those little afternoon noshes to hold you until dinner, with whole-food-based snacks, dips, and bites that are also perfect for entertaining.

One-Pot Wonders (p. 134) get dinner done in one pot, skillet, pan, or dish, featuring cozy meals with easy cleanup.

Done in 30 (p. 160) is for when you don't have time to mess around; these recipes clock in at 30 minutes or less. And yes, I'm talking 30 minutes for both prep *and* cook time!

High-Protein Hits (p. 184) delivers protein-packed meals to feed your brain and muscles, with all dishes featuring more than 30 grams of protein per serving. You'll find some surprises here, not just what you expect when you hear the "high-protein" buzz words.

Plant-Powered (p. 220) has you covered whether you're a full-on vegan, a vegetarian, or just know you need more veggies in your life. These vegan recipes have been developed for plant-based *and* meat eaters, and everyone will be coming back for seconds.

A Little Fancier (p. 248) is for when you want stylish meals for every mood, from romantic dinners to crowd-pleasers, with something for every dietary preference. While I call these dishes "fancy," they still hold to my values of efficiency, nutrition, and simple ingredients.

Standout Sides & Basics (p. 278) delivers dishes that shine, served on the side or in their own starring role, with foolproof techniques for perfect grains and more.

Everyday Elevated Sauces (p. 292) is where I share my secret sauce(s), with eight of my versatile go-tos that will transform your dishes and keep you dipping and drizzling.

Functional Sips (p. 304) takes you from lattes that will get your day started to cozy warm bevs and a bedtime tonic. Not only are they delicious, but you'll also marvel at how much money you save every week by making them at home.

Sweet Treats (p. 316) are tasty tricks—desserts that feel indulgent but are actually plant forward too. You'll find treats for every occasion, from hosting to snacking.

LET'S GET TO IT!

The beauty of this book and the recipes is that they are *customizable*! Learning to plan and prep has kept me on track, and knowing that it isn't meant to be restrictive and overly regimented is essential.

Pop Quiz!
WHAT STYLE OF PLANNER ARE YOU?
Follow the arrows based on your answers to find your best way to use this book.

start here!

- My grocery shopping strategy could use some work; every week feels like a challenge and I'm burned out from all the decisions.
- I'm the person who loves to follow a plan. I like to cook, but I'm sick of figuring out what to make for dinner every night!
- I don't have a set meal-prep routine right now, but I'm hoping to start one. I need more than just recipe ideas.
- Honestly, I don't really know what's in my pantry, fridge, and freezer right now. I end up wasting a lot of food because I don't use it all up.
- It feels like I need more than meal plans, grocery lists, and recipes. I need to start from the beginning to build a better lifestyle.
- My confidence in the kitchen is low. I don't even know where to start because I never learned the basics, like what equipment I need.
- Meal planning and prepping overwhelm me because I haven't tried it much. I need to learn some new skills to save time, money, and energy.
- I really need to build my knowledge around ingredients. I'm ready to learn everything I can to stock the pantry and start using the meal plans!
- I'm still trying to establish routines around food. I want to learn how to build a grocery list on my own so I can implement a long-term habit.

ALREADY A PRO

You've got this (or are not interested in prepping and planning, which is totally okay!). You're here for the good food, so let's get to cooking. Skip to the recipes starting on page 58 and thumb through to find what sounds best to you.

ENTHUSIASTIC PLANNER

You've got the basics down, and you're ready for more structured help. Time to put it into practice—head right to the 12 Weeks of Dinner Plans & Grocery Lists (p. 42) and get going.

ALL-IN STUDENT

You want to understand every step and suggestion, from the recipes to stocking the pantry, meal-prep basics, shopping tips, kitchen best practices, and everything in between. You're going cover to cover.

LET'S GET TO IT!

HOW TO GET IT DONE

Plan It 11

My Weekly Plan 12

What You Need to Know: Dinner Plans & Grocery Lists 15

The Anatomy of a Grocery List 16

Stock It 19

In the Pantry 19

Counterop Produce 23

In the Fridge & Freezer 24

Swap or Sub It 26

Shop It 27

Rules to Shop By 28

Quick Money-Saving Tips 28

Swap & Save 29

Prep It 30

Food Safety Guidelines 30

The Best Way to Reheat Food 31

Where to Start: Breakfast & Lunch Meal Prep 32

Tips to Make Meal Prep Easier 33

Store It 34

Meal-Prep Storage Equipment 34

Meal Storage, Freezing & Reheating Guide 35

Keep At It! 36

Roadblocks to Your Routine: The What-If? 36

Plan It

For me, the most difficult thing about eating well used to be that I didn't have a plan in mind when I'd go to the grocery store. I'd stumble in with just a vague idea of some of the recipes I'd hope to make later in the week and would end up grabbing some of my usual fallback ingredients. Flash-forward to a half hour later and I'd be in the checkout line with a bunch of items that would be useful in only one recipe, not enough beyond that day. Plus, without a plan, the bill was way higher than it needed to be. By the end of the week, I'd usually have eaten out more than once, let many of the ingredients I paid for go bad, and ended up with a jar of something random sitting in my fridge, never to be used again. I was missing a solid plan to make sure I got exactly what I needed at the grocery store for the meals I wanted for the week.

These days, by choosing a variety of recipes that use similar ingredients and pantry staples, I'm able to reduce the number of expensive one-off ingredients that I buy. I also take care to plan dishes with different vibes and flavors so I'm never bored. And knowing exactly what I'm going to cook for dinner every night not only reduces decision fatigue but also signficantly decreases the chance I'll order takeout. I recommend planning five dinners for the week, plus a once-a-week session of breakfast and lunch meal prep. Or find a combo that works for you and how you like to cook and eat.

Your plans will most likely change from week to week, depending on what's going on in your life, so it's important to allow flexibility while establishing a routine. The important piece is having *some* kind of plan! I intentionally leave the weekends unplanned, either eating leftovers, relying on what's in the freezer, or going out. But if weekend planning works for you, there are plenty of recipes to inspire you for that too.

This kind of weekly advance planning can be life-changing. It is for me, because I end up with nourishing meals for the week—meals I actually *want* to eat and can realistically make with the time I have available. But if you haven't been big into meal planning in the past, ease yourself in by trying three or four dishes for the week ahead. Or start with one. There is no right or wrong.

MY WEEKLY PLAN

My journey taught me that the best thing I could do for myself was to carve out time weekly to make a plan and write out my grocery list. Here's my usual routine:

Friday

- I check my pantry, refrigerator, and freezer for what I already have on hand.
- I choose five dinners for the following week and at least one breakfast and lunch to meal prep. I leave weekend meals unstructured for flexibility.
- I make my grocery list based on my choices, plus anything else I need to replenish.

Saturday or Sunday

- I choose my day for meal prep and shop in the morning for the ingredients on my list.
- I meal prep in the afternoon; I usually have it down to a tight 90 minutes.

THINGS TO CONSIDER WHEN PLANNING YOUR MEALS

What the upcoming week looks like: If you know you'll be out a few nights, perhaps plan lunches, breakfasts, or even just snacks like Avocado, Corn, and Black Bean Dip (p. 133) or a sweet treat like Salty Peanut Butter Pretzel Energy Balls (p. 318) instead. Every week can look different!

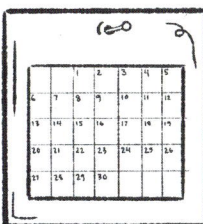

Time: Some weeknights offer more flexibility than others—factor that in when planning meals. Do you have a busy work week and expect some late nights? Choose low-prep dinners you can actually stick to. Save the more involved recipes for nights when you have time and energy to enjoy them. Making your plan achievable is important!

Budget: Finding recipes that correspond to the ingredients you already have in your pantry, freezer, and fridge helps when you're watching your food spend. Have several cans of chickpeas in your pantry? Make two or three meals using chickpeas, such as Buffalo Chickpea Stuffed Sweet Potatoes (p. 151) or Herby Chickpea and Cauliflower Bowls with Lemon-Dill Sauce (p. 174). You'll save money, prepping, and time shopping.

Special occasions: Birthday coming up? Dinner with friends? Date night? It's easy to incorporate any occasion into your planning for the week. Check out the recipes in "A Little Fancier" (p. 248) for inspo.

Health goals: Too many meals out? Coming down off the holidays? Haven't seen a veggie in a while? All of the recipes were created with plant diversity in mind so packing in veggies never gets boring. "Plant-Powered" (p. 220) is an entire chapter of plant-focused meals, with options like Sheet Pan Gnocchi with Sun-Dried Tomato Cashew Cream (p. 230) or Tomato-Basil Saucy Butter Bean Skillet (p. 243).

PUT IT INTO PRACTICE

1. **Set aside 30 minutes weekly to plan your meals and make your grocery list:** I like to do this at the end of the week, but find what works for you. Add the time to your calendar to hold yourself accountable; that's the way to develop a routine to transform your week and quiet meal stress decisions. See The Anatomy of a Grocery List (p. 16) for help.

2. **Take inventory of your pantry, refrigerator, and freezer:** A weekly inventory session before you meal-plan ensures you're using up what you have, saving money, and reducing waste. Keep a running list on your fridge, pad, phone, or whatever works for you to check things throughout the week and save time. Review your pantry and identify what you already have to put to use. Hit the fridge and freezer and do the same. Don't forget to look for open containers and approaching expiration dates.

3. **Choose and write down your weeknight dinners:** This avoids the headaches and stress during the week. Using your accurate inventory list, plan out your meals. You may have favorite recipes that align with what's in your inventory, but let this book give you some more inspiration. I intentionally developed all the dinner recipes to use simple ingredients that you'll use up, so they can be grouped on grocery lists.

4. **Add a few breakfasts and lunches for the week:** Write those choices below your dinner plan so you can see all the meals for your week. This is where flexibility and prep come in: Do you already have a batch of Broccoli, Cheddar, and Chicken Breakfast Biscuits (p. 74) in the freezer that you can use? Will this week's dinners provide leftovers for lunches? Schedule in meal-prep time to get ahead and fit your needs for the week.

5. **Write out your grocery list:** Organize your shopping list according to the store's layout for streamlined shopping: produce, proteins, dairy and substitutes, and canned and packaged. Don't forget to restock pantry staples and spices and add in anything else you'll need. Then, with list (or device) in hand, hit the aisles!

WHAT YOU NEED TO KNOW: 12 WEEKS OF DINNER PLANS & GROCERY LISTS

If you like a little help when it comes to selecting meals for planning ahead, you're in luck! On page 42 you'll find twelve different weeks of dinner plans, varying in theme, season, and dietary preferences. These meal plans are designed to cover your weeknight dinners. You can also use the recipes from the breakfast and lunch chapters, add them to your plan to fit your needs, and you're set for the week!

No matter the craving, there's something on each plan that helps nail it. From an all-plant-based heavy-duty health and recovery week to a cozier, more indulgent span of favorite comfort foods, you're covered! Each grocery list includes everything you need to make five dinners with four servings each for the week. Just grab the list, get your ingredients, and feel the decision fatigue subside as you follow each unique recipe and identify your favorites.

THE ANATOMY OF A GROCERY LIST

Here's how I break down my grocery lists. Breaking them into sections makes grocery shopping efficient. It makes building the list easier, and this way you only need to hit each aisle one time.

FRUITS apples, avocados, lemons, limes, mangoes, pineapples, oranges

VEGETABLES asparagus, broccoli, Brussels sprouts, cabbage, cauliflower, carrots, celery, corn, cucumbers, eggplant, fennel, garlic, ginger, green beans, kale, lettuce, mushrooms, onions, parsley, parsnips, peas, peppers, potatoes, shallots, spinach, squash, sweet potatoes, tomatoes

HERBS basil, chives, cilantro, dill, mint, parsley, rosemary, sage, thyme

CANNED & PACKAGED broth, coconut milk, tomatoes (crushed, sun-dried, sauce, paste), capers, olives, rice, quinoa, pasta, polenta, chipotle peppers in adobo, miso paste, curry paste, Dijon mustard, tahini, buffalo sauce, flours, breadcrumbs, nutritional yeast, tortillas

PRODUCE
fruits, vegetables, fresh herbs

PROTEINS
poultry, pork, beef, lamb, fish, shellfish, tofu, tempeh, beans, nuts, seeds, eggs

DAIRY & SUBSTITUTES
yogurt, milk, butter, cheese, dairy-free substitutes

CANNED & PACKAGED
grains, flours, jarred and canned goods, broths, sauces, pastes

PANTRY STAPLES
oils, vinegars, maple syrup, honey, coconut aminos, sriracha, tapioca flour, baking soda, baking powder

SPICES
everyday seasonings, including kosher salt and ground black pepper

CHEESES Cheddar, feta, goat, Gruyère, Parmesan, mozzarella, ricotta

MILK AND OTHER DAIRY whole milk, butter, whole-milk or low-fat Greek yogurt, cottage cheese

SUBSTITUTES soy milk, nut milk, dairy-free cheese, dairy-free yogurt, unsalted vegan butter

SPICES dried basil, cayenne pepper, chili powder, ground coriander, ground cumin, garlic powder, ground ginger, onion powder, dried oregano, dried parsley, red pepper flakes, rosemary, sage, sesame seeds, smoked paprika, ground thyme

Here's a template I like to use for my grocery lists. Scan the QR code to download it.

GROCERIES
The Plan for the Week

Date:
Budget:

THIS WEEK'S DINNER PLAN

Mon: _____
Tue: _____
Wed: _____
Thur: _____
Fri: _____
Sat: _____
Sun: _____

MEAL PREP PLAN

Breakfast: _____
_____
Lunch: _____
_____

CURRENT INVENTORY (things to use up)

Pantry: _____
_____
_____
_____

Fridge: _____
_____
_____
_____

Freezer: _____
_____
_____
_____

GROCERY LIST

PRODUCE
☐ _____ ☐ _____
☐ _____ ☐ _____
☐ _____ ☐ _____
☐ _____ ☐ _____
☐ _____ ☐ _____

DAIRY AND SUBSTITUTES
☐ _____ ☐ _____
☐ _____ ☐ _____
☐ _____ ☐ _____
☐ _____ ☐ _____
☐ _____ ☐ _____

PROTEINS
☐ _____ ☐ _____
☐ _____ ☐ _____
☐ _____ ☐ _____
☐ _____ ☐ _____
☐ _____ ☐ _____

PANTRY STAPLES AND SPICES
☐ _____ ☐ _____
☐ _____ ☐ _____
☐ _____ ☐ _____
☐ _____ ☐ _____
☐ _____ ☐ _____

CANNED/PACKAGED
☐ _____ ☐ _____
☐ _____ ☐ _____
☐ _____ ☐ _____
☐ _____ ☐ _____

OTHER
☐ _____ ☐ _____
☐ _____ ☐ _____
☐ _____ ☐ _____
☐ _____ ☐ _____

Stock It

A well-stocked pantry and freezer are essential for productive planning and meal prep. Keeping track of ingredients you already have in your kitchen will help you plan meals and make it easier to figure out what you need to buy, cut down on grocery runs, keep your meals healthier, and save money on sale items. Creating a workable pantry stocked with staples often used in your favorite recipes reduces your weekly food costs and allows you to buy in bulk or stock up when things are on sale. You'll also save space by focusing on just those key basics versus buying new specialty items every time you make a new recipe (like, when will you use lavender syrup and saffron honey again?). I make sure to shop from my pantry, refrigerator, and freezer before shopping the store.

In the Pantry

Here's a list of items that you'll always find in my pantry. There are no super-random or overly specialized items here, just the essentials you'll see on repeat throughout this book and that can be found at most grocery stores. I have them grouped by category, so take some time to evaluate your pantry and see where you may need to stock up. You can find a shoppable list on page 17.

OILS & VINEGARS

Avocado oil: I like to use avocado oil as a neutral oil because it has a higher smoke point than olive oil and works best for higher temperature cooking. Just be sure to look for a brand that uses 100% pure avocado oil, not a blend. It's more affordable to buy in bulk.

Coconut oil: I use coconut oil less than the other oils; you'll find it mostly in my baked goods or no-bake sweet treats. Refined coconut oil has a less pronounced flavor than unrefined, and you won't aggressively taste it in your sweets! This is another oil I recommend buying in bulk.

Olive oil: Healthy fats, antioxidants, and flavor! When possible, I choose monovarietal olive oil, which means the olives are all from one place. Experiment and taste test, because there are very affordable and delicious oils out there, without spending more for extra-virgin.

Toasted sesame oil: You get so much fantastic flavor from sesame oil, so I love to keep it stocked and incorporate it into savory dishes. Toasted brings the most flavor, but untoasted works too. And it's budget-friendly—just remember it's for finishing, not for frying.

Vinegars: I like to keep apple cider vinegar, balsamic vinegar, rice vinegar (I use rice vinegar without any added sodium or sugar, which some brands note on the label, or look for unseasoned), and red wine vinegar on hand, as they each have a unique flavor. You might be surprised by how much even just a splash of vinegar can elevate or balance a dish!

SAUCES, SWEETENERS & MORE

Coconut aminos: One of my most-used ingredients is coconut aminos, and for good reason: Its salty, slightly sweet taste brings umami to a variety of dishes. It's a gluten-free soy sauce substitute, and you can swap it for reduced-sodium tamari (another gluten-free option) or reduced-sodium soy sauce (note that soy sauce will contain gluten unless the label says otherwise). **Just remember that tamari and soy sauce, even with reduced sodium, are often still saltier than coconut aminos, so I recommend reducing any additional salt in a recipe first, then salting to taste to avoid oversalting.**

Hot stuff: I love to bring the heat every now and then, and hot sauces are an easy way to do it! Sriracha is the most common hot sauce on my grocery lists, but I *love* a good Buffalo sauce too. Chili garlic sauce is also an excellent sub for sriracha, and another favorite pantry item, chipotle peppers in adobo sauce, often shows up for smoky heat in my recipes.

Sweeteners: My go-to sweeteners are pure maple syrup and raw honey, but more commonly pure maple syrup, since it's vegan and easier to work with (and pours better!). Make sure it's labeled pure, as

others can contain butter or pork fat. Bonus if it's local!

& more: A few other repeat flavor enhancers I keep stocked are curry paste (specifically Thai red curry paste), white miso paste, Dijon mustard, and nutritional yeast. There are endless pantry options for elevating dishes—keep the ones you use most stocked!

CANNED GOODS & BROTH

Canned coconut milk: One of my most-used canned ingredients! I often sub this for heavy cream or other dairy products, even in Brian's Favorite Lamb Bolognese (p. 260). I usually use the full-fat version for richness, but light has its place, too, for thinner results. Certain recipes, like Coconut-Mango Chia Pudding (p. 67), call for refrigerated coconut milk because those versions (often known as coconut milk beverages), have been thinned with water and work best for setting without hardening.

Beans: Budget-friendly protein magic! Having all different types of beans on hand means the affordable and nutritious meal options are endless. You can expect black beans, butter beans, cannellini (or navy or Great Northern beans), chickpeas, kidney beans, and pinto beans to show up throughout the book and in my pantry.

Broth: I like to use low-sodium broth (veggie, chicken, or beef) whenever possible in place of water (like in rice, quinoa, or pasta) for extra flavor (and for extra protein, if you swap in bone broth)! Soups, skillets, and one-pot meals will also feature one of the three. I prefer low-sodium broths and recommend them throughout the book. **If you go for regular, taste before adding salt and adjust your added salt accordingly.**

Canned or jarred vegetables: Make eating plants easier by keeping jarred goods on hand—artichokes, roasted red peppers, pitted Kalamata olives, and capers are my favorites. They also add texture and flavor with no cooking required!

Tomatoes: Having a mix of crushed tomatoes, marinara sauce, tomato paste, and sun-dried tomatoes in the pantry will allow you to quickly whip up flavorful pastas, soups, chilis, and more. This way you can enjoy freshness and flavor no matter the season.

GOOOD TO KNOW: COCONUT MILK

As a coconut milk lover, I've had lots of practice with it, and if it's new to you, you'll be an expert after enjoying the recipes in this book. Here's what you should know: Adding canned unsweetened full-fat or light coconut milk to your savory dishes **will not make them taste like coconut when other flavors come into play.** Unless you are a total coconut hater and can't even stand a hint of it in your food, you can happily enjoy the dairy-free cream substitute in your meals. Light cream can be substituted for coconut milk in most savory dishes if you prefer it.

If you're directed to use just a portion of the coconut milk can, **always be sure it has been well shaken, because separation often does occur** (that's when there's a hardened block of coconut cream at the top of the can). If shaking doesn't do the trick (like in the winter months for me in Boston), you can always transfer the contents of the can to a microwave-safe bowl or jar and microwave it in 15-second increments until the hardened coconut cream has melted.

To store leftover canned coconut milk, I recommend transferring it to a jar with a tightly sealed lid and refrigerating for up to a week. Need ideas for what to do with that other half? There are many recipes here to use the other half, or use it in your lattes or smoothies!

SPREADS, BUTTERS, NUTS & SEEDS

Almond, cashew, peanut, and sunflower butters: My priority when looking for nut and seed butters is finding creamy ones that include only nuts or seeds and salt. That makes for the perfect drippy texture for using in recipes, without unnecessary ingredients. Sunflower butter is a great swap for nut-free diets.

Chia seeds: An omega-3 powerhouse, chia seeds are an easy way to include dietary fiber, and I always have them on hand for incorporating where I can. You can find them in my chia puddings, smoothies, and even sweet treats like Salty Peanut Butter Pretzel Energy Balls (p. 318).

Nuts: There are endless options for nuts that can bring protein and crunch to meals, but the ones I keep on hand consistently are unsalted, unroasted (raw) almonds, cashews, and walnuts. They're easy to find, tasty, and versatile and can be bought in bulk and even frozen to reduce costs. Adjust the salt if you're using salted.

Tahini: More and more, tahini has become a staple for my recipes. I love its earthy flavor and that it's more allergy-friendly than nut butters! As with nut butters, look for brands that use sesame seeds and salt as the only ingredients.

GRAINS & FLOURS

Flours: There's one flour I use most—tapioca flour. This gluten-free starch thickens sauces and improves texture. **You can substitute arrowroot starch, which acts similarly, or cornstarch if you can't access either.** I sometimes use gluten-free 1:1 baking flour, blanched almond flour, coconut flour, and oat flour in savory and sweet recipes, too, and I keep breadcrumbs (gluten-free panko is my pick) in the pantry for breading. Gluten-free options like 1:1 baking flour and GF panko can always be swapped with options like all-purpose flour and regular panko if you're not avoiding gluten. Look for recommendations in the recipes directly—alternate flours like almond and coconut can't always be substituted 1:1.

Oats: Gluten-free rolled oats are an affordable fiber source with lots of uses, including my Overnight Oats, Two Ways (p. 61), Hidden Veggie Oat Bars (p. 70) and crisps, like my Pistachio Berry Crisp (p. 328). I buy them in bulk and keep them in the pantry for when I need something quick.

Pasta: I'm all for enjoying any type of pasta, but I especially love a brown rice pasta. Rice-and-corn-based pastas are next best in my book. I also love to mix in gnocchi and stir-fry noodles. **My recipes recommend gluten-free pasta, but you can sub regular pasta if you're not avoiding gluten.** Just check my notes! I'm not usually a fan of chickpea pasta in one-pot or one-pan situations, as it tends to fall apart while cooking.

Quinoa: Perfect for meal prep, quinoa holds up well in the fridge after it's cooked. And it's also inexpensive, so it's a good value. Both white and tricolor quinoa pack a plant-based protein boost. See page 291 for my Fluffy Does-It-All Quinoa.

Rice: I absolutely love rice as a budget-friendly staple—especially in my one-pan meals—including Arborio, jasmine, brown, and wild rice. See page 290 for my basic steamed rice recipe and tips.

DRIED HERBS & SPICES

Keep the following herbs, spices, and other flavor enhancers on hand, as you'll find them throughout the book: kosher salt, ground black pepper, dried basil, cayenne pepper, chili powder, ground coriander, ground cumin, garlic powder, ground ginger, onion powder, dried oregano, dried parsley, red pepper flakes, dried rosemary, ground sage, sesame seeds, smoked paprika, and dried thyme.

COUNTERTOP PRODUCE

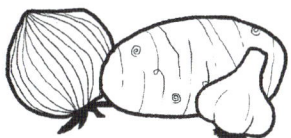

I keep my onions, garlic, shallots, potatoes, sweet potatoes, and squash on the countertop, since they don't need to be refrigerated to last longer! Seasonally, I keep fruits like peaches or melons on the counter until they are cut.

AN IMPORTANT NOTE ON SALT

Diamond kosher salt is the only salt used in this book. I'm really not a fan of fine sea or table salt. **Kosher salt is ideal for cooking because it has uniform grains and is easier to control with your fingers when seasoning**; it's also less salty than table salt. Diamond kosher salt is less salty than Morton kosher salt, so if you are using table salt or Morton kosher salt, you will need to adjust the salt levels to avoid oversalting the recipes. **As a rule, halve the amount of salt when using both table salt and Morton salt, so if a recipe in this book calls for 1 teaspoon of kosher salt, use ½ teaspoon table salt or ½ teaspoon Morton salt.**

In the Fridge & Freezer

I keep my fridge and freezer well stocked and "shoppable" by following these simple tips. I constantly take note of what's in my fridge and freezer to know what I need to buy at the grocery store. This might seem obvious, like, duh, don't buy what you already have. I can't tell you how many containers of Greek yogurt we used to let go bad in the back of our fridge before I started writing things down. I'm also always shopping sales. So rather than buy ground beef each time I go, I wait until it's on sale and stock up. If you wait to buy at the right time, you'll build up a stocked freezer while saving money. There are so many more tips like these in my Goood to Know tips and elsewhere.

You'll see from the recipes in this book that I always try to incorporate as many plants as possible into my meals and opt for in-season produce whenever possible. A lot of people don't realize that adding lots and lots of plants to your meals over higher-priced meat and fish and even packaged goods can reduce your food costs significantly. Whether you're getting fresh or frozen produce, the bulk of it is very budget-friendly and high volume, especially when you avoid precut or prepeeled items. Health benefits aside, I'm always building my meals around my produce (that's what I mean by "plant-forward").

IN THE REFRIGERATOR

I keep a consistent mix of fresh produce, dairy and dairy substitutes, thawed proteins, and eggs in my refrigerator. On any given day, I'll find some combination of the items below:

Cheese and butter: I don't eat a ton of dairy, but some recipes I make, especially higher-protein picks, include it. I'm a fan of Cheddar and mozzarella cheese and prefer to shred it myself rather than buy preshredded, which can be more expensive and sometimes contain gluten. Feta, goat, Parmesan, and ricotta are favorites too! You can usually find unsalted butter or unsalted vegan butter hanging out in my fridge.

Cottage cheese: Talk about high-protein heroes! I'm consistently amazed by how some blended cottage cheese can secretly boost the protein and flavor in a recipe (like my High-Protein Egg Muffins, Two Ways on page 77 or Dump-and-Bake Hidden Protein Pasta on page 159). You can also get lactose-free cottage cheese.

Fresh herbs: You'll always find cilantro, dill, and parsley in my fridge. I use them daily. To keep them fresher longer, store herbs wrapped in a damp paper towel or in a jar filled halfway with water, covered loosely. Other favorites are basil, rosemary, mint, and thyme! They're also easy to grow yourself, which makes them much more affordable too.

Fresh fruit: My usual staples are some sort of berry—I especially love strawberries and blueberries—and citrus fruits like oranges, lemons, and limes, which I use for their juice and zest. Depending on the season, I switch it up!

Greek yogurt: Greek yogurt (whole-milk or low-fat, whatever works for you) has so many uses, from sweet to savory, and gives a protein boost. I also love coconut- or cashew-based dairy-free yogurt as a plant-based option.

Greens: I like to keep arugula, baby spinach, butter lettuce, and curly kale on hand. I make an exception and buy curly kale shredded and bagged for ease of use. Arugula, curly kale, and spinach have versatile uses in salads, breakfast bakes, and smoothies. Butter lettuce (also known as Bibb or Boston lettuce) and romaine are staples for lettuce wraps.

Milk and substitutes: My most used milk is coconut milk (see page 21), but I sometimes use whole milk, fat-free milk, soy milk, oat milk, or some type of nut milk.

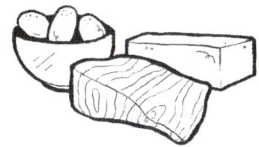

Meat, fish, tofu, and eggs: Since raw meat and fish don't last long in the fridge, I have a bigger stock in the freezer. However, right after my grocery trip, you can find both meat and fish in my fridge. Proteins that have a longer life in the fridge—like eggs, tofu, and tempeh—can often be found there.

Veggies: I like to fill my fridge with a rotating variety of vegetables to keep meals interesting, and I cut up peppers or cucumbers to grab as an easy snack throughout the day. Some veggies, like carrots and celery, are super easy to add to a meal and last a long time. I lean into seasonal picks here too!

HOW TO GET IT DONE

IN THE FREEZER

"Is this freezer-friendly?" is one of the most common questions I get when sharing recipes, so I know you're all looking for answers! It makes total sense—meal prep can be even more helpful when you know which dishes can be stored for longer, so prepping freezer-friendly recipes is a lifesaver for busy people! **With that in mind, I've included freezing and reheating tips when applicable to the recipes throughout the book.**

I always keep these items in my freezer to help with meal prep, alongside my pre-prepped frozen meals or leftovers:

Frozen produce: When fresh fruits and veggies are about to turn, I chop them up and pack them in freezer bags, then pop them in the freezer. I also always have a bag of frozen kale or spinach and plenty of frozen fruit like blueberries, strawberries, and mango. Buying already frozen fruits or veggies is a great option, too, as it's often cheaper and generally frozen before transit, preserving its nutrients. Win-win!

Frozen proteins: My go-tos are ground chicken (90%), ground pork (90%), turkey (93%), and beef (85%), but lamb (85%) is helpful too. I use a lot of chicken breast and chicken thighs and whole chickens for the best value. For seafood, I like buying my fish and shellfish frozen in bulk. My biggest budget tips for meat are to buy extra when there's a good sale and purchase your proteins in bulk for freezing. If you have the room, grabbing an extra 1 to 2 pounds of meat to enhance your freezer stock is a money-saver.

SWAP OR SUB IT

Each recipe in this book was meticulously tested using the ingredients listed, so I encourage you to follow the recipe as closely as possible for optimal results. However, I realize that whether due to dietary restrictions, allergies, preferences, or accessibility, not every ingredient works for everyone, so I suggest substitutions for the commonly used ingredients throughout the book. **Be sure to remember that changing ingredients can sometimes alter the final result, so check out the headnote for each recipe and my Goood to Know tips for more guidance.** See page 339 for quick charts for staples, proteins, and plant-based substitutions.

Shop It

Once you've chosen your meals, made your grocery list, and shopped your kitchen, it's time to hit the store for the few items you may still need for the week.

RULES TO SHOP BY

- ☐ Shop with a plan and list **already made**.
- ☐ Buy on sale **or in bulk when possible**.
- ☐ Opt for **in-season produce**.
- ☐ Go for **repeat, familiar, budget-friendly staples**.
- ☐ Prioritize **whole food ingredients** over processed foods.

Go to page 16 for my shoppable grocery list, where you can see my commonly used ingredients in one spot and build your own list from there.

QUICK MONEY-SAVING TIPS

1. **Buy in bulk:** Stock up on oils, nuts, seeds, grains, beans, frozen produce, and proteins in bulk. Depending on your budget and storage space, do this when you can.

2. **Take advantage of sales:** Buy discounted items that can be stored for extended periods of time in the pantry or freezer when you spot them. Even if it's not part of your meal plan for the week, stocking up and storing will pay off later.

3. **Go for cheaper cuts and sources of protein:** Some of my favorite budget-friendly proteins include tofu, chickpeas, chicken thighs, ground pork, and cottage cheese. Buying in bulk and freezing can also help you enjoy some pricier proteins, like fish and red meat.

4. **Utilize seasonal produce:** When fruits and vegetables are in season, they are typically priced lower (and easier to find). In general, packing your meals with plants can help bring more volume at a lower cost. See page 338 for a seasonal produce guide.

5. **Get multi-use ingredients:** Prioritize meals with ingredients that can be used in multiple ways throughout the week. For example, when a recipe leaves you with half a bag of spinach left over, find another recipe that uses up the rest. My weekly dinner plans (p. 42) were designed this way.

6. **Do a weekly fridge cleanout:** Make it a weekly habit before making your plan and heading to the store. This way you won't worry about perishable items hiding in the back, ensuring they get used up and money isn't wasted (you can even do a fridge-cleanout meal, like a stir-fry or frittata).

Swap & Save

There are endless ways to cut down your total at the grocery store, but some are easier to do than others. I try to make budget-conscious choices whenever possible—sometimes that means reaching for frozen veggies over fresh ones, and other times it's making a convenience swap, like grabbing whole fruit instead of precut. Making things like dressings, sauces, and spreads at home rather than buying them premade saves money. Evaluate your priorities: Do you want shorter prep time? Cost savings? Nutritional value? Decide what's important and go from there. Some of my suggested swaps for slashing grocery costs are below.

SUBSTITUTE GUIDE: BUDGET-FRIENDLY SWAPS

SWAP THIS	FOR THAT
Precut vegetables	Whole vegetables
Precut fruit	Whole fruit
Fresh berries	Frozen berries
Fresh vegetables	Frozen vegetables
Fresh tomatoes	Canned tomatoes
Bottled salad dressing	Homemade salad dressing
Preshredded cheese	Blocks of cheese
Chicken breasts	Chicken thighs
Canned beans	Dried beans in bulk
Microwavable rice packets	Dry rice in bulk
Fresh herbs	Dried herbs
Cartons of low-sodium broth	Water and bouillon
Cartons of nut or oat milk	Homemade nut or oat milk
Pine nuts	Walnuts

Prep It

After the planning, stocking, and shopping, it's time for meal prep. Things can get so busy during the week, but even if I'm short on time, I want tasty meals in the fridge! Meal prep is all about making things I'm *excited* to eat during the week. If I'm not psyched for what's waiting for me, I'll be tempted to let the ingredients or meals I prep sit around while I order takeout.

A little prepping gives you the power to take control of your weeks, eliminate mealtime-decision fatigue, and ensure that a nourishing option makes it to your plate at the end of the day. But even with our best intentions, meal prepping can still feel like too much work. **My strategy is simple and flexible—prepping one to two breakfast options and one to two lunch options per week makes a world of difference and creates a good routine, with easily accessible tools and directions to follow.** Dinners are planned for, but not necessarily prepped ahead—unless you want to (just follow my Store It and Reheat It directions within each recipe!). Want to add on snacks and sips for the week? You'll also find storing and reheating tips in those chapters.

Food Safety Guidelines

PROTEINS

Always prepare proteins according to USDA food safety guidelines to ensure it is cooked to the right temperature and refrigerated promptly. Cook to these minimum internal temperatures as measured with an instant-read food thermometer.

PRODUCT	MINIMAL INTERNAL TEMPERATURE
Beef and pork	145°F
Ground meats	160°F
Ground poultry	165°F
Poultry (breasts, whole, legs, thighs, wings)	165°F
Eggs	160°F
Fish and shellfish	145°F

FDA FOOD SAFETY GUIDELINES

- [ ] Keep cooked foods covered and store appropriately as soon as they are cooled.
- [ ] Store refrigerated foods in covered containers or sealed storage bags and check leftovers daily for spoilage.
- [ ] Store eggs in their carton in the refrigerator itself rather than on the door, where the temperature is warmer.
- [ ] Check canned goods for damage.
- [ ] Pack leftovers in tightly sealed containers for 3 to 4 days or freeze for up to 3 months.
- [ ] When reheating leftovers, be sure they reach 165°F as measured with an instant-read food thermometer.

For more detailed information, I recommend checking the full FDA and USDA guidelines.

THE BEST WAY TO REHEAT FOOD

An air fryer is one of my favorite ways to reheat dishes with roasted vegetables or proteins. It helps food regain some of the crispness it loses in the fridge, but an oven also works. I use the stovetop to reheat soup and sauces. A microwave oven is always a quick and easy reheating option

When reheating leftovers, be sure they reach 165°F as measured with an instant-read food thermometer. Reheat sauces, soups, and gravies by bringing them to a boil, and simmer or use immediately. Cover dishes when reheating. This retains moisture and ensures that food will heat all the way through.

WHERE TO START: BREAKFAST & LUNCH MEAL PREP

WHEN YOU'RE LOW ON TIME OR ENERGY

Hidden Protein Smashed Avocado Toast (p. 88)

Peanut Butter and Banana Smoothie (p. 63)

Banana-Chai Smoothie (p. 63)

Strawberry-Basil Smoothie (p. 63)

Orange Cream Smoothie (p. 63)

Pesto and Roasted Red Pepper Egg Casserole (p. 83)

Chipotle Sweet Potato and Black Bean Bowls (p. 113)

Greek-Style Crispy Chickpea Bowls (p. 118)

Roasted Brussels Sprouts, Sweet Potato, and Beet Salad (p. 92)

WHEN YOU NEED MORE VEGGIES IN YOUR LIFE

Hidden Veggie Oat Bars (p. 70)

Chipotle Sweet Potato Breakfast Hash (p. 84)

Leek, Potato, and Goat Cheese Frittata (p. 86)

Golden Turmeric Herby Quinoa Salad (p. 99)

Crispy Quinoa, Peanut, and Edamame Salad (p. 105)

Farmers' Market Lentil Salad (p. 96)

Cilantro-Lime Pasta Salad (p. 101)

WHEN YOU DON'T WANT TO TURN THE OVEN ON

Cookie Dough Overnight Oats (p. 61)

Lemon-Blueberry Overnight Oats (p. 62)

Coconut-Mango Chia Pudding (p. 67)

Dark Chocolate and Raspberry Chia Pudding (p. 68)

Vanilla-Almond Chia Pudding (p. 69)

Mediterranean-Inspired Chickpea Chopped Salad (p. 95)

Barbecue Chicken Chopped Salad (p. 117)

WHEN YOU'RE FOCUSING ON PROTEIN

Cheesy Pork, Pepper, and Onion Breakfast Biscuits (p. 73)

Broccoli, Cheddar, and Chicken Breakfast Biscuits (p. 74)

Bacon and Chive Egg Muffins (p. 77)

Goat Cheese and Kale Egg Muffins (p. 77)

Sheet Pan Black Bean Breakfast Burritos (p. 79)

Crunchy Pork Lettuce Wraps with Carrot Slaw (p. 108)

Spicy Tofu Crunch Bowls (p. 111)

Pineapple-Shrimp Lettuce Wraps (p. 106)

TIPS TO MAKE MEAL PREP EASIER

Get going after grocery shopping: Do some prep as soon as you get home from grocery shopping. I know that going to the store, buying groceries, lugging them home, and putting them away is a lot—and I'm sure the last thing you want to do is start prepping food. But I swear, if you do, you'll feel like a hero, and you'll be that much closer to having meals for the week ready to go.

Cook once, eat twice: As an alternative to traditional meal prep—when you're already making yourself a meal, double everything and save half for tomorrow! That's meal prep with basically no extra work.

Ingredient prep: If you're not a fan of eating the same meal multiple times, don't prep full meals ahead of time; prep individual ingredients so you can build different meals with those elements—think cooked proteins, grains, vegetables, and sauces that can be assembled in different ways.

Get ahead: Take a little bit of time the night before or in the morning you're planning to cook a meal so you can save time when you're ready to make dinner. Having partially prepped marinated proteins, chopped veggies, or sauces makes me much less likely to default to girl dinner or order takeout. No oven required!

Set a timer: When you have some free time (or right when you get back from the grocery store), set a timer for 30 to 90 minutes and just do what you can in that time—you'll be surprised by how much you can accomplish!

Loving leftovers: If you're using your leftovers for lunches the next day, pack your lunches in containers before you serve and eat dinner. Then you won't have to worry about packaging up everything after you've eaten, because everything's already perfectly portioned out and you have lunch all ready to go. Game changer!

Store It

MEAL-PREP STORAGE EQUIPMENT

The right meal-prep equipment is critical to make your work in the kitchen as efficient and effortless as possible. The following is a list of the basic meal-prep equipment I swear by, but don't worry, I've got you covered with all the gear you need. Check out my extensive kitchen equipment list on page 40, where I've broken down everything you might need into basics, specialty tools for easier prep, and storage solutions.

Sauce cups with lids: 2½-ounce cups. When I'm prepping something with a sauce or dressing that can't be mixed in until right before, small sauce cups always come in handy. I also use them for other small items I'm storing in the fridge, like chopped herbs or nuts.

Glass jars with bamboo lids: 10-ounce or 12-ounce jars. For overnight oats and chia pudding, I love using glass jars with bamboo lids. They're the perfect size, and when I'm done, they're very easy to clean. Another great option is 16-ounce mason jars. These also come in handy for sauces and dressings!

Resealable silicone storage bags: 1-gallon, ½-gallon, and sandwich-size bags. Silicone bags make prepping and transporting individual elements or meals so easy, and they're my favorite for storing muffins and biscuits, plus marinating meat.

Silicone freezer trays: 1-cup or 2-cup trays. These are handy for leftover coconut milk, broth, soups, and sauces that freeze well.

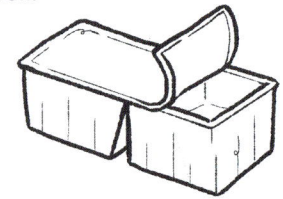

Glass container set with snap lids: 8-cup, 5-cup, and 3-cup containers. I'm passionate about these for storing prepped meals and ingredients, so they go to the top of the list. They're great because you can easily see what's inside, reheating is easy, and snap lids provide a tight seal.

See page 31 for more information on safely storing and reheating food.

MEAL STORAGE, FREEZING & REHEATING GUIDE

- Each recipe is followed by **Store It** and **Reheat It** instructions to help you prep meals and manage leftovers.

- When I'm prepping and storing something with multiple ingredients, I follow the FDA guidelines and USDA food safety rules as closely as possible. The general rule for cooked meals is to refrigerate in a tightly sealed container for 3 to 4 days or freeze for up to 3 months.

For more detailed information, I recommend checking the full FDA and USDA guidelines.

Keep At It

By implementing these planning, shopping, and prepping tools each week, you'll build your kitchen skills, stamp out mealtime dread, and create an easy routine. Like most good routines, they will become easier and more automatic over time, bringing positive change to your life. Follow the dinner plans on page 42 if you need a place to start.

Incorporating a few of or all of these steps can make your life easier, your meals tastier and healthier, and your budget on track. Remember, we're not going for perfection or pressure! Any step you take is a positive step. **"Goood enough" is an important mantra to sustain the sustainable!**

Life is about balance, and a few days or even weeks off from your healthiest habits won't make a significant difference overall. You may value your routine and the peace it brings to your life even more when you come back to it.

ROADBLOCKS TO YOUR ROUTINE: THE WHAT-IF?

WHAT IF I don't have enough time?

To cut down on time, consider using one of my twelve premade dinner plans and grocery lists, which start on page 42. If you want to meal-prep, schedule in the time you can spare and prep just one to three things; figure out where to start by checking out "Breakfast Blueprint" (page 58). It doesn't have to be all or nothing—a little bit of planning and prep can make a world of difference.

WHAT IF my plans change?

Being flexible is important, so that's why I recommend planning only five dinner options for the week, so you can account for an unexpected dinner out, a busy workday, or a surprise family commitment. You know yourself best, so make your weeks as planned out or as loose as you want. Having options that can be put into the freezer helps with this too.

WHAT IF I get bored with meal-prepped food?

Meal prep can mean making full meals ahead or just getting ahead on some veggie chopping. Do what you prefer! I always recommend ingredient prep to meal-prep skeptics—where you prep individual components like proteins, grains, veggies, or sauces rather than full meals. You can enjoy the easy, healthy meals in this book while never prepping a single step!

WHAT IF I hate reheated food?

Don't prep things that need to be reheated! Just take some extra time to chop up your produce or measure out the ingredients you'll need for meals during the week. I also have a variety of no-reheating-necessary options for you in "Breakfast Blueprint" (page 58) and "Quick Lunches, Upgraded" (page 90), as well as snacks, sips, and desserts.

WHAT IF I have dietary restrictions?

Restrictions can add an extra barrier to getting excited about meal planning and prep, but knowing what you're going to eat all week alleviates anxiety and indecision. Be sure to reference my substitution charts on page 339 and the dietary key within each recipe, which will help accommodate most diets.

WHAT IF I hate going to the grocery store?

A lot of the grocery store hate comes from panic and overwhelm, so going in with a plan is your first step. Next, romanticize your shopping routine and make it fun. Challenge yourself to include recipes in your meal plan that feature ingredients you don't normally eat, pushing you to venture down new aisles. And when you need to, there's nothing wrong with getting your items delivered.

WHAT IF I'm tired of picking out meals every week?

Well, my friend, you're definitely in the right place, because I've done the work for you! All you need to do is follow along. With more than 125 inventive recipes in this book, you'll be set with a variety of breakfast, lunch, and dinner options (plus snacks, treats, and more!).

WHAT IF I'm overwhelmed by it all?

I hear you! If you're starting from scratch, this can feel like a lot. Break it down into small pieces and take on something new each week. Start on page 11 to learn how to make a meal plan, and call that step one. From there, you'll feel more empowered to pick up a meal-prep day, start stocking up the freezer, and participate in a weekly inventory check.

Get Cooking!

Most of these recipes were created specifically for the book, but I couldn't leave out the top fan favorites from @jenneatsgoood. You'll find a range of flavors throughout, inspired by cuisines across the globe and familiar ones found in my modern takes on traditional comfort-food favorites. Every recipe is naturally gluten-free, and virtually all recipes can be modified to be dairy-free, vegetarian, and often vegan.

So now that you have a guide and tools to help you strategize, reduce stress, stay on budget, and be healthy, get ready for the nutritious, plant- and protein-forward recipes that are easy to prepare and never skimp on flavor—in other words, the dishes you will find inspiration in and become obsessed with, the same way I have.

XO, Jenn

RECIPE KEY

Dietary labels: Each recipe is labeled if it is Dairy-Free, Gluten-Free, Vegetarian, Vegan, or Nut-Free. I also have tips in the recipes for making adjustments to suit your needs.

Goood to Know: These tips follow each recipe. They're my tried-and-true shortcuts, swaps, and hacks.

Store It: These instructions show how to store prepped food and leftovers and advise which can be frozen and which should stay in the fridge.

Reheat It: I've shared the optimal way to reheat a recipe and included the best way and time range to either prep the recipe or enjoy later.

BEST PRACTICES

Read the recipe: I know it sounds obvious, but I cannot stress this enough. Read the recipe from the start of the headnote and all the Goood to Know tips, so you know exactly what you're expected to do *before* you start cooking. I packed every recipe full of helpful information!

Measure or weigh all recipe ingredients: And lay them out on the counter before you begin using them in the recipe. You'll be ahead of the game and keep a cleaner workspace. (This is what chefs call mise en place, which means "everything in its place.")

Set up your cutting board: Place a wet paper towel under your clean cutting board to keep the board from slipping around dangerously while you cut.

Lay out your knives and equipment: Pots, pans, blender, large spoons, spatulas, and whisks—have them all ready to go.

Keep the cleanup close by: Leave a bowl for food scraps next to your cutting board. Your floor will thank you.

BASIC KNIFE SKILLS

If you don't know your way around a knife or you're not sure of the difference between chopped, diced, and sliced, here's a quick guide to boost your confidence and skills. This will reduce stress, ensure a successful recipe, and make you a better cook.

Chop: Each piece is cut to a similar size. Roughly chopped pieces are generally about ¾ inch, chopped are about ½ inch, and finely chopped are about ¼ inch.

Dice: More precisely measured and carefully cut, these pieces often need to cook more evenly and consistently. Large dice are ¾ inch, medium dice are ½ inch, and small dice are ¼ inch.

Mince: A very fine dice, as small as possible, between ⅛ and 1/16 inch, often used for garlic.

Slice: Cut across the length or width of an ingredient. Slices vary in thickness depending on the effect you're going for. This can range from ⅛- to 1-inch pieces of everything from onions to steak.

HOW TO GET IT DONE

EQUIPMENT ESSENTIALS

Having the right equipment on hand is essential to make your work in the kitchen as efficient as possible. My philosophy is balance, the right tool for the right job, and consider what's frivolous and not that useful (cherry pitter? How often is that happening?), what's fun, and so on. I've broken down everything you might need into basics (including prep, tools and utensils, stovetop and oven needs, bakeware, equipment and tools, and storage solutions). For Meal-Prep Storage Equipment, see page 34.

EVERYDAY GEAR

- Cutting board, preferably 14 × 14-inch wooden
- Knives: chef's knife (8-inch), paring (4-inch), serrated (9-inch)
- Measuring cups and spoons
- Mixing bowl set: small, medium, large

STOVETOP & OVEN COOKWARE

- Small lidded saucepan or pot
- Small 3.5-quart lidded sauté pan
- Large (6-quart) lidded pot or Dutch oven
- Large (10- or 12-inch), deep, lidded, oven-safe sauté pan
- Large (10- or 12-inch) nonstick skillet

- Large (10- or 12-inch) stainless steel or cast-iron skillet
- Small (13 × 9-inch) quarter sheet pan
- Large (18 × 13-inch) half sheet pan

TOOLS & UTENSILS

- Box grater
- Kitchen shears
- Large spoons—metal and wooden
- Microplane grater
- Potato masher
- Fine-mesh sieves, large and small
- Slotted spatula or turner
- Silicone/rubber spatulas, assorted sizes
- Tongs
- Whisk

BAKEWARE & MORE

- Baking dishes: 9 × 13-inch and 9 × 9-inch ceramic or glass
- Cookie scoops: 1, 2, and 3 tablespoons
- Cooling rack

- Metal skewers: 8-inch
- 12-cup nonstick muffin pan
- Rolling pin
- 1.5- to 2-quart ceramic gratin dish

EQUIPMENT & TOOLS

- Blender and/or immersion blender
- Parchment and aluminum foil
- 5-cup (or larger) food processor
- Instant-read meat thermometer
- 6-quart slow cooker
- Stand mixer or handheld electric mixer

In addition to general kitchen tools and equipment, see more meal-prep storage solutions and equipment on page 34.

Skirt Steak with Chimichurri (p. 259)

12 WEEKS OF DINNER PLANS & GROCERY LISTS

If you're already following along with @jenneatsgoood on social media or you subscribe to my newsletter, you know how this works. If not, let me give you the lowdown! The twelve dinner plans each have an exciting theme to keep things interesting. **The plans are designed to give you five dinner recipes for the week, each serving four people.** Follow the plans that work for your lifestyle and your appetite. Household of two? Do what I do: Follow the dinner plan for each weeknight and eat the leftovers for lunch the next day. Living alone? You can absolutely follow along and take advantage of your freezer, because I've provided storage methods for every single recipe. Remember, you can always add on your breakfast and/or lunch meal prep by flipping to "Breakfast Blueprint" (page 58) or "Quick Lunches, Upgraded" (page 90) to choose from a variety of prep-ahead-friendly options. If following these plans doesn't work for you, just flip to the dinner recipe sections, which begin on page 58, to see *all* the dinner possibilities and choose what you want to make! Take the journey that works best for you.

What's extra helpful is that these plans aren't random. **They were designed so that all your groceries from the corresponding grocery lists are used, with no waste. The lists are color coded so you can easily see which ingredients are used for each recipe.** No half cans of coconut milk here! I intentionally developed each one to fit into its respective list and streamline your grocery shopping. Go in order, jump around, or pick out a list that already covers some ingredients you have on hand! Once you select your list and groceries, you can find the page numbers for the corresponding recipe.

THE DINNER PLANS

Better-Than-Takeout Week (p. 44)
Dairy-Free Favorites Week (p. 45)
Comfort Classics Week (p. 46)
Budget-Friendly Week (p. 47)
Winter Vibes Week (p. 48)
Spring Vibes Week (p. 49)

Summer Vibes Week (p. 50)
Autumn Vibes Week (p. 51)
Perfectly Plant-Based Week (p. 52)
10 Ingredients (or Less) Week (p. 53)
Vacay Mode Week (p. 54)
Jenn's Top Hits Week (p. 55)

Scan the QR code to download the grocery lists to your device.

BETTER-THAN-TAKEOUT WEEK

In the moment, ordering takeout feels like a way to make life easier, but is it? I'm challenging that with this crave-worthy menu of affordable, nutritious, and quick alternatives. When you realize you can easily whip up a steak and cheese skillet or pot of coconut curry soup in about 30 minutes, you won't even be tempted by ordering out. You'll know what ingredients are going in and you can make it your own.

DINNERS

- **Red Curry Noodles with Sautéed Green Onion and Pork** (p. 163)
- **Sticky Sesame Tofu** (p. 238) + **Jenn's Steamed Rice** (p. 290) + **Sesame-Crisped Brussels Sprouts** (p. 285)
- **Coconut Curry Soup with Tofu and Rice Noodles** (p. 224)
- **Caramelized Onion, Steak, and Cheese Skillet** (p. 152)
- **Mediterranean-Inspired Smashed Tacos** (p. 264) + **Cucumber Garlicky Sauce** (p. 299)

PRODUCE

- 2 garlic bulbs
- 2 green onion bunches
- 2 large yellow onions
- 1 pound Brussels sprouts
- 20 ounces white mushrooms
- 2 small cucumbers
- 2 green bell peppers
- 1 red bell pepper
- 2 small Roma (plum) tomatoes
- 2 lemons
- 1 lime
- 1 cilantro bunch
- ½ ounce dill
- ½ ounce mint

PROTEINS

- 1 pound ground lamb (85% lean)
- 1 pound ground pork (90% lean)
- 14 ounces shaved Angus steak
- Two 14-ounce blocks firm tofu

CANNED/PACKAGED

- 13.5-ounce can full-fat coconut milk
- Thai red curry paste (2 tablespoons needed)
- Two 32-ounce cartons low-sodium vegetable broth
- Jasmine rice (1 cup needed)
- 14 ounces stir-fry rice noodles
- Eight 6-inch corn tortillas, almond flour tortillas, or flour tortillas

DAIRY & SUBSTITUTES

- 8 ounces whole-milk or low-fat Greek yogurt or plain dairy-free yogurt
- 3 ounces crumbled feta cheese
- 6 ounces mozzarella cheese

PANTRY STAPLES

- Avocado oil
- Olive oil
- Toasted sesame oil
- Rice vinegar
- Coconut aminos*
- Pure maple syrup
- Tapioca flour or arrowroot starch†

SPICES

- Kosher salt
- Ground black pepper
- Ground cumin
- Garlic powder
- Ground ginger
- Dried oregano
- Sesame seeds
- Smoked paprika

---

* *Can substitute reduced-sodium tamari or reduced-sodium soy sauce (soy sauce typically includes gluten).*
† *Can substitute cornstarch.*

DAIRY-FREE FAVORITES WEEK

Whether or not you eat dairy, this decadent but nutritious dinner plan will leave you feeling satisfied, surely not missing the cheese and milk! While there are lots of dairy-free meals throughout the book, I compiled my top picks into one delicious menu for you. Don't blame me if you're hooked on coconut milk—my go-to sub for cream—after the week is over.

DINNERS

- **Marry Me Turkey Meatballs** (p. 182)
- **One-Pot Creamy Sun-Dried Tomato Pasta** (p. 148)
- **Skirt Steak with Chimichurri** (p. 259) + **Crispy Japanese Sweet Potato Wedges** (p. 286)
- **Salmon Bites with Coconut Rice and Chilled Cucumber Salad** (p. 217)
- **Mashed Chipotle Chickpea Quesadillas** (p. 244)*

PRODUCE

- 1 garlic bulb
- 1 medium shallot
- 1 green onion bunch
- 2-inch piece fresh ginger
- 2 large or 3 medium Japanese sweet potatoes
- 4 ounces baby spinach
- 1 English cucumber
- 1 lemon
- 1 lime
- 1 large basil bunch (3 ounces needed)
- 1 parsley bunch

PROTEINS

- 1 pound ground turkey (93% lean)
- 1½ pounds skirt steak or flank steak
- 1½ pounds skinless salmon fillets
- Two 15-ounce cans chickpeas

CANNED/PACKAGED

- 7-ounce can chipotle peppers in adobo sauce
- 13.5-ounce can full-fat coconut milk
- 13.5-ounce can light coconut milk
- 8-ounce jar sun-dried tomatoes, oil-packed
- 48-ounce carton low-sodium vegetable or chicken broth
- 12 ounces brown rice rigatoni†
- Jasmine rice (2 cups needed)
- Eight 6-inch almond flour or flour tortillas
- 4-ounce bag nutritional yeast (2 tablespoons needed)

DAIRY & SUBSTITUTES

- 6 ounces shredded dairy-free cheese or Cheddar cheese

PANTRY STAPLES

- Avocado oil
- Olive oil
- Toasted sesame oil
- Red wine vinegar
- Rice vinegar
- Coconut aminos‡
- Pure maple syrup
- Sriracha

SPICES

- Kosher salt
- Ground black pepper
- Garlic powder
- Onion powder
- Dried oregano
- Red pepper flakes (optional)
- Sesame seeds
- Smoked paprika

* *I like to serve these with Chickpea Guacamole (p. 128)—add the ingredients to your grocery list if you want to add it on!*
† *Can substitute rice-and-corn-based or regular rigatoni.*
‡ *Can substitute reduced-sodium tamari or reduced-sodium soy sauce (soy sauce typically includes gluten).*

COMFORT CLASSICS WEEK

If there's one type of recipe I love creating most, it's healthier versions of my favorite comfort foods. That's because dishes like lasagna, chili, and chicken Parm were what I grew up enjoying most (I was a picky eater!). This week is all about taking those familiar, cozy tastes and giving them a little boost. Enjoy a menu that feels decadent but actually packs in lots of plants and protein.

DINNERS

- **Deconstructed Turkey Lasagna Skillet** (p. 188)
- **Maple-Dijon Pork Tenderloin** (p. 212) + **Roasted Garlic Mashed Potatoes** (p. 280)
- **Grain-Free Chicken Parmesan** (p. 275)*
- **Spiced Lamb Meatballs with Tomato-Cucumber Salad** (p. 164)†
- **Mom's Game-Day Chili with Sweet Honey Bread** (p. 206)‡

PRODUCE

2 garlic bulbs
1 large yellow onion
2 pounds russet potatoes (about 4 medium)
4 ounces baby spinach
1 English cucumber
2 green bell peppers
1 pint cherry tomatoes
1 lemon
1 basil bunch
1 parsley bunch

PROTEINS

½ dozen (6) large eggs
1 pound ground beef (85% lean)
1 pound ground lamb (85% lean)
1 pound ground turkey (93% lean)
2 pounds boneless, skinless chicken breasts
1½ pounds pork tenderloin
15-ounce can kidney beans

CANNED/PACKAGED

28-ounce can crushed tomatoes
Dijon mustard (2 tablespoons needed)
Two 24-ounce jars marinara sauce
32-ounce carton low-sodium chicken broth
12 ounces brown rice farfalle pasta**
Blanched almond flour (3¼ cups needed)

DAIRY & SUBSTITUTES

1 pint milk of choice†† (1 cup needed)
15 ounces part-skim ricotta cheese
5 ounces grated Parmesan
3 ounces crumbled feta cheese
6 ounces mozzarella cheese
2 sticks unsalted butter or unsalted vegan butter (12 tablespoons needed)

PANTRY STAPLES

Avocado oil
Olive oil
Apple cider vinegar
Red wine vinegar
Raw honey
Pure maple syrup
Coconut aminos‡‡
Tapioca flour or arrowroot starch***
Baking powder
Baking soda

SPICES

Kosher salt
Ground black pepper
Dried basil
Chili powder
Garlic powder
Ground coriander
Ground cumin
Dried oregano
Red pepper flakes (optional)
Dried rosemary
Smoked paprika

---

* *Option to serve with cooked pasta or vegetables of your choice—just add to your grocery list!*
† *I like to serve these with Cucumber Garlicky Sauce (p. 299)—add the ingredients to your grocery list if you want it for dipping!*
‡ *Optional chili toppings include sliced green onion, shredded cheese, and sour cream—add to your grocery list if you'd like!*
** *Can substitute rice-and-corn-based or regular farfalle.*
†† *Preferably whole milk; can substitute soy milk, nut milk, or oat milk.*
‡‡ *Can substitute reduced-sodium tamari or reduced-sodium soy sauce (soy sauce typically includes gluten).*
*** *Can substitute cornstarch.*

BUDGET-FRIENDLY WEEK

While I always try to keep cost in mind when creating meal plans, this week is designed to be particularly budget-friendly. By relying on some pantry favorites like beans, rice, coconut milk, and a variety of spices, each dinner stretches your dollar while maximizing flavor.

DINNERS

- **Sweet and Spicy Tofu and Broccolini** (p. 168)*
- **Lemony Chicken Thighs and Rice** (p. 136)
- **Tomato-Basil Saucy Butter Bean Skillet** (p. 243)
- **Baked Black Bean and Poblano Tacos** (p. 215) + **Creamy Cilantro Sauce** (p. 294)
- **Herby Chickpea and Cauliflower Bowls with Lemon-Dill Sauce** (p. 174)

PRODUCE

1 garlic bulb
1 large yellow onion
1 medium shallot
16 ounces broccolini
1 medium cauliflower head (or 10-ounce bag of florets)
10 ounces shredded curly kale
2 medium poblano peppers
2 lemons
2 limes
1 basil bunch
1 cilantro bunch
½ ounce dill
1 parsley bunch

PROTEINS

1½ pounds boneless, skinless chicken thighs
16-ounce block high-protein super-firm tofu
Two 15-ounce cans black beans
Two 15-ounce cans butter beans
Two 15-ounce cans chickpeas

CANNED/PACKAGED

13.5-ounce can full-fat coconut milk
28-ounce can crushed tomatoes
16-ounce carton low-sodium chicken broth
Jasmine rice (2 cups needed)
Twelve 6-inch corn, almond flour, or chickpea flour tortillas
Nutritional yeast (¼ cup needed)

DAIRY & SUBSTITUTES

16 ounces whole-milk or low-fat Greek yogurt or plain dairy-free yogurt
6 ounces Cheddar cheese

PANTRY STAPLES

Olive oil
Toasted sesame oil
Rice vinegar
Coconut aminos†
Pure maple syrup
Sriracha
Tapioca flour or arrowroot starch‡

SPICES

Kosher salt
Ground black pepper
Dried basil
Chili powder
Ground cumin
Garlic powder
Ground ginger
Dried oregano
Dried parsley
Smoked paprika

* Option to serve with Jenn's Steamed Rice (p. 290)—just add 1 more cup of rice to your grocery list!
† Can substitute reduced-sodium tamari or reduced-sodium soy sauce (soy sauce typically includes gluten).
‡ Can substitute cornstarch.

WINTER VIBES WEEK

When the cold air hits and my windows are plastered in ice every morning, the only thing that keeps me excited is beautiful winter produce. With kale, broccoli, lemon, and carrots, plus fresh herbs and warming spices, each recipe brings the cozy flavors we all crave in the chilly months. Think spicy soup, creamy risotto—meals best enjoyed curled up on the couch.

DINNERS

- **Spicy Sausage, White Bean, and Kale Soup** (p. 172)
- **Hidden Veggie Spaghetti with Crispy Kale and Sausage** (p. 273)
- **Slow Cooker Short Ribs** (p. 253) + **"Cheesy" Polenta** (p. 282)
- **Garlicky Mushroom and Sage Risotto** (p. 256)
- **Saucy Beef and Broccoli** (p. 180)*

PRODUCE

- 1 garlic bulb
- 1 green onion bunch
- 2 large yellow onions
- 7 large carrots
- 1 celery heart
- 1 large broccoli head (or 10-ounce bag of florets)
- 10 ounces shredded curly kale
- 12 ounces mushrooms (wild, Baby Bella, shiitake, or oyster)
- ½ ounce fresh rosemary
- ½ ounce fresh thyme

PROTEINS

- 1 pound ground hot Italian sausage or chicken sausage
- 3 pounds bone-in beef short ribs (4 large ribs)
- 1 pound flank steak
- 15.5-ounce can cannellini, navy, or Great Northern beans

CANNED/PACKAGED

- 13.5-ounce can full-fat coconut milk
- 28-ounce can crushed tomatoes
- 32-ounce carton low-sodium beef broth
- 32-ounce carton low-sodium chicken or vegetable broth
- 32-ounce carton low-sodium vegetable broth
- Arborio rice (2 cups needed)
- 14 ounces brown rice spaghetti†
- Stone-ground yellow-corn instant polenta (1 cup needed)
- Nutritional yeast (¼ cup needed)
- Tomato paste (3 tablespoons needed)

DAIRY & SUBSTITUTES

- 1 pint milk of choice‡
- 5 ounces grated Parmesan

PANTRY STAPLES

- Olive oil
- Balsamic vinegar
- Coconut aminos**
- Sriracha (optional)
- Tapioca flour or arrowroot starch††

SPICES

- Kosher salt
- Ground black pepper
- Garlic powder
- Ground ginger
- Dried oregano
- Red pepper flakes (optional)
- Ground sage
- Sesame seeds (optional)
- Dried thyme

* Option to serve with Jenn's Steamed Rice (p. 290)—just add 1 cup jasmine rice to your grocery list!
† Can substitute rice-and-corn-based or regular spaghetti.
‡ Can choose preferred unsweetened milk: nut milk, soy milk, oat milk, or whole milk.
** Can substitute reduced-sodium tamari or reduced-sodium soy sauce (soy sauce typically includes gluten).
†† Can substitute cornstarch.

SPRING VIBES WEEK

Springtime brings bright flavors and zesty dishes that wake up your taste with citrus, seasonal green veggies, and unique uses of proteins. You'll use my dairy-free walnut pesto in two ways—save time and prep a double batch! Also, discover my shockingly high-protein pizza crust and one-pan dishes to make on repeat.

DINNERS

- **Mediterranean-Inspired Salmon and Orzo Bake** (p. 147)
- **Sheet Pan Pesto Pizza with Asparagus and Prosciutto** (p. 201) + **Dairy-Free Walnut Pesto** (p. 301)
- **Lemon-Caper Shrimp and Linguine** (p. 266)
- **Creamy Lemon Pesto Pasta with Walnut Crumbs** (p. 228) + **Dairy-Free Walnut Pesto** (p. 301)
- **Creamy Spinach Chicken** (p. 196)

PRODUCE

- 2 garlic bulbs
- 2 medium shallots
- 12 ounces asparagus
- 6 ounces baby spinach
- 10 ounces fresh or frozen green peas
- 1 pint cherry tomatoes
- 4 lemons
- 2 large basil bunches (5 ounces needed)*
- 1 parsley bunch

PROTEINS

- 2 pounds boneless, skinless chicken breasts
- Four 4-ounce skinless salmon fillets
- 1 pound fresh or frozen medium peeled and deveined raw shrimp
- 3 ounces prosciutto
- 8 ounces unsalted raw walnuts

CANNED/PACKAGED

- 2-ounce jar capers
- 13.5-ounce can full-fat coconut milk
- Pitted Kalamata olives (½ cup needed)
- Two 32-ounce cartons low-sodium chicken or vegetable broth
- 12 ounces brown rice linguine†
- 12 ounces brown rice spaghetti‡
- 8 ounces gluten-free orzo**
- Gluten-free 1:1 baking flour (about 2 cups needed)††
- Nutritional yeast (½ cup needed)

DAIRY & SUBSTITUTES

- 16-ounce container whole-milk or low-fat Greek yogurt (1¼ cups needed)
- 15-ounce container part-skim ricotta cheese
- 5 ounces grated Parmesan
- 8-ounce block feta cheese
- 8 ounces mozzarella cheese

PANTRY STAPLES

- Olive oil
- Tapioca flour or arrowroot starch‡‡
- Baking powder

SPICES

- Kosher salt
- Ground black pepper
- Dried basil
- Chili powder
- Garlic powder
- Dried oregano

---

* Option to use store-bought pesto and skip the fresh basil and the nutritional yeast. You will only need ½ cup walnuts total if using premade pesto for the pizza and the pasta.
† Can substitute rice-and-corn-based or regular linguine.
‡ Can substitute rice-and-corn-based or regular spaghetti.
** Can substitute regular orzo.
†† Can substitute all-purpose flour.
‡‡ Can substitute cornstarch.

SUMMER VIBES WEEK

Summer is all about a beautiful rainbow of juicy seasonal produce, best enjoyed on a patio or back porch. Dig into these shareable, warm-weather recipes that each taste like they take a lot more work than they do—so you can spend your time connecting rather than standing over the stove. This menu is so good you'll find yourself repeating it all year long! Is there ever a wrong time to make carnitas tacos and Greek chicken skewers?

DINNERS

- **Slow Cooker Carnitas Tacos with Pineapple Salsa** (p. 209)
- **Street-Corn-Inspired Shrimp Skillet** (p. 166)
- **Greek-Style Chicken and Vegetable Skewers** (p. 191) **+ Cucumber Garlicky Sauce** (p. 299)
- **Blackened Swordfish with Mango Salsa** (p. 268)
- **Sheet Pan Barbecue Chicken and Pineapple Lettuce Cups** (p. 179) **+ Tangy Maple Barbecue Sauce** (p. 298)

PRODUCE

1 garlic bulb
1 green onion bunch
2 medium red onions
1 large yellow onion
16 ounces frozen corn kernels*
1 Bibb or butter lettuce head
1 ripe avocado
1 small cucumber
1 ripe mango
1 small pineapple or two 20-ounce cans diced pineapple
3 red bell peppers
1 jalapeño pepper
1 medium zucchini
2 lemons
9 limes
2 medium oranges
2 cilantro bunches

PROTEINS

4 pounds boneless, skinless chicken thighs
2 to 2½ pounds boneless pork shoulder or butt
1 pound fresh or frozen medium peeled and deveined raw shrimp
Four 6-ounce swordfish steaks

CANNED/PACKAGED

13.5-ounce can full-fat coconut milk (1 cup needed†)
Tomato paste (¼ cup needed)
Twelve 6-inch corn, almond flour, or chickpea flour tortillas

DAIRY & SUBSTITUTES

16 ounces whole-milk or low-fat Greek yogurt
3 ounces crumbled feta

PANTRY STAPLES

Olive oil
Apple cider vinegar
Coconut aminos‡
Raw honey
Pure maple syrup

SPICES

Kosher salt
Ground black pepper
Dried basil
Cayenne pepper
Chili powder
Ground cumin
Garlic powder
Onion powder
Dried oregano
Smoked paprika
Dried thyme

* Can substitute two 15-ounce cans corn kernels or 4 to 6 ears fresh corn (2½ cups needed).
† Use the ½ cup leftover coconut milk in a smoothie, latte, overnight oats, or chia pudding!
‡ Can substitute reduced-sodium tamari or reduced-sodium soy sauce (soy sauce typically includes gluten).

AUTUMN VIBES WEEK

I do have a favorite season, and knowing I'm a New Englander, you could probably guess that it's autumn. The moment the air gets a little bit crisp, you'll find my kitchen full of fall farm favorites and scents of rosemary, sage, and thyme. I'm partial to this menu because of my love for autumn but also because of its variety. You'll look forward to dinnertime from the moment you wake up!

DINNERS

- **Sheet Pan Butternut Squash Mac and "Cheese"** (p. 233)
- **Seared Pork Chops with Apple Fennel Pan Sauce** (p. 262) + **Cauliflower and Parsnip Puree** (p. 288)
- **Garlic and Herb Spatchcock Chicken** (p. 251)
- **Miso Salmon with Acorn Squash** (p. 270)
- **One-Pot Quinoa Bake with Butternut Squash, Kale, and Feta** (p. 156)

PRODUCE

- 2 garlic bulbs
- 1 green onion bunch
- 1 large yellow onion
- 2 medium shallots
- 1 medium fennel bulb
- 1 pound parsnips (about 4)
- 4 medium Yukon Gold potatoes
- 1 medium acorn squash
- 1 large butternut squash (or 20 ounces precut)
- 1 medium cauliflower head (or 10-ounce bag of florets)
- 6 ounces shredded curly kale
- 1 red apple (like Fuji or Honeycrisp)
- 2 lemons
- 1 parsley bunch

PROTEINS

- 3- to 4-pound whole chicken
- Four 3-ounce boneless pork chops
- Four 4-ounce salmon fillets
- 8 ounces unsalted raw cashews

CANNED/PACKAGED

- White miso paste (5 tablespoons needed)
- 32-ounce carton low-sodium vegetable broth
- 12 ounces brown rice elbow macaroni*
- White or tricolor quinoa (1 cup needed)
- Nutritional yeast (2 tablespoons needed)

DAIRY & SUBSTITUTES

- 1 pint milk of choice† (1 cup needed)
- 8-ounce block feta cheese
- 1 stick unsalted butter or unsalted vegan butter (4 tablespoons needed)

PANTRY STAPLES

- Olive oil
- Toasted sesame oil
- Coconut aminos‡
- Raw honey or light brown sugar

SPICES

- Kosher salt
- Ground black pepper
- Garlic powder
- Ground ginger
- Ground sage
- Dried rosemary
- Sesame seeds (optional)
- Dried thyme

* Can substitute rice-and-corn-based or regular macaroni.
† Preferably whole milk; can substitute soy milk, nut milk, or oat milk.
‡ Can substitute reduced-sodium tamari or reduced-sodium soy sauce (soy sauce typically includes gluten).

PERFECTLY PLANT-BASED WEEK

I'm not plant-based, but that doesn't mean I don't love a good plant-based meal! Vegan recipes can be for everyone, and they ensure you're getting lots of veggies in. Make dinnertime exciting and colorful with a variety of vegan dishes, from Buffalo tempeh strips to sweet potato tacos, and don't be surprised when you find yourself adding them to your usual rotation.

DINNERS

- **Buffalo Chickpea Stuffed Sweet Potatoes** (p. 151)
- **Creamy Wild Rice and Mushroom Soup** (p. 222)
- **Crusted Buffalo Tempeh Strips** (p. 246) **with Herby Yogurt Ranch Dressing** (p. 302) **for dipping + Goes-with-Anything Kale Salad** (p. 283)
- **Sticky Balsamic Oyster Mushrooms** (p. 176) **+ Jenn's Steamed Rice** (p. 290)
- **Spiced Sweet Potato Tacos with Avocado Slaw** (p. 235)

PRODUCE

1 garlic bulb
1 large yellow onion
1 green onion bunch
3 large carrots
8 medium sweet potatoes
10-ounce bag coleslaw mix or shredded cabbage
10 ounces shredded curly kale
12 ounces oyster or portabello mushrooms
10 ounces white mushrooms
1 ripe avocado
3 lemons
1 lime
1 small chive bunch
½ ounce dill
1 cilantro bunch
1 parsley bunch

PROTEINS

Two 8-ounce tempeh blocks
Two 15-ounce cans chickpeas

CANNED/PACKAGED

16 ounces Buffalo hot sauce
13.5-ounce can full-fat coconut milk
Tahini (7 tablespoons needed)
32-ounce carton low-sodium vegetable broth
Jasmine rice (1 cup needed)
Wild rice blend or wild rice (1 cup needed)
Twelve 6-inch corn, almond flour, or chickpea flour tortillas
Nutritional yeast (10 tablespoons needed)
3 cups gluten-free panko bread crumbs (about 12 ounces)*

DAIRY & SUBSTITUTES

5.3-ounce container plain dairy-free yogurt or whole-milk or low-fat Greek yogurt (not vegan)
1 stick unsalted vegan butter or unsalted butter (not vegan) (8 tablespoons needed)

PANTRY STAPLES

Olive oil
Apple cider vinegar
Balsamic vinegar
Coconut aminos†
Pure maple syrup
Tapioca flour or arrowroot starch‡

SPICES

Kosher salt
Ground black pepper
Chili powder
Ground cumin
Garlic powder
Onion powder
Smoked paprika
Dried thyme

---

* *Can substitute regular panko bread crumbs. Depending on the brand and size of panko flakes, the ounce-to-cup measure on the panko can vary—double-check that the package includes at least 3 cups.*
† *Can substitute reduced-sodium tamari or reduced-sodium soy sauce (soy sauce typically includes gluten).*
‡ *Can substitute cornstarch.*

10 INGREDIENTS (OR LESS) WEEK

I try to balance the number of ingredients and amount of unique flavors in every recipe I create, knowing that fewer ingredients typically makes for easier prep. But this menu specifically focuses on ten or fewer, excluding spices—for those weeks where you want a short shopping list and straightforward mealtime. Despite the low ingredient count, each recipe packs in distinct elements that you may not typically prepare.

DINNERS

- **Garlic Butter Shrimp and Spaghetti Squash** (p. 142)
- **Sheet Pan Gnocchi with Sun-Dried Tomato Cashew Cream** (p. 230)
- **Weeknight Honey-Garlic Turkey Skillet** (p. 155)*
- **Spinach, Goat Cheese, and Sun-Dried Tomato Stuffed Chicken** (p. 140) **+ Fluffy Does-It-All Quinoa** (p. 291)
- **Sweet and Spicy Tempeh with Sesame Noodles** (p. 240)

PRODUCE

- 2 garlic bulbs
- 1 green onion bunch
- 10 ounces preshredded carrots (or 6 large carrots)
- 2½-inch piece fresh ginger
- 1 large spaghetti squash
- 6 ounces baby spinach
- 1 medium eggplant
- 2 pints cherry tomatoes
- 1 medium zucchini
- 12 ounces green beans
- 1 lemon
- 1 lime
- 1 cilantro bunch

PROTEINS

- 1 pound ground turkey (93% lean)
- 2 pounds boneless, skinless chicken breasts
- 1 pound fresh or frozen medium peeled and deveined raw shrimp
- Two 8-ounce tempeh blocks
- 8 ounces unsalted raw cashews

CANNED/PACKAGED

- 8-ounce jar sun-dried tomatoes, oil-packed
- 12 ounces gluten-free gnocchi (shelf-stable or frozen)†
- 8 ounces stir-fry rice noodles
- White or tricolor quinoa (1 cup needed)

DAIRY & SUBSTITUTES

- 5 ounces grated Parmesan
- 4-ounce log soft goat cheese
- 1 stick unsalted butter (3 tablespoons needed)

PANTRY STAPLES

- Olive oil
- Toasted sesame oil
- Rice vinegar
- Coconut aminos‡
- Raw honey
- Pure maple syrup
- Sriracha

SPICES

- Kosher salt
- Ground black pepper
- Dried basil
- Chili powder
- Garlic powder
- Dried oregano
- Red pepper flakes (optional)
- Sesame seeds

* To bulk it up, you can pair this with Jenn's Steamed Rice (p. 290) or an additional batch of Fluffy Does-It-All Quinoa (p. 291)—just add the additional ingredients to your grocery list!
† Can substitute regular shelf-stable or frozen gnocchi.
‡ Can substitute reduced-sodium tamari or reduced-sodium soy sauce (soy sauce typically includes gluten).

VACAY MODE WEEK

Vacay Mode is a state of mind more than a physical place, although this menu lends itself perfectly to a week away in a rental house with limited ingredients. It means you want your meals to be incredibly simple yet exciting! For dishes that are perfect for sharing and relaxing. Because a vacation mindset is much easier to achieve while digging into a beef and bean taco skillet, right?

DINNERS

- **Dump-and-Bake Hidden Protein Pasta** (p. 159)
- **Cauliflower Pizza Skillet** (p. 204)
- **Not-Your-Average Burrito Bowls with Sheet Pan Salsa** (p. 193) + **Jenn's Steamed Rice** (p. 290)
- **Pantry Staples Spicy Black Bean Soup** (p. 226)
- **Stovetop Beef and Bean Taco Skillet** (p. 144)

PRODUCE

- 1 garlic bulb
- 1 medium red onion
- 1 large yellow onion
- 2 large carrots
- 1 celery heart (4 ribs needed)
- 1 medium cauliflower head or 10-ounce bag of florets
- 6 ounces baby spinach
- 20 ounces Baby Bella mushrooms
- 3 green bell peppers
- 1 red bell pepper
- 1 jalapeño pepper
- 3 small Roma (plum) tomatoes
- 4 limes
- 1 cilantro bunch

PROTEINS

- 1 pound ground beef (85% lean)
- 1 pound ground pork (90% lean)
- 4 ounces uncured pork and beef pepperoni
- 16-ounce block high-protein super-firm tofu
- Two 15-ounce cans black beans
- Two 15-ounce cans pinto beans

CANNED/PACKAGED

- 7-ounce can chipotle peppers in adobo sauce
- Two 24-ounce jars marinara sauce
- 16-ounce carton low-sodium beef broth
- 32-ounce carton low-sodium vegetable broth
- 12 ounces brown rice penne*
- Jasmine rice (1¾ cups needed)

DAIRY & SUBSTITUTES

- 16 ounces 4% milkfat small-curd cottage cheese
- 4 ounces Cheddar cheese
- 12 ounces mozzarella cheese

PANTRY STAPLES

- Olive oil

SPICES

- Kosher salt
- Ground black pepper
- Dried basil
- Chili powder
- Ground cumin
- Garlic powder
- Onion powder
- Dried oregano
- Red pepper flakes (optional)
- Smoked paprika

* Can substitute rice-and-corn-based or regular penne.

JENN'S TOP HITS WEEK

Only a select number of existing Jenn Eats Goood recipes made it to this book, and it was a really tough decision to make. At the end of the day, I chose my most-loved recipes—the ones I get daily tags in over on Instagram. The book just wouldn't be complete without them! This menu turns five of those top hits into your dinner plans. I can confidently say you'll love them, knowing millions already do (maybe even you!).

DINNERS

- **Jenn's Viral Baked Feta, Chicken, Quinoa, and Veggies** (p. 187)
- **French Onion Meatball Skillet** (p. 199)
- **One-Pot Chicken Sausage, Spinach, and Rice** (p. 171)
- **Chicken Pot Pie Soup** (p. 138)
- **Brian's Favorite Lamb Bolognese** (p. 260)

PRODUCE

2 garlic bulbs
4 large yellow onions
5 large carrots
1 celery heart
3 medium Yukon Gold potatoes
1 medium broccoli head or 10 ounces broccoli florets
4 ounces baby spinach
8 ounces fresh or frozen green peas
8 ounces white mushrooms
1 pint cherry tomatoes
1 lemon
1 basil bunch
2 parsley bunches
½ ounce fresh rosemary
½ ounce fresh sage
1 ounce fresh thyme

PROTEINS

1 pound ground beef (85% lean)
1 pound ground lamb (85% lean)
2½ pounds boneless, skinless chicken breasts
12 ounces fully cooked Italian-style chicken sausage

CANNED/PACKAGED

13.5-ounce can full-fat coconut milk
28-ounce can crushed tomatoes
Tomato paste (¼ cup needed)
32-ounce carton low-sodium beef broth
Two 32-ounce cartons low-sodium chicken broth
12 ounces brown rice tagliatelle pasta*
Jasmine rice (2½ cups needed)
White or tricolor quinoa (½ cup needed)

DAIRY & SUBSTITUTES

8-ounce block feta cheese
6 ounces Gruyère or mozzarella cheese

PANTRY STAPLES

Olive oil
Coconut aminos†
Tapioca flour or arrowroot starch‡

SPICES

Kosher salt
Ground black pepper
Garlic powder
Onion powder
Dried oregano
Red pepper flakes (optional)

*Can substitute rice-and-corn-based or regular tagliatelle.
†Can substitute reduced-sodium tamari or reduced-sodium soy sauce (soy sauce typically includes gluten).
‡Can substitute cornstarch.

PART TWO:
THE RECIPES

BREAKFAST BLUEPRINT

Breakfast may be the most important meal of the day, but let's be real—it's also the easiest to skip when you're rushing out the door. Having a satisfying breakfast option ready to go takes the mental weight off and makes it less likely you'll find yourself ravenous at the drive-thru later. This chapter lays out your blueprint for better mornings. It's packed with make-ahead, protein-forward, flavor-filled options that keep mornings delicious and stress-free—whether you're a meal-prepper or just need something quick and satisfying to start your day right.

Cookie Dough Overnight Oats 61

Lemon-Blueberry Overnight Oats 62

Orange Cream Smoothie 63

Banana-Chai Smoothie 63

Strawberry-Basil Smoothie 63

Peanut Butter and Banana Smoothie 63

Coconut-Mango Chia Pudding 67

Dark Chocolate and Raspberry Chia Pudding 68

Vanilla-Almond Chia Pudding 69

Hidden Veggie Oat Bars 70

Cheesy Pork, Pepper, and Onion Breakfast Biscuits 73

Broccoli, Cheddar, and Chicken Breakfast Biscuits 74

Bacon and Chive Egg Muffins 77

Goat Cheese and Kale Egg Muffins 77

Sheet Pan Black Bean Breakfast Burritos 79

Pesto and Roasted Red Pepper Egg Casserole 83

Chipotle Sweet Potato Breakfast Hash 84

Leek, Potato, and Goat Cheese Frittata 86

Hidden Protein Smashed Avocado Toast 88

Lemon-Blueberry Overnight Oats (p. 62)

Cookie Dough Overnight Oats (p. 61)

OVERNIGHT OATS, TWO WAYS

Gluten-free, dairy-free option, vegetarian, vegan option, nut-free option

Overnight oats are my go-to breakfast because they're easy to prep, taste delicious, and keep me satisfied all morning long. The ratio of oats, chia seeds, and milk I use is a blank canvas, so you can add whatever flavors you're craving and make these your own! Here are two versions that always make me happy to see when I open the fridge. Don't forget to add a scoop of vanilla protein powder for that extra boost. It's the perfect way to level up your morning routine and give you a sweet, energizing kick start to your day.

COOKIE DOUGH OVERNIGHT OATS

SERVES 4

Prep time: 10 minutes, plus 6 hours chilling

Cook time: none

Special equipment: Four 10- or 12-ounce lidded jars or containers

To make this dairy-free, nut-free, and vegan: Use plant milk; vegan vanilla protein powder, such as pea protein; vegan chocolate; nut-free milk and sunflower butter.

GOOOD TO KNOW: Adding vanilla protein powder will also make these taste sweeter. If you choose to leave it out, I recommend upping the maple syrup.

Prepping these always serves as motivation to get out of bed in the morning. Dessert for breakfast! What else is there to say? Protein powder adds a hint of vanilla and an extra boost to keep you satiated longer.

2 cups gluten-free rolled oats

One 50 g scoop (3½ tablespoons) vanilla vegetarian protein powder (optional but recommended)

¼ cup chia seeds

¼ cup mini chocolate chips

½ teaspoon kosher salt

2½ cups milk of your choice

2 tablespoons cashew butter, almond butter, or sunflower butter

1 tablespoon pure maple syrup

1 teaspoon pure vanilla extract

1. In a medium bowl, whisk together the oats, protein powder (if using), chia seeds, chocolate chips, and salt. Whisk in the milk, cashew butter, maple syrup, and vanilla until combined.

2. Dividing evenly, spoon the oat mixture into four 10- or 12-ounce lidded containers and refrigerate for at least 6 hours.

STORE IT: Refrigerate in sealed containers for up to 4 days.

REHEAT IT: If you prefer warm oats, transfer to a microwave-safe bowl and microwave until warm, 1 to 1½ minutes.

BREAKFAST BLUEPRINT

LEMON-BLUEBERRY OVERNIGHT OATS

Gluten-free, vegetarian, dairy-free option, vegan option, nut-free option

SERVES 4

Prep time: 10 minutes, plus 6 hours chilling

Cook time: none

Special equipment: Four 10- or 12-ounce lidded jars or containers

To make this dairy-free, and vegan: Use plant milk and vegan vanilla protein powder, such as pea protein; nut-free milk.

GOOOD TO KNOW: For an extra protein boost, I love to top these off with Greek yogurt after they've set.

This lemon-blueberry version is a real winner. Lemon gives the oats a bright, fresh citrus flavor while blueberries add just the right amount of tart natural sweetness and texture.

2 cups gluten-free rolled oats

One 50 g scoop (3½ tablespoons) vanilla vegetarian protein powder (optional but recommended)

¼ cup chia seeds (about 1 ounce)

½ teaspoon kosher salt

2½ cups milk of your choice

Grated zest and juice of 1 lemon

1 tablespoon pure maple syrup

1 teaspoon pure vanilla extract

1 cup fresh or frozen blueberries

1. In a medium bowl, whisk together the oats, protein powder (if using), chia seeds, and salt. Whisk in the milk, lemon zest and juice, maple syrup, and vanilla until fully incorporated. Fold in the blueberries.

2. Dividing evenly, spoon the oat mixture into four 10- or 12-ounce lidded containers and refrigerate for at least 6 hours.

STORE IT: Refrigerate in sealed containers for up to 4 days.

REHEAT IT: If you prefer warm oats, transfer to a microwave-safe bowl and microwave until warm, 1 to 1½ minutes.

GREEN SMOOTHIES, FOUR WAYS

Gluten-free, dairy-free option, vegetarian, vegan option, nut-free variations

Back in college, I worked part-time at a smoothie bar, and after countless hours I perfected a foolproof smoothie formula—1 cup greens, 1 cup milk of choice, a scoop of protein powder, a banana, and chia seeds. Use whatever greens you like, but my go-to is a 50/50 blend of spinach and kale—mostly because they're always in my fridge or freezer. When you hit the right combo of fat, fiber, and protein, a good smoothie can keep you full and satisfied for hours. These are my go-to blends, each with its own twist.

EACH VARIATION SERVES 2

Prep time: 10 minutes
Cook time: none

To make this vegan and dairy-free: Use plant milk, swap in vanilla pea protein for the protein powder, and swap the syrup for honey.

GOOOD TO KNOW: You can prep and store smoothie bags in advance by measuring everything but the milk and freezing the ingredients in sealed bags for up to 3 months.

FOR THE SMOOTHIE BASE
1 cup greens (I like ½ cup curly shredded kale and ½ cup baby spinach)
1 cup milk of your choice
1 large banana, halved
2 tablespoons chia seeds
One 50 g scoop (3½ tablespoons) vanilla vegetarian protein powder (optional but recommended)
Pinch of kosher salt

VARIATION 1: FOR THE ORANGE CREAM SMOOTHIE
½ cup frozen cauliflower rice
Grated zest of 1 orange
½ cup orange juice

VARIATION 2: FOR THE BANANA-CHAI SMOOTHIE
1 cup frozen cauliflower rice
2 teaspoons ground cinnamon
1 teaspoon ground cardamom
½ teaspoon ground ginger
½ teaspoon ground nutmeg
¼ teaspoon ground cloves
Pinch of ground black pepper
1 teaspoon pure vanilla extract

VARIATION 3: FOR THE STRAWBERRY-BASIL SMOOTHIE
½ cup chopped frozen strawberries (about 6 strawberries)
½ ripe avocado, pitted, peeled, and roughly chopped
⅓ cup chopped fresh basil
1 tablespoon raw honey

VARIATION 4: FOR THE PEANUT BUTTER AND BANANA SMOOTHIE
1 large banana, halved
2 tablespoons creamy natural peanut butter

In a blender, combine the smoothie base ingredients. Add the variation ingredients and blend on high until smooth, 30 to 60 seconds. Serve immediately.

From left to right (p. 63):
Orange Cream, Banana-Chai,
Strawberry-Basil,
Peanut Butter and Banana

CHIA PUDDING, THREE WAYS

Chia pudding is one of my meal-prep staples. Just throw a few ingredients together and you've got a fiber-packed, omega-3-rich breakfast ready to go, no heating required. It's so versatile that narrowing it down to just three recipes for this book was *seriously* tough. But these combos are my absolute favorites. Each one also sneaks in a protein boost—whether it's Greek yogurt or almond butter—so you can start your day feeling fueled and energized!

From left to right: Coconut-Mango Chia Pudding (p. 67), Dark Chocolate and Raspberry Chia Pudding (p. 68), Vanilla-Almond Chia Pudding (p. 69)

COCONUT-MANGO CHIA PUDDING

Gluten-free, dairy-free option, vegetarian, vegan option, nut-free

SERVES 4

Prep time: 10 minutes, plus 6 hours chilling

Cook time: none

Special equipment: Four 10- or 12-ounce lidded jars or containers

To make this dairy-free and vegan: Swap the Greek yogurt for a plain dairy-free yogurt of your choice, like a cashew- or coconut-based yogurt.

GOOOD TO KNOW: Steal my chia pudding ratios and make any flavor you want by adding mix-ins of your choice. Use ¾ cup chia seeds and 3 cups liquid—the options are endless from there!

A spoonful of this combination of luxurious tropical flavors is all it takes to transport you to this side of your paradise.

¾ cup chia seeds (about 3 ounces)
¼ cup unsweetened shredded coconut
½ teaspoon kosher salt
1¼ cups unsweetened coconut milk (refrigerated in the carton, not canned)
1 cup whole-milk or low-fat Greek yogurt
1 ripe mango, peeled, seeded, and medium-diced, or frozen chunks, thawed (about 2 cups)
2 tablespoons pure maple syrup

1. In a large bowl, whisk together the chia seeds, coconut, and salt.

2. In a blender or food processor, combine the coconut milk, yogurt, ¾ cup of the diced mango, and the maple syrup and blend until smooth, about 30 seconds. Pour the mixture into the bowl with the chia seeds and whisk vigorously until no chia seeds are settled on the bottom of the bowl, about 1 minute. Fold in the remaining 1¼ cups diced mango.

3. Dividing evenly, spoon the pudding into four 10- to 12-ounce jars. If there are chia seeds settled at the bottom of the jars, stir for 30 seconds, until incorporated into the mixture.

4. Cover the jars with their lids and refrigerate for at least 6 hours to set, or overnight for best results.

STORE IT: Refrigerate in a sealed jar or container for up to 4 days.

DARK CHOCOLATE AND RASPBERRY CHIA PUDDING

Gluten-free, dairy-free option, vegetarian, vegan option, nut-free

SERVES 4

Prep time: 10 minutes, plus 6 hours chilling

Cook time: none

Special equipment: Four 10- or 12-ounce lidded jars or containers

To make this dairy-free, vegetarian, and vegan: Use plant milk; vegan vanilla protein powder, such as pea protein; and vegan chocolate.

The delicious bitterness of the chocolate gets an undertone of juicy brightness from the raspberries.

¾ cup chia seeds (about 3 ounces)
¼ cup finely chopped dark chocolate
½ teaspoon kosher salt
2¼ cups milk of your choice
¾ cup fresh or frozen raspberries
One 50 g scoop (3½ tablespoons) vanilla protein powder, preferably whey- or pea-based
1 tablespoon pure maple syrup
1 teaspoon pure vanilla extract

1. In a large bowl, whisk together the chia seeds, dark chocolate, and salt.

2. In a blender or food processor, combine the milk, raspberries, protein powder, maple syrup, and vanilla and blend until smooth, about 1 minute. Pour the mixture into the chia seeds and whisk vigorously until no chia seeds are settled on the bottom of the bowl, about 30 seconds.

3. Dividing evenly, spoon the pudding into four 10- or 12-ounce jars. If there are chia seeds settled at the bottom of the jars, stir for 30 seconds, until incorporated into the mixture. Cover the jars with their lids.

4. Refrigerate for at least 6 hours to set, or overnight for best results.

STORE IT: Refrigerate in a sealed jar or container for up to 4 days.

VANILLA-ALMOND CHIA PUDDING

Gluten-free, dairy-free option, vegetarian, vegan option

SERVES 4

Prep time: 10 minutes, plus 6 hours chilling

Cook time: none

Special equipment: Four 10- or 12-ounce lidded jars or containers

To make this dairy-free and vegan: Use plant milk and swap the Greek yogurt for a plain dairy-free yogurt of your choice, like a cashew- or coconut-based yogurt.

The savory and nutty flavors of Greek yogurt and almond extract result in a cheesecake-like flavor that doubles down on richness while adding a refreshing tang.

¾ cup chia seeds (about 3 ounces)
¼ cup finely chopped unsalted raw almonds
½ teaspoon kosher salt
2 cups milk of your choice
1¼ cups plain or vanilla whole-milk or low-fat Greek yogurt
2 tablespoons pure maple syrup
1½ teaspoons pure vanilla extract
1 teaspoon almond extract
¼ cup creamy almond butter

1. In a large bowl, whisk together the chia seeds, almonds, and salt. Add the milk, yogurt, maple syrup, vanilla, and almond extract and whisk vigorously until no chia seeds are settled on the bottom of the bowl, about 30 seconds.

2. Dividing evenly, spoon the pudding into four 10- or 12-ounce jars. If there are chia seeds settled at the bottom of the jars, stir for 30 seconds, until incorporated into the mixture. Top each jar with 1 tablespoon of the almond butter and cover with its lid.

3. Refrigerate for at least 6 hours to set, or overnight for best results.

STORE IT: Refrigerate in a sealed jar or container for up to 4 days.

HIDDEN VEGGIE OAT BARS

Gluten-free, dairy-free, vegetarian

Sneaking veggies into recipes is my love language. Thanks to 2 cups of zucchini, you get loads of antioxidants and fiber—without even noticing it's in there. The warm, cozy flavors make these bars the ideal treat for a crisp fall morning, giving you that comforting *yet* energized start to your day. Great from the fridge, or stash them in the freezer.

MAKES 8 BARS

Prep time: 15 minutes
Cook time: 30 minutes

GOOOD TO KNOW:

Add about ⅔ cup of chopped nuts or chocolate chips (or both!) or dried fruit to add texture.

Crumble the bar over Greek yogurt like a parfait for added protein.

These can be prepped ahead.

Reserve any remaining zucchini for my favorite smoothies (page 63) or Overnight Oats (page 61).

STORE IT: Refrigerate in a sealed container for up to 4 days or freeze for up to 3 months.

REHEAT IT: To reheat from the refrigerator, microwave until warm, 30 to 45 seconds. To reheat from the freezer, microwave until warm, 2 to 2½ minutes.

1 cup gluten-free rolled oats
⅔ cup blanched almond flour
½ cup coconut sugar or light brown sugar
⅓ cup tapioca flour or arrowroot starch (can substitute cornstarch)
¼ cup ground flaxseed
2 teaspoons ground cinnamon
1 teaspoon baking soda
1 teaspoon kosher salt
½ teaspoon ground allspice
1 large or 2 small zucchini (10 to 12 ounces)
½ cup canned pumpkin puree
2 large eggs, beaten
1 teaspoon pure vanilla extract

1. Preheat the oven to 350°F. Line a 9 × 9-inch baking dish with parchment paper and fold the excess over the rim. Set aside.

2. In a large bowl, whisk together the oats, almond flour, coconut sugar, tapioca flour, flaxseed, cinnamon, baking soda, salt, and allspice. Set aside.

3. Shred the zucchini using the large holes of a box grater set over a clean kitchen towel. Tightly close all corners and squeeze the wrapped zucchini over the sink to release as much liquid as possible.

4. Add 2 cups of the zucchini to the bowl with the dry ingredients. Add the pumpkin puree, eggs, and vanilla and stir the batter until no dry streaks remain and everything is evenly combined.

5. Transfer the mixture to the prepared baking dish and spread the batter evenly to all corners. Bake until the top is golden brown and a toothpick inserted into the center comes out clean, 25 to 30 minutes.

6. Cool until the oat bars are no longer hot to the touch, 10 to 15 minutes.

7. Lift the oat bars from the pan and slice in a 4 × 2-inch grid to make 8 bars.

HIGH-PROTEIN BREAKFAST BISCUITS, TWO WAYS

Gluten-free, dairy-free option

It's no surprise these cheesy breakfast biscuits went viral—they're everything a morning bite should be: easy to prep ahead, quick to reheat, packed with protein, and ridiculously satisfying. Once you master the basics (like my pork and peppers or chicken and broccoli variations), the sky's the limit—swap in ground turkey and chiles, or whatever leftovers are hanging out in your fridge.

A huge shout-out to my blog followers who've been making and tweaking these weekly since day one! They freeze like a dream, so stash a batch for the ultimate grab-and-go breakfast—ready in minutes in the oven, microwave, or air fryer.

CHEESY PORK, PEPPER, AND ONION BREAKFAST BISCUITS

EACH RECIPE MAKES 12 BISCUITS

Prep time: 20 minutes
Cook time: 30 minutes

To make this dairy-free: Use dairy-free cheese.

GOOOD TO KNOW: These biscuits are wonderfully forgiving and easy to customize. Prefer all almond flour? Use 2½ cups blanched almond flour and skip the coconut flour. You can also swap both for 2¾ cups gluten-free or regular all-purpose flour (you'll lose some protein). Even the ground meat is flexible—try a block of pressed, shredded tofu instead.

1 tablespoon olive oil
1 large yellow onion, small-diced (about 1½ cups)
1 red bell pepper, cored, seeded, and small-diced (about 1 cup)
1 pound 90% lean ground pork
2 teaspoons kosher salt
1 teaspoon ground black pepper
1 teaspoon ground sage
6 large eggs
8 ounces Cheddar, shredded (1½ cups)
1½ cups blanched almond flour
⅓ cup coconut flour
2 teaspoons baking powder

1. Preheat the oven to 400°F. Line a large sheet pan with parchment paper and set aside.

2. In a large skillet, heat the oil over medium heat. Add the onion and bell pepper and cook, stirring occasionally, until softened, 6 to 8 minutes.

3. Push the onion and pepper to thin the refrigerator e sides of the skillet to make a hole in the center. Add the ground pork in the center and cook, breaking up any large chunks with a wooden spoon, until the pork is browned and the onion is translucent, about 8 minutes.

(continues)

BREAKFAST BLUEPRINT

STORE IT: Refrigerate in a sealed container for up to 4 days or freeze for up to 3 months.

REHEAT IT: To reheat from the refrigerator, bake or air-fry at 325°F until warm, 5 to 7 minutes. Alternatively, microwave until warm, 1 to 2 minutes. To reheat from the freezer, either thaw in the refrigerator overnight in the fridge, then bake or air-fry at 325°F for 5 to 7 minutes or, if wholly frozen, bake or air-fry at 325°F for 10 to 12 minutes. From the freezer, microwave until warm, 2 to 3 minutes.

4. Remove from the heat, season with the salt, black pepper, and sage and mix well. Carefully pour off any excess oil and set the mixture aside to cool in the pan for 10 minutes.

5. In a large bowl, whisk the eggs until no streaks remain. Add the pork mixture and 1 cup of the Cheddar and mix well. Add the almond flour, coconut flour, and baking powder and mix until just combined. Do not overmix.

6. Using a lightly oiled large cookie scoop, a spoon, or your clean hands, scoop about 12 balls of dough onto the sheet pan, spacing them 1 to 2 inches apart. Press down gently on the top of each ball to form a biscuit. Evenly sprinkle the top of the biscuits with the remaining ½ cup Cheddar.

7. Bake for 13 to 15 minutes, until the cheese is melted and the biscuits are baked through and lightly browned all over.

BROCCOLI, CHEDDAR, AND CHICKEN BREAKFAST BISCUITS

1 tablespoon olive oil
1 large yellow onion, small-diced (about 1½ cups)
2 cups finely chopped broccoli florets (about 1 medium head)
1 pound 90% lean ground chicken
2 teaspoons kosher salt
1 teaspoon ground black pepper
1 teaspoon garlic powder
6 large eggs
8 ounces Cheddar, shredded (1½ cups)
1½ cups blanched almond flour
⅓ cup coconut flour
2 teaspoons baking powder

1. Preheat the oven to 400°F. Line a large sheet pan with parchment paper and set aside.

2. Heat the oil in a large skillet over medium heat. Add the onion and cook, stirring occasionally, until translucent, 4 to 5 minutes. Add the broccoli and cook, stirring occasionally, until softened, 2 to 3 minutes.

3. Push the onion and broccoli to the sides of the skillet to create a hole in the center. Add the ground chicken in the center and cook, breaking up any large chunks with a wooden spoon, until the chicken is browned, the onion is trans-

lucent, and the broccoli is fork-tender, about 8 minutes. Remove from the heat and season with the salt, black pepper, and garlic powder. Carefully pour off any excess oil and set the mixture aside to cool in the pan for 10 minutes.

4. In a large bowl, whisk the eggs until no streaks remain. Add the chicken mixture and 1 cup of the Cheddar and mix well. Add the almond flour, coconut flour, and baking powder and mix until just combined. Do not overmix.

5. Using a lightly oiled large cookie scoop, a spoon, or your clean hands, scoop about 12 balls of dough onto the sheet pan, spacing them 1 to 2 inches apart. Press down gently on the top of each ball to form a biscuit. Evenly sprinkle the top of the biscuits with the remaining ½ cup Cheddar.

6. Bake for 13 to 15 minutes, until the cheese is melted and the biscuits are baked through and lightly browned all over.

HIGH-PROTEIN EGG MUFFINS, TWO WAYS

Gluten-free, vegetarian variation, nut-free

These egg muffins are my homemade Starbucks dupe without the Starbucks price tag. I used to be a total cottage cheese skeptic, but once I blended it seamlessly with eggs, I was hooked—and now I'm living my best cottage cheese life! This little trick not only cranks up the protein, but it also nixes the heavy, curd-like texture for a silky bite. No wonder this is one of my most popular meal-prep recipes—low-sugar, low-carb, and packed with staying power to keep that midmorning crash at bay. Use the base recipe as a blank canvas for any chopped mix-ins you love!

MAKES 12 MUFFINS

Prep time: 15 minutes, plus 15 minutes cooling
Cook time: 30 minutes

GOOOD TO KNOW: My pro tip for perfect bacon is to line a sheet pan with parchment, lay out the bacon evenly, and bake at 425°F for 14 to 16 minutes, until crispy. It comes out perfect every time, without the usual spatter and mess!

FOR THE EGG MUFFIN BASE

Olive oil for the pan
10 large eggs
1½ cups 4% milkfat small-curd cottage cheese
½ teaspoon ground black pepper
½ teaspoon garlic powder
½ teaspoon kosher salt

VARIATION 1: FOR THE BACON AND CHIVE EGG MUFFINS

6 strips uncured bacon (about 6 ounces), cooked and finely chopped
3 ounces Cheddar, coarsely shredded (½ cup)
¼ cup finely chopped chives

VARIATION 2: FOR THE GOAT CHEESE AND KALE EGG MUFFINS

1 cup shredded curly kale, finely chopped (about 1½ ounces)
¾ cup crumbled soft goat cheese (about 3 ounces)

1. Preheat the oven to 325°F. Lightly oil a 12-muffin pan. See Goood to Know for tips to prevent sticking.

2. In a blender, combine the eggs, cottage cheese, black pepper, garlic powder, and salt and blend on high until smooth, about 30 seconds. Evenly distribute the variation mixture in the bottom of the muffin cups, then fill each to the top with the egg muffin base.

3. Bake until the tops are golden brown and a toothpick inserted into the center comes out clean, about 25 minutes. Let cool in the pan completely, about 15 minutes. The muffins will deflate slightly as they cool.

4. Once cooled, use a small spatula to remove the muffins from the pan.

(continues)

BREAKFAST BLUEPRINT

STORE IT: Refrigerate in a sealed container for up to 3 days or freeze for up to 3 months.

REHEAT IT: To reheat from the refrigerator, microwave until warm, 45 to 60 seconds. Alternatively, bake or air-fry at 325°F for 4 to 6 minutes. To reheat from the freezer, microwave in 30-second increments until warm. For better results, defrost for at least 8 hours in the refrigerator first.

PRO TIPS

- **Don't overblend:** Once the egg mixture is blended smooth, don't continue blending. You want to limit the amount of air bubbles in the mixture.

- **Strain the mixture:** After you've blended, strain the eggs through a fine-mesh sieve into a separate vessel. This optional extra step helps remove any air bubbles that resulted from blending.

- **Invest in a good muffin pan:** I won't lie to you—a reliable nonstick muffin pan can be life-changing. I personally love my nonstick ceramic muffin pan, which can cost more, but you won't need to buy liners and your egg muffins won't get stuck in the pan (no waste!). If you don't have one, greased silicone muffin liners work, but avoid basic parchment liners—they tend to warp and leave you with funky-shaped muffins once they cool down.

- **Fill to the top and don't overbake:** Make sure you're filling each muffin well to the top, until they are just about full, so the cook time is appropriate. This prevents overbaking; overcooked egg muffins can get spongy or rubbery. You know they are done when you shake the muffin tin and the centers of each muffin jiggle.

- **Try a water bath:** This one little step makes a huge difference! Before you preheat the oven, fill a baking dish halfway with water and place it on the bottom rack to heat up while you preheat. The water bath will steam the muffins and create the fluffiest eggs.

- **Don't heat the oven too high:** 325°F is the max temperature I'd suggest for egg muffins. You want the eggs to cook slowly, so if your oven tends to run hot, cut back to 300°F. The muffins will rise as they bake and then deflate back down slightly, which is normal!

SHEET PAN BLACK BEAN BREAKFAST BURRITOS

Gluten-free, dairy-free option, vegetarian, nut-free

Have you ever cooked eggs on a sheet pan? When I first tried it, it felt like I was breaking the breakfast rules, but these no-fuss breakfast burritos totally convinced me that this sheet pan egg situation is kind of a life hack. Start by roasting your beans and veggies on the pan, then pour in the eggs, scramble them, finish baking, and roll everything up in warm tortillas. Storing a batch of these in the freezer and knowing I can just pop them in the microwave lowers the "what's for breakfast?" stress. Stress-free breakfast, sorted!

SERVES 6

Prep time: 20 minutes
Cook time: 20 minutes

To make this dairy-free: Omit the Cheddar or use a dairy-free alternative.

GOOOD TO KNOW: If you're not avoiding gluten, you can use 10-inch flour tortillas for the burritos and follow the same instructions.

2 teaspoons ground cumin
1 teaspoon chili powder
1 teaspoon garlic powder
1 teaspoon smoked paprika
Kosher salt
One 15.5-ounce can black beans, drained and rinsed
1 green or red bell pepper, cored, seeded, and roughly chopped (about 1 cup)
1 large yellow onion, roughly chopped (about 1½ cups)
1 jalapeño pepper, seeded and finely chopped
2 tablespoons olive oil
10 large eggs
Six 9- or 10-inch gluten-free tortillas
2 ounces Cheddar, shredded (⅔ cup)

1. Preheat the oven to 400°F. Line a sheet pan with parchment paper and set aside. If you're prepping for the fridge or freezer, pull out six 12-inch lengths of aluminum foil for wrapping. Skip this step if serving all six at once.

2. In a medium bowl, mix the cumin, chili powder, garlic powder, smoked paprika, and 1 teaspoon salt. Add the black beans, bell pepper, onion, jalapeño, and oil and mix well. Transfer the mixture to the sheet pan and spread it in one even layer. Roast until the onions and peppers are softened, 10 to 12 minutes.

3. Meanwhile, in the same medium bowl, whisk the eggs and a pinch of salt until no streaks remain.

4. Use a spatula to push the vegetables to the outer edges of the sheet pan, creating about a 10 × 6-inch rectangle in the middle of the tray. Pour the egg mixture into the center of the rectangle.

(continues)

5. Return the pan to the oven, stirring to scramble halfway through with a fork or spatula, until the eggs are opaque and fluffy, 7 to 9 minutes. Mix the vegetables and eggs together with a spatula until evenly combined.

6. Wrap the tortillas in one or two damp paper towels and microwave until softened and pliable, about 1 minute.

7. To assemble, place the six 12-inch sheets of aluminum foil on the counter. Place 1 tortilla on top of each foil sheet. Dividing evenly, spoon the shredded Cheddar into the middle of each tortilla and top with the egg mixture. To wrap up the burrito, fold the sides of the tortilla into the center. Then, starting at the bottom, roll tightly toward the top into a cigar shape. Immediately wrap the burrito tightly in the foil sheet.

8. Transfer to the refrigerator or freezer for storage.

STORE IT: Refrigerate the burritos tightly wrapped in foil for up to 4 days or freeze for up to 3 months.

REHEAT IT: From the refrigerator, remove the foil and microwave until warm, 1½ to 2 minutes. From the freezer, remove the foil and microwave until warm, 2½ to 3 minutes. If desired, heat 1 tablespoon oil in a skillet and pan-fry the burrito over medium heat for 2 minutes on each side.

PESTO AND ROASTED RED PEPPER EGG CASSEROLE

Gluten-free, dairy-free, vegetarian

I've been whipping up these big egg casseroles for breakfast meal prep since college, when I switched to a protein-packed breakfast with plenty of veggies! Now they're my go-to for just about everything—group trips, bachelorette weekends, even vacations. The pesto is a total game changer (I'm obsessed with my dairy-free walnut version), but if you're missing that cheese, a handful of shredded mozzarella does the trick. Feeling extra hungry? Toss in some cooked chicken sausage, which adds both substance and protein. However you spin it, this one's a keeper!

SERVES 8

Prep time: 10 minutes
Cook time: 35 minutes

GOOOD TO KNOW: You can swap the milk for 1 cup 4% small-curd cottage cheese for a higher-protein, extra-fluffy egg casserole. Just blend with the eggs and salt on high speed instead of whisking to incorporate.

Olive oil for the pan
12 large eggs
¾ cup milk of your choice
½ teaspoon kosher salt
1 cup thinly sliced roasted red peppers, drained if using jarred
3 cups firmly packed baby spinach, finely chopped (about 4 ounces)
¾ cup Dairy-Free Walnut Pesto (p. 301) or store-bought dairy-free pesto

1. Preheat the oven to 350°F. Lightly oil a 9 × 13-inch baking dish and set aside.

2. In a large bowl, whisk the eggs until no streaks remain. Whisk in the milk and salt until combined. Stir in the roasted red peppers and spinach.

3. Pour the egg mixture into the prepared baking dish and use a spatula to evenly disperse the vegetables. Lightly whisk the pesto and dollop heaping tablespoons on top of the egg mixture. (Don't skip the whisking; if the pesto isn't whipped it will sink!) Gently spread the pesto with a rubber spatula into a thin layer over the egg mixture. This doesn't have to be perfect, but again you're avoiding having the pesto sink to the bottom of the pan.

4. Bake for 30 to 35 minutes, until a toothpick inserted into the center comes out clean.

5. Let cool for about 5 minutes in the baking dish so the eggs can firm up before serving. To serve, slice into 8 pieces.

STORE IT: Refrigerate slices in a sealed container for up to 3 days or freeze for up to 3 months.

REHEAT IT: From the refrigerator, microwave until warm, 1 to 1½ minutes. From the freezer, thaw in the refrigerator overnight, then microwave in 30-second increments until completely warm.

CHIPOTLE SWEET POTATO BREAKFAST HASH

Gluten-free, dairy-free, vegetarian, vegan option, nut-free

Jump-start your morning with a rainbow of veggies and a solid protein boost in every bite! Swapping starchy spuds for sweet potatoes adds extra fiber and antioxidants. Meal-prep it into effortless grab-and-go portions or make it the star of a leisurely Sunday brunch alongside a Salted Tahini-Maple Latte (page 307) or Dreamy Blueberry Matcha Latte (page 309). Trust me, your mornings are about to get a major upgrade!

SERVES 4

Prep time: 20 minutes
Cook time: 40 minutes

To make this vegan: Omit the eggs.

GOOOD TO KNOW: This skillet is perfect for clearing out the fridge before your weekly grocery trip! Swap in any leftover greens, root vegetables, peppers, or onions that need to be used up, and let the spices and sauce shine.

STORE IT: Refrigerate the hash and chipotle sauce separately in sealed containers; up to 3 days for the hash and up to 7 days for the sauce.

REHEAT IT: Transfer the hash to a microwave-safe dish and microwave until warm, 1 to 2 minutes. Drizzle with chipotle sauce.

FOR THE SWEET POTATO HASH

- 1 teaspoon chili powder
- 1 teaspoon ground cumin
- 1 teaspoon garlic powder
- 1 teaspoon smoked paprika
- 1 teaspoon kosher salt
- 2 tablespoons olive oil
- 1 red bell pepper, cored, seeded, and roughly chopped (about 1 cup)
- ½ large yellow onion, roughly chopped (about ¾ cup)
- 1 jalapeño pepper, seeded and finely chopped
- 2 medium sweet potatoes, peeled and medium-diced (about 3 cups)
- 2 cups shredded curly kale (about 3 ounces)
- 4 large eggs

FOR SERVING

- Smoky Chipotle Sauce (p. 296)
- Chopped fresh cilantro
- 1 ripe avocado, halved, pitted, peeled, and sliced

1. **Make the sweet potato hash:** In a small bowl, whisk the chili powder, cumin, garlic powder, smoked paprika, and salt until combined. Set aside.

2. Heat the oil in a large lidded skillet over medium heat. Add the bell pepper, onion, and jalapeño and cook, stirring occasionally, until softened, about 5 minutes. Add the sweet potatoes and stir to combine. Cover the skillet and continue to cook, stirring every few minutes, until the sweet potatoes are fork-tender, 20 to 30 minutes.

3. Uncover, add the spice mixture, and cook, stirring occasionally, until fragrant, about 1 minute. Add the kale, stir, and cover the pan again. Cook for about 1 minute, until the kale is wilted.

4. Using the back of a spoon, make four evenly spaced, round indentations on top of the hash. Carefully crack an egg into each one. Reduce the heat to low, cover the pan, and cook until the yolk is just set, 3 to 4 minutes. For firmer yolks, cook for 2 minutes more. If omitting eggs, skip this step and cook for an additional 2 minutes once the kale has wilted.

5. **To serve:** Divide the hash and eggs among four plates. Drizzle some chipotle sauce on top, sprinkle with the cilantro, and top with the avocado slices.

LEEK, POTATO, AND GOAT CHEESE FRITTATA

Gluten-free, dairy-free option, vegetarian, nut-free

Italian technique meets French flavors in this crowd-pleasing egg dish. Unlike an omelet, the Italian frittata is baked in the oven. My version uses potatoes, leeks, and soft goat cheese for a little French flair, but feel free to mix and match with your favorite veggie and cheese combo, like red bell peppers and Parm. Serve as part of a brunch spread with Hidden Veggie Oat Bars (page 70) and Broccoli, Cheddar, and Chicken Breakfast Biscuits (page 74) for a lineup that's equal parts wholesome and delicious. Effortless, versatile, and always a hit—what's not to love?

SERVES 6

Prep time: 15 minutes
Cook time: 40 minutes

To make this dairy-free: Use plant milk and skip the cheese or sub in a dairy-free alternative.

GOOOD TO KNOW: Leeks can be very sandy, so it's important to wash them well. Cut them lengthwise through the root and rinse them under cold water, gently pulling back the layers to remove the grit. It's worth the minor effort for their sweet, oniony flavor.

2 tablespoons olive oil
2 medium Yukon Gold potatoes, peeled and medium-diced (about 2 cups)
2 leeks, white and light green parts only, halved lengthwise and thinly sliced crosswise (about 2 cups)
10 large eggs
½ cup milk of your choice
1 teaspoon garlic powder
1½ teaspoons kosher salt
½ teaspoon ground black pepper
¾ cup crumbled soft goat cheese (about 3 ounces)
Fresh thyme (optional)

1. Preheat the oven to 350°F.

2. Heat the oil in a 10-inch cast-iron or ovenproof skillet over medium-low heat until shimmering. Add the potatoes in a single layer, cover, and cook without disturbing until the potatoes begin to soften and caramelize, about 10 minutes.

3. Turn the potatoes over using tongs or a spatula. Spread the leeks evenly over the potatoes, cover, and cook until the potatoes are fork-tender, 8 to 10 minutes.

4. Meanwhile, crack the eggs into a large bowl. Whisk in the milk until combined. Set aside.

5. When the potatoes and leeks are tender, add the garlic powder, salt, and black pepper and cook, uncovered, stirring often, until fragrant, 2 to 3 minutes. Remove the pan from the heat, spread the vegetables out evenly, and pour in the egg mixture. Sprinkle the goat cheese evenly across the top.

6. Transfer to the oven and bake until a toothpick inserted in the center comes out clean, 15 to 18 minutes. Sprinkle with thyme (if using).

7. Let cool for 5 minutes in the skillet. To serve, slice into 6 wedges.

STORE IT: Refrigerate slices in a sealed container for up to 3 days or freeze for up to 3 months.

REHEAT IT: From the refrigerator, microwave slices until warm, 1 to 1½ minutes. From the freezer, thaw in the refrigerator overnight, then microwave in 30-second increments until completely warm.

HIDDEN PROTEIN SMASHED AVOCADO TOAST

Gluten-free, dairy-free, vegetarian, vegan, nut-free

When that avocado toast craving hits, this version delivers—fancy enough for Sunday brunch, simple enough for a hectic Monday morning. The secret? Cannellini beans. They sneak in a protein boost without stealing the show, turning your avo toast into a truly balanced meal. Not into the tomato and basil combo? No problem—switch it up with roasted red peppers, crumbled feta, my Pickled Onions (page 114), or a crunchy sprinkle of toasted nuts and seeds with a drizzle of good olive oil. You might never go back to basic avocado toast again.

SERVES 2

Prep time: 5 minutes
Cook time: 5 minutes

GOOOD TO KNOW: For even more protein, add a fried egg on top. You can also add a sprinkle of microgreens for added nutrients or swap the bread for thinly sliced sweet potato "toasts."

One 15-ounce can cannellini or navy beans, drained and rinsed
1 ripe avocado, halved and pitted
Juice of ½ lemon
1 teaspoon kosher salt
½ teaspoon ground black pepper
½ teaspoon garlic powder
4 thick-cut slices of your favorite bread (gluten-free as needed), toasted
½ cup drained oil-packed sun-dried tomatoes, finely chopped
½ cup chopped fresh basil
Balsamic glaze, for drizzling (optional)

1. In a medium bowl, mash the beans with a fork or potato masher until no whole beans remain (it won't be perfectly smooth, which is okay!). Scoop the avocado flesh into the bowl and add the lemon juice, salt, black pepper, and garlic powder and continue to mash until the mixture is uniform, about 30 seconds.

2. Dividing evenly, spread the avocado mash over the four pieces of the toast. Top with the sun-dried tomatoes and basil. Drizzle with balsamic glaze, if desired.

STORE IT: While this is best enjoyed right away, you can refrigerate the avocado mash in a sealed container with a piece of aluminum foil, plastic wrap, or parchment pressed directly on top for up to 3 days.

QUICK LUNCHES, UPGRADED

A midday lunch break can either boost energy or leave you sluggish—it all comes down to what's on your plate. That's why I swear by meal prep to save time and make healthier choices effortless. The plant-forward lunches in this chapter are designed for easy prep ahead, but they come together just as seamlessly in the moment. Think hearty salads, nourishing bowls, and flavor-packed bites that make weekdays easier and potlucks more exciting. Because let's be real—healthy can (and should!) never be boring.

Roasted Brussels Sprouts, Sweet Potato, and Beet Salad 92

Mediterranean-Inspired Chickpea Chopped Salad 95

Farmers' Market Lentil Salad 96

Golden Turmeric Herby Quinoa Salad 99

Cilantro-Lime Pasta Salad 101

Crispy Quinoa, Peanut, and Edamame Salad 105

Pineapple-Shrimp Lettuce Wraps 106

Crunchy Pork Lettuce Wraps with Carrot Slaw 108

Spicy Tofu Crunch Bowls 111

Chipotle Sweet Potato and Black Bean Bowls 113

Barbecue Chicken Chopped Salad 117

Greek-Style Crispy Chickpea Bowls 118

ROASTED BRUSSELS SPROUTS, SWEET POTATO, AND BEET SALAD

Gluten-free, dairy-free, vegetarian, vegan

This hearty salad is the ultimate in coziness—loaded with roasted veggies that bring gorgeous color to your table. Toss it all together with a creamy maple-tahini dressing that's nutty, salty, and just sweet enough to keep things interesting. Whether you're hosting a laid-back weeknight dinner or setting the table for Thanksgiving, this dish always gets rave reviews. Serve it warm right after assembling or let it cool to room temp—either way, it's a winning dish, especially alongside autumn dinners like Miso Salmon with Acorn Squash (page 270). If you can't find preshaved Brussels sprouts, trim the bottoms and slice them as thinly as possible.

SERVES 4

Prep time: 15 minutes, plus 10 minutes resting

Cook time: 30 minutes

GOOOD TO KNOW: Feel free to up the protein by adding crumbled goat cheese or feta, chickpeas, or shredded rotisserie chicken.

REHEAT IT: Heat the salad on a sheet pan and bake in a 350°F oven for 8 to 10 minutes to bring the veggies back to life (alternatively, microwave until warm, 1 to 2 minutes), then toss with the dressing.

STORE IT: Refrigerate the salad and dressing in separate sealed containers, up to 4 days for the salad and up to 7 days for the dressing. Dress the salad right before serving.

2 teaspoons dried thyme
1 teaspoon garlic powder
1 teaspoon dried rosemary
1 teaspoon kosher salt
½ teaspoon ground black pepper
4 cups shaved Brussels sprouts (about 7 ounces)
2 medium sweet potatoes, peeled and medium-diced (about 3 cups)
2 medium beets, peeled and medium-diced (about 1½ cups)
1 cup roughly chopped unsalted raw walnuts
2 tablespoons olive oil
⅔ cup dried cranberries
Maple-Tahini Dressing (recipe follows)

1. Preheat the oven to 400°F. Line a sheet pan with parchment paper.

2. In a large bowl, combine the thyme, garlic powder, rosemary, salt, and black pepper. Add the Brussels sprouts, sweet potatoes, beets, walnuts, and oil and mix well. Transfer the mixture to the prepared sheet pan.

3. Bake until the vegetables are fork-tender and browned, 20 to 25 minutes. Let cool on the sheet pan for 5 to 10 minutes.

4. Transfer the cooled vegetables to the bowl, add the dried cranberries, and toss with the dressing until everything is evenly coated.

5. To serve, spoon the salad onto four plates.

MAPLE-TAHINI DRESSING

Gluten-free, dairy-free, vegetarian, vegan, nut-free

MAKES ABOUT ¾ CUP

GOOOD TO KNOW: Add a few tablespoons of warm water if the dressing is too thick and doesn't pour easily.

STORE IT: Refrigerate in a sealed container for up to 7 days.

3 tablespoons olive oil
3 tablespoons tahini
2 tablespoons apple cider vinegar
Juice of 1 lemon
1 tablespoon pure maple syrup
1 tablespoon Dijon mustard
1 teaspoon kosher salt
½ teaspoon garlic powder
½ teaspoon ground black pepper

In a large bowl, whisk together all the ingredients until smooth.

MEDITERRANEAN-INSPIRED CHICKPEA CHOPPED SALAD

Gluten-free, dairy-free option, vegetarian, vegan option, nut-free

Who says a salad has to have lettuce? This viral fan favorite is a hit because the meal prep is effortless and the flavor combinations and textures always hit the mark. The lemony red wine vinaigrette is more of a marinade than a dressing, as the flavors deepen after a few hours or overnight in the fridge. It's Italian pasta salad without the pasta! You probably have all the ingredients hanging out in your pantry too.

SERVES 4

Prep time: 20 minutes
Cook time: none

To make this dairy-free and vegan: Omit the mozzarella.

GOOOD TO KNOW: It's normal for the liquid to separate when marinating. Discard any excess liquid at the bottom of the container before serving.

- One 14-ounce can water-packed artichoke hearts, drained, rinsed, and roughly chopped
- 3 roasted red peppers, drained if jarred, medium-diced
- 1 large English cucumber, unpeeled, medium-diced
- ½ cup pitted Kalamata olives, roughly chopped
- One 15-ounce can chickpeas, drained and rinsed
- One 8-ounce mozzarella ball, cut into small cubes
- 1 cup packed fresh basil, finely chopped
- ⅔ cup Lemony Red Wine Vinaigrette (p. 303)

1. In a large bowl, combine the artichoke hearts, roasted peppers, cucumber, and olives. Add the chickpeas, mozzarella, and basil and mix well. Toss with the vinaigrette until evenly coated.

2. Enjoy immediately or let the salad marinate in the vinaigrette in a sealed container in the refrigerator for 8 to 12 hours.

STORE IT: Refrigerate in a sealed container for up to 4 days.

FARMERS' MARKET LENTIL SALAD

Gluten-free, dairy-free option, vegetarian, vegan option, nut-free

Saturday-morning trips to the Union Square farmers' market in Somerville, Massachusetts, with Brian are some of our most cherished moments—exploring and poking around in the bins bursting with in-season produce, discovering new ingredients, and finding fresh inspiration for our meals. That's exactly how this salad came to be. The punchy dressing wakes everything up, the lentils bring staple protein power, and the rainbow of veggies make it as stunning as it is satisfying. Customize it with whatever catches your eye at the market, and when the weather cools, try roasting the veggies for a whole new depth of flavor (see Goood to Know).

SERVES 4

Prep time: 20 minutes
Cook time: 30 minutes

To make this dairy-free and vegan: Omit the goat cheese. Use maple syrup for vegan.

GOOOD TO KNOW: For a variation, toss the veggies on a sheet pan with a drizzle of olive oil, salt, and black pepper to taste and roast at 425°F for about 15 minutes, until golden.

1 cup dried green lentils
1 medium yellow summer squash, roughly chopped
1 medium zucchini, roughly chopped
1 orange bell pepper, cored, seeded, and roughly chopped (about 1 cup)
1 red bell pepper, cored, seeded, and roughly chopped (about 1 cup)
5 cups (5 ounces) arugula
⅔ cup packed fresh basil, finely chopped
⅔ cup Lemony Red Wine Vinaigrette (p. 303)
¾ cup crumbled soft goat cheese (about 3 ounces)
2 tablespoons raw honey or pure maple syrup

1. Combine 3 cups water and the lentils in a small pot and bring to a boil over medium-high heat. Cover, reduce the heat to low, and cook until the lentils are tender, 25 to 30 minutes. Drain and rinse with cold water for 45 to 60 seconds, then transfer to a large bowl.

2. Add the summer squash, zucchini, bell peppers, arugula, and basil to the lentils. Right before serving, add the vinaigrette, goat cheese, and honey and toss lightly until just combined.

STORE IT: Refrigerate the salad and dressing in separate sealed containers: up to 4 days for the salad and up to 7 days for the dressing.

GOLDEN TURMERIC HERBY QUINOA SALAD

Gluten-free, dairy-free, vegetarian, vegan, nut-free option

I created this salad after I read a study from the American Gut Project recommending a diverse range of plants for optimal gut health. So I packed in more than ten—yes, even spices count—in this dish! With roasted carrots, sweet dates, crunchy almonds, and bold fresh herbs, this quinoa salad channels Moroccan-inspired flavors, whether you're enjoying it for lunch or as a side with dinner (like Garlic and Herb Spatchcock Chicken, page 251). A turmeric-infused dressing ties it all together with warm, earthy depth. It's a vibrant explosion of nourishing plant power and protein—and it just so happens to be vegan.

SERVES 4

Prep time: 20 minutes
Cook time: 25 minutes

To make this nut-free: Omit the slivered almonds.

GOOOD TO KNOW: This salad shines on its own with plant-based protein, but adding rotisserie chicken bulks it up if you're looking for even more protein, or to stretch it to 6 servings.

FOR THE ROASTED VEGETABLES

2 teaspoons ground cumin
1 teaspoon chili powder
1 teaspoon smoked paprika
1 teaspoon kosher salt
½ teaspoon ground black pepper
½ teaspoon ground cinnamon
3 large carrots, cut into ¼-inch coins
One 15-ounce can chickpeas, drained and rinsed
6 Medjool dates, pitted and roughly chopped
2 tablespoons olive oil

FOR THE TURMERIC–MAPLE DRESSING

3 tablespoons olive oil
3 tablespoons tahini
2 tablespoons apple cider vinegar
2 tablespoons pure maple syrup
2 teaspoons ground turmeric
1 teaspoon kosher salt
½ teaspoon ground black pepper
½ teaspoon ground cumin

FOR ASSEMBLY

White or tricolor Fluffy Does-It-All Quinoa (p. 291)
⅔ cup slivered almonds
¼ cup chopped fresh parsley
¼ cup chopped fresh mint
¼ cup chopped fresh cilantro

(continues)

1. Preheat the oven to 400°F. Line a sheet pan with parchment paper.

2. **Roast the veggies:** In a large bowl, combine the cumin, chili powder, smoked paprika, salt, black pepper, and cinnamon. Add the carrots, chickpeas, dates, and oil and mix until everything is fully and evenly coated. Spread the mixture on the sheet pan in a single layer.

3. Roast until the carrots are fork-tender and begin to crisp at the edges, 20 to 25 minutes.

4. **Meanwhile, make the dressing:** In a small bowl, whisk together all the ingredients plus 2 tablespoons warm water until smooth.

5. **To assemble:** In a large bowl, combine the quinoa, roasted carrot mixture, and dressing. Add the slivered almonds, parsley, mint, and cilantro, tossing until evenly combined.

STORE IT: Refrigerate the dressed salad in a sealed container for up to 4 days or refrigerate the dressing separately for up to 7 days.

CILANTRO-LIME PASTA SALAD

Gluten-free, dairy-free option, vegetarian option, nut-free

Fresh, bright, and bursting with herby-citrus goodness, this easy, no-reheat pasta salad has become my go-to for warm-weather meals. The cilantro-lime dressing is my "everything sauce," perfect on salads, grilled fish, or roasted veggies.

SERVES 4

Prep time: 20 minutes
Cook time: 10 minutes, plus 15 minutes chilling

To make this dairy-free: Use dairy-free yogurt.

To make this vegetarian: Swap the shredded chicken for a can of chickpeas or cannellini beans.

GOOOD TO KNOW: Mix in any of your extra summer produce for even more color and nutrients, such as chopped bell peppers, zucchini, or summer squash.

STORE IT: Refrigerate in a sealed container for up to 4 days.

FOR THE CILANTRO-LIME DRESSING
¾ cup chopped fresh cilantro
½ cup whole-milk or low-fat Greek yogurt
1 tablespoon apple cider vinegar
1 tablespoon pure maple syrup
1 tablespoon olive oil
Grated zest and juice of 1 lime
½ jalapeño pepper, seeded and roughly chopped
1 teaspoon kosher salt, plus more to taste
½ teaspoon garlic powder
½ teaspoon ground black pepper

FOR THE PASTA SALAD
12 ounces brown rice farfalle, rice-and-corn-based farfalle, or regular farfalle
3 cups medium-diced No-Fail Baked Chicken (recipe follows) or store-bought rotisserie chicken
1½ cups cooked fresh corn kernels (from 2 ears), thawed frozen corn, or one 15-ounce can, drained
1 pint cherry tomatoes, halved (about 1½ cups)
3 green onions, finely chopped
¼ cup finely chopped fresh cilantro

1. **Make the cilantro-lime dressing:** In a blender or food processor, combine the cilantro, yogurt, vinegar, maple syrup, oil, lime zest and juice, jalapeño, salt, garlic powder, and black pepper and blend on high speed until completely smooth, about 1 minute. If needed, season with more salt. Transfer to a small bowl and set aside.

2. **Make the pasta salad:** In a pot of boiling water, cook the pasta until al dente according to package directions. Drain and rinse with cold water.

3. In a large bowl, combine the pasta, chicken, corn, cherry tomatoes, green onions, and cilantro. Pour in half of the dressing and toss until everything is fully coated. Place in the refrigerator to chill for at least 15 minutes before serving.

4. Serve the salad in bowls and drizzle with more dressing, if desired.

NO-FAIL BAKED CHICKEN

Gluten-free, dairy-free, nut-free

MAKES ABOUT 3 CUPS

Prep time: 10 minutes

Cook time: 30 minutes, plus 10 minutes cooling

GOOOD TO KNOW: If you prefer boneless, skinless chicken thighs, bake for 25 to 30 minutes.

Use this chicken for salads, bowls, wraps, and tacos.

1 pound boneless, skinless chicken breasts
1 tablespoon olive oil
1 teaspoon garlic powder
1 teaspoon kosher salt
½ teaspoon ground black pepper

1. Preheat the oven to 400°F and line a sheet pan with parchment paper.

2. In a large bowl, combine the chicken, oil, garlic powder, salt, and black pepper. Toss with tongs or clean hands until evenly coated. Set the chicken on the sheet pan and bake until it reaches an internal temperature of 165°F, 20 to 30 minutes.

3. Let cool on the sheet pan for 10 to 15 minutes. Transfer the chicken to a clean large bowl and shred using two forks or an electric mixer. Alternatively, slice or cube the chicken for salads and bowls.

STORE IT: Refrigerate in a sealed container for up to 4 days or freeze for up to 3 months.

CRISPY QUINOA, PEANUT, AND EDAMAME SALAD

Gluten-free, dairy-free, vegetarian, vegan

I love that a follower called this salad their gateway into the JennEatsGoood community. First introduced in my viral budget grocery series, it's quickly become a fan favorite—and I credit that to the utterly irresistible Lick-the-Bowl Peanut Sauce. Whether it's a meal-prepped lunch or a dinner party showstopper, I've yet to meet anyone who doesn't fall in love with this vibrant dish. If you're in a hurry, permission granted to skip roasting the quinoa—but just know, crisping it up really takes it to the next level, adding a deeper, nutty flavor that elevates the whole dish, even for meal prep.

SERVES 4

Prep time: 15 minutes
Cook time: 45 minutes

GOOOD TO KNOW: This plant-based favorite pairs beautifully with some crispy tofu on top, providing extra protein and another unique texture. Try it with Sweet and Spicy Tofu and Broccolini (page 168)—you won't regret it!

1 cup uncooked white or tricolor quinoa
2 tablespoons olive oil
1 teaspoon kosher salt
½ teaspoon ground black pepper
12 ounces fresh or thawed frozen shelled edamame
5 ounces preshredded carrots, or 3 large carrots, coarsely shredded (about 1½ cups)
1 English cucumber, unpeeled, halved lengthwise, and sliced into thin half-moons
¾ cup packed chopped fresh cilantro
4 green onions, thinly sliced
¾ cup Lick-the-Bowl Peanut Sauce (p. 295)

1. Preheat the oven to 350°F. Line a large sheet pan with parchment paper and set aside.

2. Bring 2 cups water to a boil in a small pot over medium-high heat. Add the quinoa, cover, and reduce the heat to low. Cook until the water is absorbed and the quinoa is fluffy, 15 to 18 minutes.

3. Drizzle the quinoa with the oil, season with the salt and black pepper, and toss to mix well. Spread the quinoa onto the prepared sheet pan in one even layer. Bake until crispy, about 30 minutes, stirring halfway through.

4. Combine the crispy quinoa, edamame, carrots, cucumber, cilantro, and green onions in a large bowl and mix. Add the peanut sauce and mix well.

5. Serve in bowls.

STORE IT: Refrigerate the dressed salad in a sealed container for up to 4 days or store the dressing separately for up to 7 days.

QUICK LUNCHES, UPGRADED

PINEAPPLE-SHRIMP LETTUCE WRAPS

Gluten-free, dairy-free, nut-free

These lettuce wraps are fully giving island vibes, no matter what time of year you serve them. A hot summer day? Absolutely! A cold and stormy winter afternoon, so you can pretend you're on an island? Why not! The tender Bibb lettuce leaves surround the tropical-flavored crunch inside. Fresh pineapple in the slaw and marinade brings sweetness and tang to each bite, anchored by savory, toasty sesame oil. Whether served immediately or marinated overnight to enhance the flavor—you can't go wrong!

SERVES 4

Prep time: 30 minutes
Cook time: 10 minutes

GOOOD TO KNOW: Prefer to eat this with a fork? Make it a salad: Chop up the lettuce leaves and mix in the slaw and cooked shrimp.

STORE IT: Refrigerate the leftovers in a sealed container for up to 4 days. If prepping ahead of time, store the shrimp, slaw, and lettuce cups separately until ready to serve.

REHEAT IT: Transfer the shrimp to a microwave-safe dish and microwave until warm, 1 to 2 minutes, then assemble the wraps.

FOR THE PINEAPPLE SLAW

One 10-ounce bag coleslaw mix or shredded cabbage
1 cup small-diced fresh pineapple
⅓ cup chopped fresh cilantro
2 tablespoons coconut aminos (or reduced-sodium tamari or reduced-sodium soy sauce)
Juice of 1 lime
2 tablespoons apple cider vinegar
1 tablespoon toasted sesame oil
1 tablespoon pure maple syrup
½ teaspoon kosher salt

FOR THE SHRIMP

¼ cup coconut aminos (or reduced-sodium tamari or reduced-sodium soy sauce)
¼ cup fresh or canned pineapple juice
2 tablespoons olive oil
1 teaspoon chili powder
1 teaspoon garlic powder
1 teaspoon ground ginger
1 teaspoon smoked paprika
½ teaspoon kosher salt
1 pound fresh or thawed frozen medium shrimp, peeled and deveined, tails off

FOR ASSEMBLY

16 leaves Bibb lettuce or other butter lettuce (about 1 head)
Chopped fresh cilantro

1. **Make the pineapple slaw:** In a large bowl, toss together the coleslaw mix, pineapple, cilantro, coconut aminos, lime juice, vinegar, sesame oil, maple syrup, and salt. Let chill while making the shrimp.

2. **Cook the shrimp:** In a medium bowl, mix together the coconut aminos, pineapple juice, oil, chili powder, garlic powder, ground ginger, smoked paprika, and salt. Add the shrimp and stir until evenly coated. Refrigerate for at least 15 minutes to allow the shrimp to marinate.

3. Heat a large dry skillet over medium heat. Working in batches to avoid overcrowding, carefully arrange the shrimp in a single layer, shaking off any excess marinade. Cook until lightly pink and browned around the edges, 2 to 3 minutes. Using tongs, flip and cook until pink and opaque throughout, 2 to 3 minutes more. Transfer to a large plate or sheet pan and repeat with the remaining shrimp.

4. **To assemble:** Place 4 lettuce cups on each of four plates. Divide the pineapple slaw among the lettuce cups and top each with 4 or 5 shrimp. Sprinkle with chopped cilantro.

CRUNCHY PORK LETTUCE WRAPS WITH CARROT SLAW

Gluten-free, dairy-free, nut-free option

These pork lettuce wraps are the kind of midday diversion that makes the workweek a little more exciting. Each bite delivers crunchy carrot slaw, savory pork, and toasted cashews—all wrapped up in crisp lettuce leaves. Need a more portable option? Turn it into an on-the-go bowl with Fluffy Does-It-All Quinoa (page 291), rice, or cauliflower rice. Hosting? Lay out all the components and let everyone build their own—it's interactive, effortless, and always a hit!

SERVES 4

Prep time: 15 minutes
Cook time: 15 minutes

To make this nut-free: Omit the cashews.

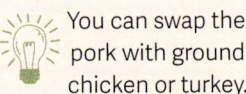

GOOOD TO KNOW: You can swap the pork with ground chicken or turkey.

STORE IT: Refrigerate the components in separate sealed containers for up to 4 days.

REHEAT IT: Microwave the pork mixture until warm, 1 to 2 minutes, then assemble the wraps.

FOR THE CARROT SLAW

10 ounces preshredded carrots, or 6 large carrots, coarsely shredded (about 3 cups)

4 green onions, thinly sliced

Juice of 1 lime

2 tablespoons toasted sesame oil

1 tablespoon coconut aminos (or reduced-sodium tamari or reduced-sodium soy sauce)

1 tablespoon pure maple syrup

1 tablespoon rice vinegar

FOR THE PORK FILLING

⅓ cup coconut aminos (or reduced-sodium tamari or reduced-sodium soy sauce)

1 tablespoon rice vinegar

1 tablespoon sriracha

1 tablespoon olive oil

1 pound 90% lean ground pork

2 teaspoons ground ginger

1 teaspoon garlic powder

⅔ cup unsalted raw cashews, roughly chopped

FOR ASSEMBLY

16 leaves Bibb lettuce or other butter lettuce (about 1 head), separated into leaves

Chopped fresh cilantro

1. **Make the carrot slaw:** In a large bowl, toss together all the slaw ingredients and set aside.

2. **Make the pork filling:** In a small bowl, whisk together the coconut aminos, vinegar, and sriracha. Set aside.

3. Heat the oil in a large skillet over medium heat. Add the ground pork and cook, breaking it up into small pieces with a wooden spoon, until golden

brown all over and no pink remains, 8 to 10 minutes. Using a large spoon, carefully drain and discard any excess fat. Add the ginger and garlic powder, and cook, stirring occasionally, until aromatic, 1 to 2 minutes more.

4. Pour the reserved coconut aminos mixture into the pan and stir to combine. Simmer, stirring often, until slightly thickened, about 5 minutes. Stir in the cashews and remove from the heat.

5. **To assemble:** Divide the lettuce cups among four plates. Place a heaping spoonful or two of the pork mixture inside each, followed by a spoonful or two of slaw. Garnish with chopped cilantro.

SPICY TOFU CRUNCH BOWLS

Gluten-free, dairy-free, vegetarian, vegan, nut-free

I pride myself on the number of skeptics I have converted into full-on tofu lovers. Tofu is one of my favorite budget-friendly proteins, and these crispy tofu bowls are worth the extra effort to get a crunch that rivals fried chicken. A crunch you can *literally* hear when you bite into it. The sauce is heavenly as is, or change things up and swap in peanut butter, almond butter, or cashew butter—whatever you have on hand. Want more tasty tofu? Flip to some other favorites like Coconut Curry Soup with Tofu and Rice Noodles (page 224), Sweet and Spicy Tofu and Broccolini (page 168), or Sticky Sesame Tofu (page 238).

SERVES 4

Prep time: 30 minutes
Cook time: 20 minutes

GOOOD TO KNOW: Make a spice-free variation by swapping the sauce for Lick-the-Bowl Peanut Sauce (page 295)—absolutely delicious!

FOR THE SPICY SUN BUTTER SAUCE

⅓ cup creamy natural sunflower butter

2 tablespoons coconut aminos (or reduced-sodium tamari or reduced-sodium soy sauce)

2 tablespoons sriracha

1 teaspoon garlic powder

1 teaspoon ground ginger

½ teaspoon kosher salt

¼ teaspoon red pepper flakes

FOR THE CORNFLAKE-CRUSTED TOFU

One 14-ounce block firm tofu

1½ cups gluten-free cornflakes

1 teaspoon garlic powder

½ teaspoon kosher salt

½ teaspoon ground black pepper

⅓ cup tapioca flour or arrowroot starch (can substitute cornstarch)

⅔ cup milk of choice

FOR THE BOWLS

Jenn's Steamed Rice (p. 290), or 3 cups cooked brown rice

6 ounces preshredded carrots, or 4 large carrots, coarsely shredded (about 2 cups)

1 red bell pepper, cored, seeded, and sliced into ⅛-inch-thick strips (about 1 cup)

1 English cucumber, unpeeled, halved lengthwise, and sliced into thin half-moons

Chopped fresh cilantro

3 green onions, thinly sliced

1. **Make the sun butter sauce:** In a small bowl, whisk the sunflower butter, coconut aminos, sriracha, garlic powder, ginger, salt, red pepper flakes, and ¼ cup warm water until you reach a pourable consistency. If the sauce is still too thick to easily pour, add up to 3 tablespoons more water. Set aside.

(continues)

2. **Prepare the cornflake-crusted tofu:** Preheat the oven to 375°F. Line a large sheet pan with parchment paper and set aside.

3. Press the tofu block with a tofu press or wrap it in a clean kitchen towel or paper towels. Place the block on a plate and top with a heavy object, like a cast-iron pan or large can of tomatoes. Let sit until the excess liquid has drained, 15 to 20 minutes.

4. Meanwhile, in a food processor or blender, combine the cornflakes, garlic powder, salt, and black pepper and pulse until an even, sand-like texture is formed, about 30 seconds. (Alternatively, combine the ingredients in a large sealable plastic bag and crush using a meat mallet or rolling pin.)

5. Set up a dredging station with three medium shallow bowls. Add the tapioca flour to one bowl. Add the milk to the second bowl. Transfer the cornflake crumbs to the third bowl.

6. Slice the pressed tofu block horizontally in half. Cut each half in a 4 × 4-inch grid into 16 cubes (32 cubes total). Coat each cube in the tapioca flour, then the milk, and finally in the cornflake mixture. Evenly space the coated cubes on the prepared sheet pan to prevent steaming in the oven. Bake until the outsides are golden brown and crispy, 15 to 20 minutes.

7. **Assemble the bowls:** Spoon the cooked rice into four bowls. Top with the carrots, bell peppers, and cucumber. Set 8 pieces of tofu on top of the vegetables in each bowl. Drizzle with the spicy sun butter sauce and garnish with cilantro and green onions.

STORE IT: Refrigerate the tofu, bowl components, and sauce in separate sealed containers, up to 4 days for the tofu bowl components and up to 7 days for the sauce.

REHEAT IT: Warm the tofu in a 400°F oven or air fryer until crisp, about 6 minutes right before serving, for optimal results. Alternatively, microwave the tofu until warm, 1 to 2 minutes, then assemble.

CHIPOTLE SWEET POTATO AND BLACK BEAN BOWLS

Gluten-free, dairy-free, vegetarian, vegan, nut-free

I do really love a good plant-based meal, and seasonings and sauces are my secret to leveling up vegan and vegetarian dishes. The nonnegotiable is that they're both satisfying and protein-packed. Canned black beans are a simple, budget-friendly way to get there. My smoky, slightly spicy chipotle sauce brings the heat to everything from tacos to eggs to burrito bowls.

SERVES 4

Prep time: 15 minutes
Cook time: 30 minutes

GOOOD TO KNOW: If you're not feeling the bowl, ditch the quinoa and grab some tortillas to assemble chipotle sweet potato and black bean tacos instead. Either way, you can't go wrong!

STORE IT: Refrigerate the quinoa, sweet potatoes, and beans in separate sealed containers for up to 4 days.

REHEAT IT: Microwave the quinoa, sweet potatoes, and black beans until warm, 1½ to 2 minutes, or transfer to a sheet pan and bake at 350°F for 10 to 12 minutes to crisp.

FOR THE SWEET POTATOES

1 teaspoon chili powder
1 teaspoon garlic powder
1 teaspoon dried oregano
1 teaspoon smoked paprika
1 teaspoon kosher salt
4 medium sweet potatoes, peeled and cut into ¾-inch cubes (about 6 cups)
2 tablespoons olive oil

FOR THE BOWLS

White or tricolor Fluffy Does-It-All Quinoa (p. 291)
Two 15.5-ounce cans black beans, drained and rinsed
1 cup coleslaw mix or shredded green cabbage (about 2 ounces)
Smoky Chipotle Sauce (p. 296)
Pickled Onions (recipe follows; optional)

1. **Roast the sweet potatoes:** Preheat the oven to 400°F. Line a sheet pan with parchment paper.

2. In a large bowl, whisk the chili powder, garlic powder, oregano, smoked paprika, and salt. Add the sweet potatoes and oil and toss until coated. Transfer the sweet potatoes to the sheet pan and spread them out evenly.

3. Bake until the outsides are crispy and the insides are fork-tender, 25 to 30 minutes.

4. **Assemble the bowls:** Spoon the quinoa into four bowls. Top with the sweet potatoes, black beans, and coleslaw mix in separate sections over the quinoa. Drizzle with chipotle sauce. Garnish with pickled onions (if using).

PICKLED ONIONS

Gluten-free, dairy-free, vegetarian, vegan, nut-free

MAKES 1 CUP

Prep time: 5 minutes
Marinating time: 25 minutes

> **GOOOD TO KNOW:** If you're a spice lover, add a pinch of cayenne or a few red pepper flakes for a sweet and spicy twist.

Keeping a jar of pickled onions in the fridge is an easy way to add punchy flavor to so many dishes. In our house we love the pretty pink onions on grain, on tacos—like Spiced Sweet Potato Tacos with Avocado Slaw (page 235), or even on top of soups, like Pantry Staples Spicy Black Bean Soup (page 226). Here's an easy, refined-sugar-free recipe to instantly level up your meals.

1 medium red onion, thinly sliced
¾ cup distilled white vinegar or apple cider vinegar
2 tablespoons pure maple syrup
2 teaspoons kosher salt

1. Pack the onion slices into a 16-ounce heatproof glass jar or lidded container.

2. In a small saucepan, combine ¾ cup water, the vinegar, maple syrup, and salt and bring to a boil over high heat. Remove from the heat.

3. Carefully pour the hot vinegar mixture over the onions in the jar. Use a spoon to push down any uncovered onions.

4. Let the onions sit for 25 to 30 minutes, until at room temperature.

STORE IT: Refrigerate in a sealed container for up to 2 weeks.

BARBECUE CHICKEN CHOPPED SALAD

Gluten-free, dairy-free option, vegetarian option, nut-free

I'm *obsessed* with chopped salads—especially the kind that deliver big on contrast. Think savory and sweet, crunchy and creamy, all in one bite. This one is a total warm-weather MVP, perfect for BBQs, picnics, or any gathering where you want a salad that actually holds up. No sad, wilted greens here—sturdy kale and cabbage keep everything crisp and fresh, even if you make it ahead. And the real stars? My homemade BBQ sauce and ranch dressing, which take it straight to ten out of ten territory. No weird ingredients, no refined sugars—just bold, delicious flavor. Bonus: My husband swears the leftovers wrapped in a warm tortilla make the ultimate next-day burrito.

SERVES 4

Prep time: 25 minutes, plus 15 minutes chilling

Cook time: none

To make this dairy-free: Omit the Cheddar and use dairy-free yogurt in the ranch dressing.

To make this vegetarian: See Goood to Know.

GOOOD TO KNOW: Vegetarians can enjoy this salad too! Toss two 15.5-ounce drained and rinsed cans of chickpeas with olive oil, kosher salt, garlic powder, and onion powder. Spread on a large sheet pan and roast at 425°F until crispy, 20 to 25 minutes. Toss with the BBQ sauce just as with the chicken.

3 cups medium-diced No-Fail Baked Chicken (page 102) or store-bought rotisserie chicken

2/3 cup Tangy Maple Barbecue Sauce (p. 298) or store-bought barbecue sauce, plus more for serving

4 cups shredded curly kale (about 6 ounces)

7 ounces packed coleslaw mix or shredded green cabbage (about 3 cups)

1 pint cherry tomatoes, halved (about 1½ cups)

One 15.5-ounce can black beans, drained and rinsed

1½ cups cooked fresh corn kernels (from 2 ears), thawed frozen corn, or from one 15-ounce can, drained

2/3 cup small-diced Cheddar (about 4 ounces)

1/3 cup chopped fresh cilantro

4 green onions, finely chopped

2/3 cup Herby Yogurt Ranch Dressing (p. 302) or store-bought ranch dressing

1. In a large bowl, combine the chicken and barbecue sauce. Mix until the chicken is evenly coated in the sauce. Set aside.

2. In a second large bowl, combine the kale, coleslaw mix, cherry tomatoes, black beans, corn, Cheddar, cilantro, and green onions. Add half of the ranch dressing and mix well. Let the salad sit for 10 minutes to allow the kale to soften.

3. Add the chicken to the kale mixture and mix well. Add more dressing if desired. Refrigerate for at least 15 minutes or chill for up to 4 hours.

4. Serve the salad in bowls and drizzle with more barbecue sauce.

STORE IT: Refrigerate in a sealed container for up to 4 days.

GREEK-STYLE CRISPY CHICKPEA BOWLS

Gluten-free, dairy-free option, vegetarian, vegan option, nut-free

Chickpeas make frequent appearances in my kitchen—and for good reason. They're nutrient-packed, easy on the wallet, and ridiculously versatile. Their mild flavor is ready for any seasoning you throw at them. My absolute favorite way to enjoy them? Roasted on a sheet pan with fragrant herbs and spices until golden and crispy—perfect for snacking. Here they bring a Mediterranean twist to a plant-based bowl that's so good your coworkers *will* be envious!

SERVES 4

Prep time: 15 minutes
Cook time: 30 minutes

To make this dairy-free and vegan: Use dairy-free feta and dairy-free yogurt.

GOOOD TO KNOW: Transform these bowls into a plant-packed wrap (or lettuce wraps) with the yogurt sauce inside when you want to switch it up.

STORE IT: Refrigerate the quinoa salad, chickpeas, and sauce in separate sealed containers, up to 4 days for the salad and chickpeas and up to 7 days for the sauce.

REHEAT IT: Optionally, to recrisp the chickpeas, warm them in a 400°F oven or air fryer for 5 to 10 minutes.

FOR THE CRISPY CHICKPEAS
1 teaspoon dried oregano
1 teaspoon kosher salt
½ teaspoon dried basil
½ teaspoon ground cumin
½ teaspoon garlic powder
½ teaspoon smoked paprika
½ teaspoon dried thyme
½ teaspoon ground black pepper
Two 15-ounce cans chickpeas, drained and rinsed
2 tablespoons olive oil

FOR THE BOWLS
White or tricolor Fluffy Does-It-All Quinoa (p. 291)
1 pint cherry tomatoes, halved (about 1½ cups)
1 English cucumber, unpeeled, medium-diced (about 1 cup)
¾ cup crumbled feta (about 3 ounces)
½ cup Kalamata olives, pitted and chopped
Cucumber Garlicky Sauce (p. 299)
Chopped fresh cilantro

1. **Make the crispy chickpeas:** Preheat the oven to 400°F. Line a sheet pan with parchment paper and set aside.

2. In a small bowl, whisk together the oregano, salt, basil, cumin, garlic powder, smoked paprika, thyme, and black pepper. Add the chickpeas, oil, and spice mixture and toss until the chickpeas are fully coated in the spices. Transfer to the prepared sheet pan.

3. Bake until golden brown and crispy, 25 to 30 minutes.

4. In a large bowl, mix the quinoa, tomatoes, cucumber, feta, and olives. Spoon into four bowls and top each with a big spoonful of the crispy chickpeas. Drizzle the cucumber sauce over the top and garnish with cilantro.

NOURISHING SNACKS & DIPS

Snacks are little bites of joy—quick, satisfying, and sometimes, a chance to sneak in extra veggies while you're at it. This chapter is packed with crave-worthy bites—salty, cheesy, spicy, and creamy—perfect for make-ahead munching. Whether you're fueling up between meals, hosting friends, or just need a little something to keep the hanger at bay, these snacks have your back. Bonus: They double as easy ways to impress with minimal effort. Snack happy!

Crispy Ranch Chickpea Snack Mix 122

Baked Sweet Potato Crackers 124

High-Protein Cilantro-Edamame Dip 125

Whipped Feta and Beet Dip 126

Chickpea Guacamole 128

Garlicky Hummus 129

Dairy-Free Spinach and Artichoke Dip 130

Avocado, Corn, and Black Bean Dip 133

CRISPY RANCH CHICKPEA SNACK MIX

Gluten-free, dairy-free option, vegetarian, vegan option

The zippy tang of homemade ranch seasoning + the crispy, savory crunch of roasted chickpeas = the ultimate afternoon snack win. This mix is the kind of thing you'll want to keep on hand for when cravings strike—or when you've got good friends, great conversation, and a refreshing drink like Tart Raspberry-Honey Lemonade (page 313) in the mix. Bonus: It's way more affordable than the fancy store-bought stuff, and the flavor possibilities are endless. Swap up the dried herbs and spices, get creative, and discover a new favorite snack!

SERVES 8

Prep time: 10 minutes, plus 15 minutes cooling
Cook time: 40 minutes

To make this dairy-free and vegan: Use unsalted vegan butter.

GOOOD TO KNOW: The drier the chickpeas, the crispier they will get in the oven. Take an extra minute to pat them dry as best you can, and if you have the time, remove the skins to make them even crispier.

STORE IT: Keep in a sealed container in a cool, dry place for up to 5 days.

- 1 tablespoon nutritional yeast
- 2 teaspoons dried parsley
- 1 teaspoon dried dill
- 1 teaspoon garlic powder
- 1 teaspoon onion powder
- 1 teaspoon kosher salt
- ½ teaspoon ground black pepper
- 4 tablespoons (½ stick) unsalted butter, melted
- 2 tablespoons coconut aminos (or reduced-sodium tamari or reduced-sodium soy sauce)
- One 15-ounce can chickpeas, drained and rinsed
- 3 cups salted gluten-free pretzels (twists, sticks, or a mix of both)
- 1 cup unsalted raw cashews
- 2 cups Rice Chex cereal

1. Preheat the oven to 300°F.

2. In a small bowl, whisk together the nutritional yeast, parsley, dill, garlic powder, onion powder, salt, and black pepper. Add the butter and coconut aminos and mix well. Set aside.

3. Line a large sheet pan with paper towels. Transfer the rinsed chickpeas to the paper towels and pat with additional paper towels until they are as dry as possible.

4. In a large bowl, combine the chickpeas, pretzels, cashews, and Rice Chex. Add the reserved spice/butter mixture and toss with clean hands or a rubber spatula until everything is evenly coated. Discard the paper towels from the sheet pan and evenly spread the mixture onto the sheet pan.

5. Bake until crisp, 35 to 40 minutes, tossing halfway through. Let cool completely on the pan before serving, 10 to 15 minutes.

DON'T THINK ABOUT DINNER

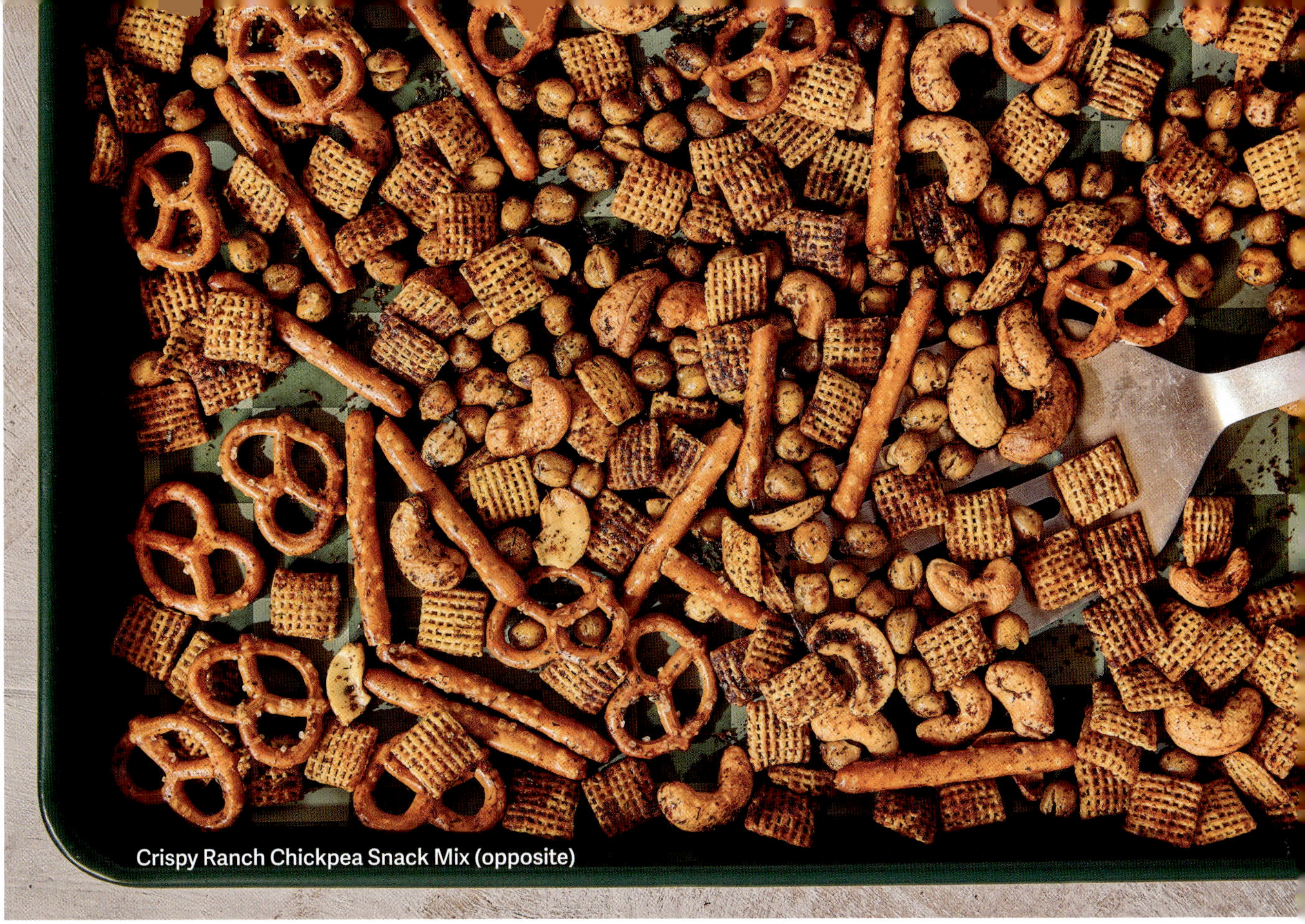

Crispy Ranch Chickpea Snack Mix (opposite)

Baked Sweet Potato Crackers (p. 124)

BAKED SWEET POTATO CRACKERS

Gluten-free, dairy-free, vegetarian, vegan

Homemade crackers might *sound* fancy, but don't let that scare you off—they're way easier to make than you think! This crunchy, nutrient-packed snack is loaded with fiber and potassium, and best of all, it tastes amazing. I'll be honest, I usually snack on these straight off the pan, but they're also the ultimate dip-delivery vehicle. Pair them with Garlicky Hummus (page 129) or Dairy-Free Spinach and Artichoke Dip (page 130), or pile them onto a cheese and fruit board for instant snack-time success. Want to mix things up? Try adding rosemary, nutritional yeast, finely chopped sun-dried tomatoes, a sprinkle of ranch seasoning, everything bagel seasoning… you get the idea!

MAKES ABOUT 56 CRACKERS

Prep time: 15 minutes
Cook time: 20 minutes

GOOOD TO KNOW: Sweet potato puree is easy to make at home and will save you money! For the ½ cup of puree needed for this recipe, bake 1 small sweet potato in a 375°F oven until fork-tender, 45 minutes to 1 hour. Let cool to room temperature before peeling and mashing.

STORE IT: Keep the crackers in a sealed container in a cool, dry place for up to 5 days.

¾ cup blanched almond flour

⅔ cup tapioca flour or arrowroot starch (can substitute cornstarch), plus more as needed and for rolling

2 tablespoons ground flaxseed

½ teaspoon kosher salt, plus more for sprinkling

½ teaspoon garlic powder

Generous pinch of baking soda

½ cup sweet potato puree, canned, thawed frozen, or home-cooked (see Goood to Know)

1. Preheat the oven to 350°F. Line a sheet pan with parchment paper and set aside.

2. In a large bowl, whisk together the almond flour, tapioca flour, flaxseed, salt, garlic powder, and baking soda until evenly combined. Add the sweet potato puree and mix with a spatula until a very thick, uniform dough forms. The dough should be soft and thick but not sticky. If it is still sticky, add more tapioca flour a tablespoon at a time and mix it in until it is no longer sticky.

3. Sprinkle a clean surface with tapioca flour. Place the dough on top of the flour and sprinkle with more tapioca flour. Roll the dough with a tapioca-floured rolling pin into a ⅛-inch-thick 12 × 10½-inch rectangle. Use your hands to create an even rectangular shape, adding pieces of dough where needed and flattening with your rolling pin.

4. Use a pizza cutter or knife to cut the rectangle into about fifty-six 1½ × 1½-inch squares. Carefully transfer them to the sheet pan, leaving space between them.

5. Bake until golden and crisp, 16 to 20 minutes. Sprinkle with salt and let cool completely in the pan on the counter before serving or storing.

HIGH-PROTEIN CILANTRO-EDAMAME DIP

Gluten-free, dairy-free option, vegetarian, vegan option, nut-free

Keeping an eye on your protein intake makes it easier to stay mindful about what you're eating—and trust me, I *feel* the difference when I'm getting enough. More energy, better focus, all-around good vibes. That's why this dip is a total winner for anyone looking to sneak in more protein throughout the day. It's just as yummy as it is satisfying, and since we *always* have a bag of edamame in the freezer, it's on constant rotation in our house. Scoop it up with veggies, dunk in some store-bought crackers or Baked Sweet Potato Crackers (opposite), or use it as a topper for a loaded grain bowl. However you snack, this dip is here for it.

MAKES ABOUT 2 CUPS

Prep time: 15 minutes

To make this dairy-free or vegan: Use dairy-free yogurt.

GOOOD TO KNOW: Swap the yogurt with my other sneaky high-protein fave, cottage cheese, for a similar taste.

STORE IT: Refrigerate in a sealed container for up to 4 days.

12 ounces fresh or thawed frozen shelled edamame
½ cup packed chopped fresh cilantro
1 clove garlic, minced
1 teaspoon kosher salt, plus more to taste
½ teaspoon ground black pepper
⅓ cup whole-milk or low-fat Greek yogurt
Juice of 1 lemon
¼ cup olive oil

FOR SERVING

1 English cucumber, unpeeled, cut into spears
2 cups crackers of your choice (I prefer gluten-free rice or almond flour crackers)

1. In a food processor or blender, combine the edamame, cilantro, garlic, salt, and black pepper and process on high, occasionally scraping down the sides with a rubber spatula, until the edamame is blitzed into small pieces, 30 to 45 seconds. Scrape down the sides, add the yogurt and lemon juice, and process on high until smooth, about 30 seconds.

2. With the machine running, slowly pour in the oil and ¼ cup cold water, alternating between the two liquids until smooth. If needed, season with more salt.

3. Transfer the dip to a small bowl and serve with the cucumber slices and crackers.

WHIPPED FETA AND BEET DIP

Gluten-free, vegetarian, nut-free

When you need an easy appetizer or snack *fast*—as in, toss everything into the blender and enjoy two minutes later—this citrusy whipped beet and feta dip is about to become your new best friend. It's creamy, tangy, and just the right amount of sweet, with a color so bold it practically demands a spot at the table. Serve it alongside a rainbow of crisp crudités or pita chips and watch it disappear. Impressive but practically effortless, it also shines as a side dish or starter—because who doesn't love a dip that does it all?

MAKES ABOUT 2 CUPS

Prep time: 10 minutes

GOOOD TO KNOW: Try the dip smeared on a piece of toast with arugula and a fried egg on top for an unexpectedly tasty and colorful breakfast option.

One 8-ounce block feta, broken into 3 to 4 large pieces, plus more for topping
Grated zest and juice of ½ lemon
1 cup medium-diced peeled precooked beets (8 ounces precooked)
½ teaspoon garlic powder
½ teaspoon kosher salt
½ teaspoon ground black pepper
¼ cup olive oil
Chopped fresh dill

1. In a food processor, combine the feta and lemon zest and juice and blend on high speed until thick and smooth, 30 to 60 seconds. Scrape down the sides with a spatula. Add the beets, garlic powder, salt, and black pepper and pulse until the beets are pulverized into very small pieces, about 10 pulses. Scrape down the sides with a spatula.

2. With the machine running, slowly stream in the oil, scraping down the sides as necessary, until smooth and uniformly pink in color, about 60 seconds.

3. Transfer the dip to a shallow serving bowl, top with more crumbled feta, and garnish with chopped fresh dill.

STORE IT: Refrigerate the dip in a sealed container for up to 4 days.

High-Protein Cilantro-Edamame Dip (p. 125)

Whipped Feta and Beet Dip (opposite)

Chickpea Guacamole (p. 128)

Garlicky Hummus (p. 129)

CHICKPEA GUACAMOLE

Gluten-free, dairy-free, vegetarian, vegan, nut-free

I wanted to sneak a little extra protein into my go-to guac—because let's be real, a big bowl of guac is *always* a crowd pleaser. So I did what any resourceful snacker would do: rummaged through my pantry. And there they were—chickpeas! Not only do they add a creamy, protein-packed boost, but they also help stretch your avocado supply (avocados aren't exactly budget-friendly). No chickpeas? No problem. Cannellini, navy, or Great Northern beans all work just as well. While this guac is perfect for scooping up with tortilla chips, try slathering it onto Mashed Chipotle Chickpea Quesadillas (page 244) or spooning it over Not-Your-Average Burrito Bowls with Sheet Pan Salsa (page 193) for next-level plant-based goodness.

MAKES ABOUT 3 CUPS

Prep time: 10 minutes

GOOOD TO KNOW: You can push this in any flavor direction you dare to go, from the classic Mexican lime and cilantro to Mediterranean oregano, lemon, and garlic; you can even add a spoonful of smoky adobo sauce from a can of chipotles to spice things up.

1 teaspoon kosher salt
½ teaspoon garlic powder
½ teaspoon onion powder
¼ teaspoon red pepper flakes (optional)
One 15-ounce can chickpeas, drained and rinsed
2 avocados, halved and pitted
¼ cup finely chopped fresh cilantro

1. In a small bowl, combine the salt, garlic powder, onion powder, and pepper flakes (if using).

2. In a large bowl, use a fork to mash the chickpeas until roughly smashed. Scoop the avocado flesh into the bowl and continue mashing until the avocado and chickpeas are evenly combined. Stir in the cilantro. Add the spice mix and mash again until well incorporated. Serve immediately.

STORE IT: Refrigerate in a sealed container with plastic wrap or aluminum foil pressed directly on top of the guacamole before covering the container to reduce its exposure to oxygen. It will keep for up to 3 days.

GARLICKY HUMMUS

Gluten-free, dairy-free, vegetarian, vegan, nut-free

Homemade hummus is worth the effort because you control what goes into it (no weird additives!), plus, as I'm always a fan of money-saving hacks, it's much more economical than pricey store-bought versions. Serve with Baked Sweet Potato Crackers (page 124), or try it as a topping for Herby Chickpea and Cauliflower Bowls with Lemon-Dill Sauce (page 174), Mediterranean-Inspired Smashed Tacos (page 264), or Mediterranean-Inspired Salmon and Orzo Bake (page 147).

MAKES ABOUT 3 CUPS

Prep time: 15 minutes

GOOOD TO KNOW: Swap ½ cup of the chickpeas with roasted red peppers for a roasted red pepper hummus.

Two 15.5-ounce cans chickpeas, with their liquid
⅓ cup tahini
Juice of 2 lemons
3 tablespoons olive oil, plus more for serving
2 garlic cloves
1 teaspoon ground cumin
½ teaspoon kosher salt
Smoked paprika
Pine nuts (optional)
Chopped fresh dill (optional)

1. Set a fine-mesh sieve over a small bowl. Pour the chickpeas into the sieve and drain the aquafaba liquid into the bowl, reserving the liquid. You should have ⅓ cup liquid. If not, make up the difference with cold water. Rinse the chickpeas thoroughly under cold water.

2. In a food processor or blender, combine the tahini and lemon juice and blend on high speed until smooth, about 2 minutes, scraping down the sides. Add the oil, garlic, cumin, and salt and blend again until no big pieces of chickpea or garlic are left, 1 to 2 minutes. Scrape the sides down again. With the machine running, slowly stream in the reserved aquafaba until combined. Continue to blend until the hummus is completely smooth and uniform, 2 to 3 minutes. If needed, season with more salt to taste.

3. To serve, transfer the hummus to a shallow bowl. Garnish with smoked paprika and a drizzle of oil. If desired, also sprinkle with some pine nuts and dill.

STORE IT: Refrigerate in a sealed container for up to 7 day (best within 4 days).

DAIRY-FREE SPINACH AND ARTICHOKE DIP

Gluten-free, dairy-free, vegetarian, vegan

This spinach and artichoke dip is *that* appetizer—the one you spot on a menu and instantly want to order. It's a classic, never-fail dip. I wanted a dairy-free version that still delivered on all the creamy, rich, and savory goodness. Enter: a high-protein vegan cream made from blended cashews and water.

Perfect for parties, tailgates, impressing the in-laws, or just leveling up a chill movie night, this dip does it all. *One little note*—make sure your guests know cashews are the secret ingredient, in case of allergies!

MAKES ABOUT 4 CUPS

Prep time: 40 minutes

Cook time: 20 minutes, plus 10 minutes cooling

Special equipment: 1½- or 2-quart gratin dish or baking pan

GOOOD TO KNOW: To thaw frozen spinach, place in a microwave-safe bowl and microwave 3 to 4 minutes. Transfer to a kitchen towel and squeeze out excess water.

STORE IT: Refrigerate in a sealed container for up to 4 days or freeze for up to 3 months.

REHEAT IT: From the refrigerator, transfer to a baking dish in a 400°F oven for about 15 minutes. From the freezer, thaw in the refrigerator overnight, transfer to a baking dish, then warm as above.

1 cup unsalted raw cashews
1½ cups boiling water
Neutral oil spray
One 16-ounce bag frozen spinach, thawed and squeezed dry (see Goood to Know)
One 14-ounce can water-packed artichoke hearts, drained and roughly chopped
4 ounces dairy-free or regular cream cheese, at room temperature
2 tablespoons nutritional yeast
2 tablespoons olive oil
3 garlic cloves, minced
1½ teaspoons kosher salt (if using salted cashews, reduce to 1 teaspoon)
½ teaspoon ground black pepper
½ teaspoon red pepper flakes (optional)

1. Place the cashews in a heatproof glass bowl or jar and cover with the boiling water. Soak until the cashews are softened, 25 to 30 minutes, or let cool and soak overnight in the fridge. (A longer soak creates a smoother blend.)

2. Preheat the oven to 400°F. Lightly grease a 1½- or 2-quart baking dish with neutral oil spray.

3. Reserving the soaking liquid, drain the soaked cashews. In a food processor or blender, combine the cashews and half the soaking liquid and blend on high speed until creamy and uniform, about 45 seconds. If the mixture is too thick, add more of the soaking water, 1 tablespoon at a time, until smooth.

4. Transfer the cashew cream to a large bowl and add the spinach, artichokes, cream cheese, nutritional yeast, olive oil, garlic, salt, black pepper, and red pepper flakes (if using). Mix well. Transfer to the baking dish and smooth.

5. Bake until golden brown and bubbling, 20 to 25 minutes. Let cool for 10 minutes before serving. Serve warm or at room temperature.

AVOCADO, CORN, AND BLACK BEAN DIP

Gluten-free, dairy-free, vegetarian, vegan, nut-free

Whether you serve it on its own with tortilla chips or as a salsa accompaniment, this recipe is a *must*-have. When I can't bear turning on the oven or even pulling out a skillet, this dip is a lifesaver, as it's more about combining some of my favorite ingredients and less about having to fuss with "cooking." It truly sings in the summer when you can hit the corn stands, but it can be made in any season with frozen corn. This comes together in a flash and can be used in so many ways: in a salad; as a crunchy, refreshing dip for chips; spooned into tacos; or as a topping for rice bowls, grilled chicken, or fish.

MAKES ABOUT 5 CUPS

Prep time: 15 minutes, plus 30 minutes chilling

GOOOD TO KNOW: Rinse the beans well before tossing with the rest of the ingredients.

1 teaspoon kosher salt
½ teaspoon chili powder
½ teaspoon garlic powder
½ teaspoon smoked paprika
Two 15-ounce cans black beans, drained and rinsed
1½ cups cooked fresh corn kernels (from 2 ears), thawed frozen corn, or from one 15-ounce can, drained
1 pint cherry tomatoes, halved (about 1½ cups)
1 ripe avocado, halved, pitted, peeled, and small-diced
1 red bell pepper, cored, seeded, and small-diced (about 1 cup)
¼ cup apple cider vinegar
Juice of 1 lime

1. In a small bowl, whisk the salt, chili powder, garlic powder, and smoked paprika.

2. In a large bowl, combine the black beans, corn, cherry tomatoes, avocado, bell pepper, vinegar, and lime juice. Mix well. Add the spice mixture and toss until all the vegetables are evenly coated.

3. Refrigerate for at least 30 minutes before serving.

STORE IT: Refrigerate in a sealed container for up to 5 days.

ONE-POT WONDERS

One and done—that's the beauty of a great one-pot (or one-pan) meal. From the very start, Jenn Eats Goood has been all about dishes that pack maximum flavor with minimal effort. These recipes prove that simplicity doesn't mean sacrificing taste—or creativity. Whether it's a simmering soup with an unexpected spice blend, a skillet meal with a bold flavor twist, or a sheet-pan dinner that reinvents weeknight staples, these no-fuss, no-mess meals deliver big on comfort, nutrition, and deliciousness—all while keeping cleanup blissfully easy.

Lemony Chicken Thighs and Rice 136

Chicken Pot Pie Soup 138

Spinach, Goat Cheese, and Sun-Dried Tomato Stuffed Chicken 140

Garlic Butter Shrimp and Spaghetti Squash 142

Stovetop Beef and Bean Taco Skillet 144

Mediterranean-Inspired Salmon and Orzo Bake 147

One-Pot Creamy Sun-Dried Tomato Pasta 148

Buffalo Chickpea Stuffed Sweet Potatoes 151

Caramelized Onion, Steak, and Cheese Skillet 152

Weeknight Honey-Garlic Turkey Skillet 155

One-Pot Quinoa Bake with Butternut Squash, Kale, and Feta 156

Dump-and-Bake Hidden Protein Pasta 159

LEMONY CHICKEN THIGHS AND RICE

Gluten-free, dairy-free, nut-free

Every dream come true has an origin story, and this is mine. With tens of millions of views and thousands of remakes, this recipe is one of the reasons you're reading this book right now (it's even on the cover!). It really is that good—and once you try this all-in-one dinner, you'll be hooked too. It practically cooks itself, bursting with flavor while sneaking in veggies and boasting creamy, lemony goodness in every mouthwatering bite. An "I can't believe it's gluten- *and* dairy-free" favorite.

SERVES 4

Prep time: 15 minutes
Cook time: 35 minutes

GOOOD TO KNOW: Play with this base recipe—swap in sage, thyme, and butternut squash in the fall; mushrooms and rosemary in the winter; and fresh corn kernels, tomatoes, and lime in the summer.

STORE IT: Refrigerate in a sealed container for up to 4 days or freeze for up to 3 months.

REHEAT IT: From the refrigerator, microwave until warm, 2 to 3 minutes. From the freezer, thaw in the refrigerator overnight, then microwave in 30-second increments until warm.

2 teaspoons dried oregano
2 teaspoons smoked paprika
Kosher salt
½ teaspoon ground black pepper
1½ pounds boneless, skinless chicken thighs
2 tablespoons olive oil
½ large yellow onion, small-diced (about ¾ cup)
3 garlic cloves, minced
1 cup uncooked jasmine rice
2 cups low-sodium chicken broth
¾ cup full-fat coconut milk (about half a well-shaken 13.5-ounce can)
3 cups shredded curly kale (about 4½ ounces)
Juice of 1 lemon
Chopped fresh parsley

1. Preheat the oven to 375°F.

2. In a small bowl, combine the oregano, smoked paprika, 1½ teaspoons salt, and the black pepper. Pat the chicken thighs dry with a paper towel and season both sides evenly with the herb-spice mixture.

3. Heat the oil in a large ovenproof sauté pan or large Dutch oven over medium-high heat until shimmering. Working in batches to avoid overcrowding, add the chicken and cook until golden brown and cooked through on the inside, 5 to 7 minutes per side. Transfer to a plate and set aside.

4. In the same pan, add the onion and cook over medium heat, stirring occasionally, until softened, about 3 minutes. Add the garlic and cook, stirring frequently, until fragrant, 1 to 2 minutes.

5. Add the rice and toast, stirring frequently, until golden brown, 1 to 2 minutes. Add the broth, coconut milk, and a big pinch of salt and stir to combine. Bring to a simmer over medium heat. Add the kale and lemon juice, mix

well, and cook until wilted, about 1 minute. Place the chicken on top and transfer to the oven. Bake, uncovered, until the liquid is absorbed and the rice is fluffy, 15 to 20 minutes.

6. Divide among four plates or shallow bowls and garnish with parsley.

CHICKEN POT PIE SOUP

Gluten-free, dairy-free, nut-free

When I was growing up, chicken pot pie was a staple in my Irish American household. We had it almost every week, and it's become my shorthand for the warmth and coziness of childhood. I wanted to access those same feelings without sacrificing lots of time and effort prepping ingredients and making pies, so I came up with this chicken pot pie soup. It has all the classic pot pie flavors, and the number-one comment I still receive is that people can't believe it's dairy-free.

SERVES 4

Prep time: 15 minutes
Cook time: 30 minutes

GOOOD TO KNOW: The tapioca flour is what makes the soup nice and thick and keeps it gluten-free, so don't skip it!

STORE IT: Refrigerate in a sealed container for up to 4 days or freeze for up to 3 months.

REHEAT IT: From the refrigerator, heat in a saucepan over medium heat until warm or microwave for 2 to 3 minutes. From the freezer, thaw in the refrigerator overnight, then heat in a saucepan over medium heat or microwave in 30-second increments until warm.

3 tablespoons olive oil
3 large carrots, chopped (about 1½ cups)
3 celery ribs, small-diced (about 1½ cups)
1 large yellow onion, small-diced (about 1½ cups)
8 ounces white mushrooms, small-diced (about 2 cups)
4 garlic cloves, minced
1 tablespoon finely chopped fresh rosemary, or 1 teaspoon dried
1 tablespoon finely chopped fresh sage, or 1 teaspoon dried
1 tablespoon finely chopped fresh thyme, or 1 teaspoon dried
1½ teaspoons kosher salt
½ teaspoon ground black pepper
¼ cup tapioca flour or arrowroot starch (can substitute cornstarch)
4 cups low-sodium chicken broth
2½ cups medium-diced peeled Yukon Gold potatoes (about 3 medium potatoes)
3 cups No-Fail Baked Chicken (page 102) or store-bought rotisserie chicken, shredded
¾ cup full-fat coconut milk (about half a well-shaken 13.5-ounce can)
1 cup fresh or frozen green peas (8 ounces)
Chopped fresh parsley

1. Heat the oil in a large pot over medium heat. Add the carrots, celery, and onion and cook, stirring occasionally, until softened, about 7 minutes. Add the mushrooms and garlic and cook, stirring occasionally, until softened, 4 to 5 minutes. Add the rosemary, sage, thyme, salt, black pepper, and tapioca flour, stir, and cook, stirring constantly to form a paste, 2 to 3 minutes.

2. Add the broth and potatoes and bring to a boil over high heat. Reduce the heat to low, stir, cover, and simmer until the vegetables are tender, about 15 minutes.

3. Add the shredded chicken, coconut milk, and peas and stir until combined. Simmer until the peas are heated through, about 2 minutes.

4. Divide the soup among four bowls and garnish with parsley.

SPINACH, GOAT CHEESE, AND SUN-DRIED TOMATO STUFFED CHICKEN

Gluten-free, nut-free

I love a recipe that looks fancy but is secretly easy—like a culinary magic trick. Enter this stuffed chicken: the ultimate date-night dish that delivers big on wow without keeping you chained to the stove. There are endless ways to spin a stuffed chicken breast (see Goood to Know), but this combo? A total showstopper. Sweet, creamy goat cheese melts into velvety spinach, while sun-dried tomatoes bring that bright, tangy punch. Bulk it up with Fluffy Does-It-All Quinoa (page 291) on the side.

SERVES 4

Prep time: 15 minutes
Cook time: 30 minutes

GOOOD TO KNOW: Use this as a base recipe and make it your own! Try making a spinach, cream cheese, and garlic variation; a broccoli and Cheddar variation; or a pesto, roasted red pepper, and mozzarella variation.

STORE IT: Refrigerate in a sealed container for up to 4 days or freeze up to 3 months.

REHEAT IT: From the refrigerator, microwave until warm, 1 to 2 minutes. From the freezer, thaw in the refrigerator overnight, then microwave in 30-second increments until warm.

2 cups baby spinach, finely chopped (about 3 ounces)
One 4-ounce log soft goat cheese
½ cup drained oil-packed sun-dried tomatoes, finely chopped
Kosher salt
1 teaspoon dried basil
1 teaspoon garlic powder
1 teaspoon dried oregano
½ teaspoon ground black pepper
¼ teaspoon red pepper flakes (optional)
2 pounds boneless, skinless chicken breasts
1 tablespoon olive oil

1. Preheat the oven to 375°F.

2. In a large bowl, mash the spinach, goat cheese, and sun-dried tomatoes with a fork until it holds together when pressed. Season with a big pinch of salt and set aside.

3. In a small bowl, combine the basil, garlic powder, oregano, 1 teaspoon salt, black pepper, and red pepper flakes (if using). Pat the chicken dry with a paper towel and season all over with the spice mixture.

4. Starting on the fat end of the breast, carefully cut a 3-inch-long horizontal slit to create a big pocket without slicing the chicken in half. Evenly spoon the goat cheese mixture into each pocket. Press down firmly on the top to seal.

5. Heat the oil in a large cast-iron or ovenproof skillet over medium heat. Add the chicken and cook until golden brown on each side, 3 to 4 minutes per side. Immediately transfer the skillet to the oven.

6. Bake until the chicken reaches an internal temperature of 165°F, 14 to 16 minutes.

7. To serve, slice the breasts on an angle and fan one breast on each plate.

GARLIC BUTTER SHRIMP AND SPAGHETTI SQUASH

Gluten-free, dairy-free option, nut-free

I'm always on the hunt for that weeknight dinner—elevated and flavorful but without a kitchen disaster in its wake. Enter my healthier take on shrimp scampi. Spaghetti squash steps in for pasta, keeping things light yet satisfying, while garlic and butter do their magic. And the best part? It's all about the timing—once I nailed that, I cracked the code on a one-pan dump-and-bake version. It's so easy, you'll wonder why you ever put up with boiling pasta water in the first place.

SERVES 4

Prep time: 10 minutes
Cook time: 40 minutes

To make this dairy-free: Swap out the butter for unsalted vegan butter and use ¼ cup nutritional yeast in place of the Parmesan.

GOOOD TO KNOW: Save those spaghetti squash seeds! To minimize waste and get a deliciously crispy salad topping, wash them, toss them in oil and salt on a sheet pan, and roast them at 400°F for 10 to 15 minutes.

2 tablespoons olive oil
5 garlic cloves, minced
Kosher salt
1 large spaghetti squash (about 3 pounds)
1 pint cherry tomatoes, halved (about 1½ cups)
2 teaspoons dried basil
2 teaspoons dried oregano
1 teaspoon chili powder
½ teaspoon ground black pepper
1 pound fresh or thawed frozen medium shrimp, peeled and deveined, tails off
3 tablespoons unsalted butter, cut into small cubes
2 cups roughly chopped baby spinach (about 3 ounces)
⅔ cup grated Parmesan, plus more for garnish
Juice of 1 lemon

1. Preheat the oven to 400°F. Coat a 9 × 13-inch baking dish with the oil. Sprinkle the garlic and a few pinches of salt on the bottom and set aside.

2. Poke the spaghetti squash all over with a fork, 8 to 10 times. Microwave until softened, about 5 minutes, to make it easier to halve the squash. (The squash will be very hot, so use oven mitts to remove it from the microwave.) Allow the squash to cool on a cutting board for 5 to 10 minutes before handling.

3. Cut the squash in half lengthwise and scoop out and discard the seeds (or roast them—see Goood to Know). Place both halves, cut side down, over the chopped garlic in the baking dish. (Push the garlic under the squash halves; this will keep it from burning while the squash bakes.) Arrange the cherry tomatoes around the squash.

4. Bake until the tomatoes burst and soften and the skin of the squash is fork-tender, 25 to 30 minutes.

DON'T THINK ABOUT DINNER

STORE IT: Refrigerate in a sealed container for up to 3 days.

REHEAT IT: Microwave until warm, 1 to 2 minutes, or toss in a skillet over medium heat with a tablespoon of olive oil until warm.

5. Meanwhile, in a medium bowl, stir together the basil, oregano, chili powder, 1 teaspoon salt, and the black pepper. Add the shrimp and mix until well coated.

6. When the squash is ready, arrange the shrimp in a single layer around the spaghetti squash. Top the shrimp and tomatoes with the butter cubes. Bake until the shrimp are pink and opaque, 10 to 12 minutes.

7. Using tongs or oven mitts, transfer the squash to a cutting board. Scrape out the insides with a fork to create spaghetti-like strands. Return the strands to the baking dish, discarding the squash skins. Add the spinach, Parmesan, and lemon juice to the baking dish and mix until combined.

8. Divide among four plates and garnish with more grated Parmesan.

STOVETOP BEEF AND BEAN TACO SKILLET

Gluten-free, dairy-free option, vegetarian option, vegan option, nut-free

Get ready to get obsessed! This warming one-pan rice dish is a twist on quick chili in a skillet and is packed with protein. Between the beef, beans, and veggies, it's a full meal that'll leave you very satisfied. Ground turkey or chicken? Those work just as well. Pinto beans or black beans? Your call. No matter how you play with it, one thing's for sure: Even picky eaters won't turn down this easy, cheesy skillet.

SERVES 4

Prep time: 10 minutes
Cook time: 35 minutes

To make this dairy-free, vegetarian, and vegan: Skip the Cheddar and ground beef, and use vegetable broth. Add an extra can of beans for more protein, if desired.

GOOOD TO KNOW: Giving the rice a good rinse washes away excess starch, meaning less sticky cooking water and grains that stay separate and perfectly tender. Place the rice in a fine-mesh sieve and run under cold water for about 30 seconds. Let the water drain thoroughly and gently shake the sieve to remove any dripping water.

STORE IT: Refrigerate in a sealed container for up to 4 days or freeze for up to 3 months.

1½ teaspoons chili powder
1½ teaspoons ground cumin
1½ teaspoons kosher salt
1 teaspoon garlic powder
1 teaspoon smoked paprika
½ teaspoon dried oregano
1 tablespoon olive oil, plus more as needed
1 pound 85% lean ground beef
½ medium red onion, medium-diced (about ½ cup)
1 green bell pepper, cored, seeded, and medium-diced (about 1 cup)
1 red bell pepper, cored, seeded, and medium-diced (about 1 cup)
¾ cup uncooked jasmine rice, rinsed (see Goood to Know)
2 cups low-sodium beef broth
½ cup marinara sauce
One 15-ounce can pinto beans, drained and rinsed
About 4 ounces Cheddar, shredded (1 cup)
Chopped fresh cilantro
1 lime, quartered

1. In a small bowl, whisk together the chili powder, cumin, salt, garlic powder, smoked paprika, and oregano.

2. Heat the oil in a large lidded skillet or Dutch oven over medium heat. Add the ground beef and cook, stirring occasionally to break up the large chunks, until browned, 5 to 7 minutes. Stir in half the spice mixture and cook until fragrant, about 1 minute. Transfer the ground beef to a plate.

3. Return the skillet to medium heat and add a drizzle of oil if the pan is dry. Add the onion and bell peppers and cook, stirring occasionally, until softened, 5 to 7 minutes. Stir in the remaining spice mixture.

4. Stir in the rice and toast it until lightly golden and fragrant, 1 to 2 minutes. Stir in the broth, marinara sauce, and pinto beans and bring to a simmer.

REHEAT IT: From the refrigerator, microwave until warm, 1 to 2 minutes. From the freezer, thaw in the refrigerator overnight, then microwave in 30-second increments until warm.

Reduce the heat to medium-low, cover, and cook until the rice is fluffy and most of the liquid is absorbed, 12 to 14 minutes, stirring occasionally.

5. Stir in the reserved ground beef until combined. Sprinkle the Cheddar over the top, cover, and cook until melted, 2 to 3 minutes more.

6. Spoon onto four plates and garnish with cilantro. Serve with a lime wedge.

MEDITERRANEAN-INSPIRED SALMON AND ORZO BAKE

Gluten-free, dairy-free option, nut-free

When I need a dinner that's fast but still fancy enough to serve to guests, this is the one. Think flaky salmon baked with briny olives, creamy feta, juicy tomatoes, and fragrant oregano—all the Mediterranean flavors you love, no extra effort required. It's one of those meals that makes you feel like you really did something—when, in reality, you just let the oven do all the work.

SERVES 4

Prep time: 15 minutes
Cook time: 35 minutes

To make this dairy-free: Use dairy-free feta or omit the cheese altogether. The result will be a lightly coated orzo rather than a creamy sauce, but both are delicious!

GOOOD TO KNOW: My gluten-free orzo of choice is a corn-and-rice-based version, or substitute the orzo with rice.

STORE IT: Refrigerate the salmon and orzo mixture in separate sealed containers for up to 4 days.

REHEAT IT: From the refrigerator, microwave until warm, 1 to 2 minutes.

2½ tablespoons olive oil
2 teaspoons dried basil
2 teaspoons dried oregano
2 teaspoons garlic powder
1½ teaspoons kosher salt
1 teaspoon chili powder
½ teaspoon ground black pepper
Four 4-ounce skinless salmon fillets
2½ cups low-sodium vegetable or low-sodium chicken broth
1 cup gluten-free orzo or regular orzo
One 8-ounce block feta cheese
1 pint cherry tomatoes, halved (about 1½ cups)
½ cup pitted Kalamata olives
1½ cups roughly chopped baby spinach (about 2 ounces)
Juice of ½ lemon

1. Preheat the oven to 400°F.

2. In a 9 × 13-inch baking dish, whisk together the oil, basil, oregano, garlic powder, salt, chili powder, and black pepper.

3. Pat the salmon dry and place in the baking dish. Swirl the fish to coat with the spiced oil. Transfer to a plate.

4. Mix the broth and orzo in the dish. Set the feta block in the center of the dish and surround with the cherry tomatoes and olives. Bake until the orzo is al dente and the tomatoes are softened, 23 to 25 minutes.

5. Stir in the spinach and lemon juice, breaking up the feta and incorporating it into the orzo as you stir. Arrange the fish over the orzo.

6. Bake until the salmon is opaque and easily flakes with a fork, 9 to 11 minutes.

7. Divide the orzo among four plates and top each with a piece of salmon.

ONE-POT CREAMY SUN-DRIED TOMATO PASTA

Gluten-free, dairy-free, vegetarian, vegan, nut-free

Creamy, dreamy, and entirely vegan in just over 30 minutes? Yes, this pasta is a weeknight must. It's on permanent residence in my weekly dinner rotation when I'm short on time but still want something comforting. And the best part? It's gluten-free, dairy-free, and packed with veggies—without tasting like a "healthified" version of anything. My dairy-loving parents were on their third helping before I told them it was vegan—their looks were priceless!

SERVES 4

Prep time: 10 minutes
Cook time: 35 minutes

GOOOD TO KNOW:
The rigatoni cook time may vary based on what brand you use. Check the instructions for al dente pasta.

The sauce will thicken as it cools down, so for a thicker coating, let cool off heat for 15 minutes. I recommend waiting—it's worth it!

STORE IT: Refrigerate in a sealed container for up to 4 days.

REHEAT IT: Microwave until warm, 1 to 2 minutes, or return to a pot or skillet over medium heat with a splash of broth until glossy and warm.

2 tablespoons olive oil
1 medium shallot, minced
2 garlic cloves, minced
1 teaspoon kosher salt, plus more to taste
½ teaspoon ground black pepper
½ teaspoon dried oregano
¼ teaspoon red pepper flakes (optional)
3 cups low-sodium vegetable or low-sodium chicken broth, plus more as needed
12 ounces brown rice rigatoni, rice-and-corn-based rigatoni, or regular rigatoni
3 cups packed baby spinach (about 4 ounces)
1¼ cups chopped fresh basil
½ cup drained oil-packed sun-dried tomatoes, finely chopped
¾ cup full-fat coconut milk (about half a well-shaken 13.5-ounce can)

1. Heat the oil in a large lidded sauté pan or Dutch oven over medium heat. Add the shallot and cook, stirring occasionally, until translucent and aromatic, about 2 minutes. Add the garlic, salt, black pepper, oregano, and red pepper flakes (if using) and cook, stirring occasionally, until fragrant, 2 to 3 minutes.

2. Add the broth and rigatoni and mix well. The pasta should mostly be submerged in the liquid. If more than half of the individual pieces of pasta are above the liquid, add broth or water to cover. Bring to a boil, cover, and lower the heat to a simmer, stirring occasionally until the pasta is al dente, 12 to 15 minutes (see Goood to Know).

3. Stir in the spinach, 1 cup of the chopped basil, and the sun-dried tomatoes and cook until the spinach is wilted, about 2 minutes. Add the coconut milk and cook until the sauce is warmed and slightly thickened and the pasta is evenly coated, 1 to 2 minutes. If needed, season with more salt.

4. Divide among four bowls and garnish with the remaining ¼ cup basil.

BUFFALO CHICKPEA STUFFED SWEET POTATOES

Gluten-free, dairy-free, vegetarian, vegan, nut-free

When I've been running around all day, the last thing I want is a complicated dinner. Enter these stuffed sweet potatoes—a sheet pan miracle where chickpeas get crispy and sweet potatoes caramelize at the same time, and the whole thing comes together with a fiery Buffalo sauce drizzle. Kid-friendly? Swap Buffalo for barbecue sauce. More protein? Toss in some shredded rotisserie chicken. Extra sauce? Herby Yogurt Ranch Dressing (page 302) has your back.

SERVES 4

Prep time: 15 minutes
Cook time: 30 minutes

GOOOD TO KNOW: I strongly prefer sweet potatoes for this recipe—I just think they pair best with Buffalo sauce—but you can swap them for russet potatoes.

STORE IT: Refrigerate the sweet potatoes, chickpeas, and sauce separately in sealed containers, up to 4 days for the sweet potatoes and chickpeas and up to 7 days for the sauce.

REHEAT IT: Assemble the stuffed sweet potatoes and microwave until warm, 1 to 2 minutes. Or transfer the chickpeas to a sheet pan and recrisp in a 425°F oven. Warm the sweet potatoes and sauce separately.

2 tablespoons olive oil
1 teaspoon chili powder
1 teaspoon garlic powder
1 teaspoon smoked paprika
1 teaspoon kosher salt, plus more for sprinkling
½ teaspoon ground black pepper
Two 15-ounce cans chickpeas, drained and rinsed
4 medium sweet potatoes, halved lengthwise
⅓ cup Buffalo hot sauce
¼ cup tahini
Chopped fresh parsley
1 lemon, quartered

1. Preheat the oven to 425°F.

2. In a small bowl, mix together 1 tablespoon of the oil, the chili powder, garlic powder, smoked paprika, salt, and black pepper. Set aside.

3. Place the chickpeas on the prepared sheet pan and pat dry with a paper towel. Toss with the oil until fully coated. Push them to one side of the pan and place the sweet potatoes on the other. Coat the sweet potatoes with the remaining up to 1 tablespoon oil. Sprinkle with salt and turn them cut side down on the pan.

4. Bake until the sweet potatoes are fork-tender and the chickpeas are crispy, 28 to 30 minutes.

5. Meanwhile, in a small bowl, whisk together the Buffalo hot sauce and tahini until smooth. Set aside.

6. To serve, flip the sweet potatoes cut side up, and mash the insides with a fork. Evenly divide the crispy chickpeas among the potato halves. Place two halves on each plate and drizzle with the Buffalo/tahini sauce. Garnish with parsley and a squeeze of lemon.

ONE-POT WONDERS

CARAMELIZED ONION, STEAK, AND CHEESE SKILLET

Gluten-free, dairy-free option, nut-free

This skillet is basically a deconstructed Philly cheesesteak, and I'm obsessed. Caramelized onions bring sweetness, savory shaved steak keeps things juicy, and melty cheese ties it all together. I first made this for my meat- and cheese-loving brother-in-law, who normally dodges anything remotely plant-forward—and he was hooked. Eat it straight from the skillet for a low-carb dinner and stuff any leftovers into a hoagie roll for the full-on veggie cheesesteak situation.

SERVES 4

Prep time: 15 minutes
Cook time: 30 minutes

To make this dairy-free: Omit the mozzarella.

GOOOD TO KNOW: Shaved steak can be made from a few different cuts of meat. Ask the butcher to thinly shave a top round, rib eye cap, or sirloin. Or buy the same weight, freeze the steak for about 1 hour, and carefully slice thinly with a sharp knife.

STORE IT: Refrigerate in a sealed container for up to 4 days or freeze for up to 3 months.

REHEAT IT: From the refrigerator, microwave until warm, 1 to 2 minutes. From the freezer, thaw in the refrigerator overnight, then microwave in 30-second increments until warm.

- 3 tablespoons avocado oil
- 1 large yellow onion, thinly sliced into half-moons
- 2 green bell peppers, cored, seeded, and thinly sliced (about 2 cups)
- 10 ounces white mushrooms, thinly sliced (about 3 cups)
- 4 garlic cloves, minced
- 14 ounces shaved Angus steak (see Goood to Know)
- 2 teaspoons tapioca flour or arrowroot starch (can substitute cornstarch)
- ½ teaspoon kosher salt
- ½ teaspoon ground black pepper
- ¼ cup coconut aminos (or reduced-sodium tamari or reduced-sodium soy sauce)
- About 6 ounces mozzarella, shredded (1 cup)

1. Heat 2 tablespoons of the avocado oil in a large cast-iron skillet over medium heat. Add the onion and bell peppers and cook, stirring occasionally, until the onion is caramelized and the peppers are soft, 25 to 30 minutes, taking care not to burn them (reduce the heat to medium-low if needed). Add a splash of water if the onion and peppers brown too quickly.

2. Reduce the heat to medium-low. Add the mushrooms and garlic and cook, stirring occasionally, until the mushrooms are softened, about 5 to 7 more minutes.

3. Create a well in the center of pan and add the remaining 1 tablespoon oil. Carefully add the steak and cook, stirring frequently, until it is cooked through and browned, about 2 minutes.

4. Add the tapioca flour, salt, and black pepper and mix until well combined. Stir in the coconut aminos and reduce the heat to low. Sprinkle the mozzarella over the top, cover, and cook until the sauce is thickened and the cheese is melted, about 5 minutes.

5. Divide the steak and vegetables among four plates and serve.

WEEKNIGHT HONEY-GARLIC TURKEY SKILLET

Gluten-free, dairy-free, nut-free

Some nights, the urge to order takeout is strong. But this sweet-spicy ground turkey dish? It's just as fast, more affordable, and better for you. Plus, it's endlessly flexible—swap in whatever veggies need using up, grab whatever ground meat you have on hand, and pair it with your grain of choice to stretch it further. It's the kind of weeknight recipe that makes you feel like you took a shortcut.

SERVES 4

Prep time: 15 minutes
Cook time: 25 minutes

GOOOD TO KNOW: Get a delicious variation of this same recipe by swapping the turkey for pork, green beans for sliced red bell peppers, and carrot for sliced yellow onion. There are so many options!

STORE IT: Refrigerate in a sealed container for up to 4 days or freeze for up to 3 months.

REHEAT IT: From the refrigerator, microwave until warm, 1 to 2 minutes. From the freezer, thaw in the refrigerator overnight, then microwave in 30-second increments until warm. Alternatively, reheat in a skillet over medium heat until warm.

2 tablespoons olive oil
1 pound 93% lean ground turkey
12 ounces green beans, ends trimmed
6 ounces preshredded carrots, or 4 large carrots, cut into thin matchsticks (about 2 cups)
4 garlic cloves, minced
1½ tablespoons minced peeled fresh ginger (or 1½ teaspoons ground ginger)
Kosher salt
⅓ cup coconut aminos (or reduced-sodium tamari or reduced-sodium soy sauce)
¼ cup raw honey
1 tablespoon sriracha (optional)
Chopped fresh cilantro
Thinly sliced green onions
Sesame seeds

1. Heat the oil in a large lidded skillet over medium heat until shimmering. Add the ground turkey and cook, stirring often to break up large chunks, until no pink remains, 4 to 6 minutes.

2. Stir in the green beans and carrots, cover, and steam the vegetables until softened, about 5 minutes, stirring halfway through to prevent sticking.

3. Uncover and increase the heat to medium-high. Continue to cook, stirring often, until the turkey and vegetables are lightly browned, 2 to 3 minutes more.

4. Reduce the heat to medium, stir in the garlic, ginger, a pinch of salt, and cook until soft and fragrant, 1 to 2 minutes. Stir in the coconut aminos, honey, and sriracha (if using) and cook until the sauce is slightly reduced, 3 to 4 more minutes.

5. Serve the turkey and vegetables on plates or in bowls. Garnish with cilantro, green onions, and sesame seeds.

ONE-POT WONDERS

ONE-POT QUINOA BAKE WITH BUTTERNUT SQUASH, KALE, AND FETA

Gluten-free, vegetarian

This dish is my answer to a question I'm frequently asked online: "How can I eat more veggies and actually enjoy it?" It's a homey, layered bake that shines in fall—when butternut squash is at its best and readily available at the farmers' market—but works year-round. I love making it on Sundays for a feel-good dinner, knowing the leftovers will hold up beautifully all week. Want to mix it up? Swap feta for soft goat cheese. Want to bring it to Thanksgiving? It's the perfect potluck harvest-vibe dish.

SERVES 4

Prep time: 10 minutes
Cook time: 30 minutes

GOOOD TO KNOW: For extra protein, add rotisserie chicken, chickpeas, or cooked salmon after baking.

STORE IT: Refrigerate in a sealed container for up to 4 days or freeze for up to 3 months.

REHEAT IT: From the refrigerator, microwave until warm, 1 to 2 minutes. From the freezer, thaw in the refrigerator overnight, then microwave in 30-second increments until warm.

1 tablespoon olive oil, plus more for the pan
2 teaspoons dried rosemary
2 teaspoons dried thyme
2 teaspoons kosher salt
1 teaspoon ground black pepper
1 teaspoon ground dried sage
3 cups low-sodium vegetable broth
2 cups medium-diced peeled butternut squash (about ½ large squash or 10 ounces precut squash)
1 cup uncooked white or tricolor quinoa
3 garlic cloves, minced
1 medium shallot, minced
4 cups shredded curly kale, finely chopped (about 6 ounces)
One 8-ounce block feta cheese

1. Preheat the oven to 400°F. Lightly coat a 9 × 13-inch baking dish with oil.

2. In the baking dish, mix the rosemary, thyme, salt, black pepper, and sage. Add the broth, squash, quinoa, garlic, shallot, and the tablespoon of oil, and stir with a wooden spoon or spatula to mix well. Be sure to evenly distribute the squash for even baking.

3. Add the kale and submerge it in the liquid. Place the block of feta in the middle of the dish, wiggling the block slightly so it sits flat on the bottom. Loosely cover the dish with aluminum foil.

4. Bake until the squash is fork-tender and the quinoa has absorbed the liquid, 28 to 30 minutes. If liquid remains in the dish after 30 minutes, remove from the oven and rest, covered, until absorbed, up to 15 minutes. Mix well.

5. Spoon onto four plates or into bowls.

DUMP-AND-BAKE HIDDEN PROTEIN PASTA

Gluten-free, vegetarian, nut-free

I love a sneaky protein boost, and many times blended cottage cheese is the move. (Don't freak out! You'll have *no* idea it's in there, just like in the wildly popular High-Protein Egg Muffins on page 77. Stay with me—it's life-changing.) In this tomato-spinach pasta, it disappears seamlessly, adding creaminess and extra protein without a trace. It's kid-friendly and weeknight-friendly. What's not hidden is the delicious factor!

SERVES 4

Prep time: 5 minutes
Cook time: 40 minutes

GOOOD TO KNOW: Serve as is or top the pasta with cooked meat like chicken or sausage for some "unhidden" protein, if you'd like. Different pasta types, especially wheat pasta, can vary in cook time, so adjust for more time as needed.

STORE IT: Refrigerate in a sealed container for up to 4 days or freeze for up to 3 months.

REHEAT IT: From the refrigerator, microwave until warm, 1 to 2 minutes. From the freezer, thaw in the refrigerator overnight, then microwave in 30-second increments until warm.

Olive oil for the pan
16 ounces 4% small-curd cottage cheese
2 cups marinara sauce
1¾ cups low-sodium vegetable broth
2 teaspoons dried basil
1 teaspoon dried oregano
1 teaspoon garlic powder
1 teaspoon kosher salt
½ teaspoon ground black pepper
12 ounces brown rice penne, rice-and-corn-based penne, or regular penne
3 cups packed baby spinach (about 4 ounces)
About 8 ounces mozzarella, shredded (1½ cups)

1. Position an oven rack 3 to 4 inches from the broiler and preheat the oven to 400°F. Lightly coat a 9 × 13-inch baking dish with oil and set aside.

2. In a food processor or blender, combine the cottage cheese, marinara sauce, broth, basil, oregano, garlic powder, salt, and black pepper and process on high speed until completely smooth.

3. Pour the blended mixture into the baking dish. Add the penne and spinach and mix until the penne is submerged in the sauce. Cover the baking dish with aluminum foil.

4. Bake until the pasta is al dente, about 30 to 40 minutes, stirring halfway through.

5. Turn the oven to high broil. Remove the foil and sprinkle the mozzarella over the top of the penne. Broil until the cheese is golden and bubbling, about 5 minutes, taking care not to burn the cheese.

6. Let rest for at least 10 minutes to continue allowing liquid to absorb, and up to 30 minutes for best results. Evenly divide among four bowls.

DONE IN 30

How many so-called 30-minute meals have you tried that actually took closer to 90 minutes? I've definitely found myself mired in more than a few, which is why a quick-dinners chapter was a nonnegotiable for this book. This chapter's recipes have a *combined* prep and cook time of 30 minutes. You'll want to keep these recipes at the ready for busy nights when you need to get something great on the table without getting sucked into a time vortex.

Red Curry Noodles with Sautéed Green Onion and Pork 163

Spiced Lamb Meatballs with Tomato-Cucumber Salad 164

Street-Corn-Inspired Shrimp Skillet 166

Sweet and Spicy Tofu and Broccolini 168

One-Pot Chicken Sausage, Spinach, and Rice 171

Spicy Sausage, White Bean, and Kale Soup 172

Herby Chickpea and Cauliflower Bowls with Lemon-Dill Sauce 174

Sticky Balsamic Oyster Mushrooms 176

Sheet Pan Barbecue Chicken and Pineapple Lettuce Cups 179

Saucy Beef and Broccoli 180

Marry Me Turkey Meatballs 182

RED CURRY NOODLES WITH SAUTÉED GREEN ONION AND PORK

Gluten-free, dairy-free, nut-free

You'll always find at least one—okay, usually three—jars of Thai red curry paste in my pantry. Thai flavors have a hold on me, and if you haven't cooked with curry paste yet, consider this your nudge to join the party. This dish is all about big flavors with hacks to cut down on time and effort. The pork gets a quick sear, then the pasta cooks right in the sauce, soaking up all that savory, spicy goodness—which means fewer dishes. Fast, flavorful, and low mess. It's a win-win!

SERVES 4

Prep time: 10 minutes
Cook time: 20 minutes

GOOOD TO KNOW: You can use green or yellow curry paste in place of red. The red is spicier, so adjust accordingly to your taste. If you want a milder taste, use 1 teaspoon of the red.

STORE IT: Refrigerate in a sealed container for up to 4 days.

REHEAT IT: Microwave until warm, 1 to 2 minutes, or return to a skillet over medium heat with a generous splash of broth until warm.

1 tablespoon avocado oil
1 pound 90% lean ground pork
1½ teaspoons ground ginger
½ teaspoon kosher salt
½ teaspoon ground black pepper
5 green onions, sliced into 1-inch pieces
4 garlic cloves, minced
1 tablespoon Thai red curry paste (or more for added spice)
3 cups low-sodium vegetable broth
¾ cup full-fat coconut milk (about half a well-shaken 13.5-ounce can)
2 tablespoons coconut aminos (or reduced-sodium tamari or reduced-sodium soy sauce)
8 ounces stir-fry rice noodles (such as pad Thai noodles)
Chopped fresh cilantro
Sesame seeds
1 lime, quartered

1. Heat the oil in a large lidded nonstick skillet over medium-high heat until shimmering. Add the ground pork and cook, stirring occasionally to break up the large chunks, until browned, 5 to 6 minutes. Stir in the ginger, salt, and black pepper. Add the green onions and cook, stirring occasionally until softened, 2 to 3 minutes. Add the garlic and cook until fragrant, about 1 minute. Transfer the mixture to a bowl with a slotted spoon and set aside.

2. Add and stir in the curry paste until fragrant, 20 to 30 seconds. Add the broth, coconut milk, and coconut aminos and bring to a simmer. Add the rice noodles and stir until the noodles are fully submerged in the liquid. (If needed, add up to ½ cup water or additional broth.) Reduce the heat to medium, cover, and simmer, stirring occasionally to prevent sticking, until the noodles are softened, 5 to 7 minutes. Return the pork to the skillet and stir until combined.

3. Spoon the curried noodles into four bowls. Garnish with cilantro, a sprinkle of sesame seeds, and lime wedges.

SPICED LAMB MEATBALLS WITH TOMATO-CUCUMBER SALAD

Gluten-free, dairy-free option

I hadn't cooked with ground lamb until I met Brian, who's Greek, and now I'm basically making up for lost time. Lamb meatballs are now my favorite type of meatballs (which is saying a lot if you've taken a look at all of the different meatballs in this book)! These are juicy, flavorful, and begging for a drizzle of Cucumber Garlicky Sauce (page 299). Make extra—these meatballs can be frozen, too!

SERVES 4

Prep time: 15 minutes
Cook time: 15 minutes

To make this dairy-free: Use dairy-free feta or omit the cheese.

GOOOD TO KNOW: If lamb isn't your thing, you can use lean ground beef. The spices will still work perfectly!

STORE IT: Refrigerate the meatballs and salad separately in sealed containers for up to 4 days or freeze the meatballs for up to 3 months.

REHEAT IT: From the refrigerator, microwave the meatballs, 1 to 2 minutes, or transfer to a sheet pan to bake in a 400°F oven until warm. From the freezer, thaw the meatballs in the refrigerator overnight. Microwave in 30-second increments until warm.

FOR THE LAMB MEATBALLS
1 large egg
1 pound 85% lean ground lamb
¼ cup blanched almond flour
1 teaspoon ground coriander
1 teaspoon ground cumin
1 teaspoon garlic powder
1 teaspoon dried oregano
1 teaspoon kosher salt
½ teaspoon ground black pepper
Olive oil, for rolling

FOR THE TOMATO-CUCUMBER SALAD
1 English cucumber, unpeeled, small-diced
1 pint cherry tomatoes, halved (about 1½ cups)
¾ cup crumbled feta (about 3 ounces)
2 tablespoons olive oil
2 tablespoons red wine vinegar
Juice of ½ lemon
1 teaspoon dried oregano
1 teaspoon kosher salt

Chopped fresh parsley

1. Preheat the oven to 400°F. Line a sheet pan with parchment paper.

2. **Make the lamb meatballs:** In a large bowl, whisk the egg until no streaks remain. Add the ground lamb, almond flour, coriander, cumin, garlic powder, oregano, salt, and black pepper and mix until evenly combined.

3. Rub the oil onto clean hands and pinch off about 1 tablespoon of the meat mixture. Roll loosely between your palms until round and smooth. Place the meatball on the prepared sheet pan. Repeat with the rest of the mixture, forming about 20 equal-size meatballs and leaving about 1 inch of space between each.

4. Bake until lightly browned on the outside and with an internal temperature of 160°F, 12 to 14 minutes. There may be some excess fat on the pan, which you can discard after cooling.

5. **Meanwhile, make the salad:** In a medium bowl, combine the cucumber, tomatoes, feta, oil, vinegar, lemon juice, oregano, and salt. Mix well and chill until serving.

6. To serve, plate the lamb meatballs with the tomato cucumber salad alongside. Garnish with chopped parsley.

STREET-CORN-INSPIRED SHRIMP SKILLET

Gluten-free, dairy-free option, nut-free

Two freezer staples—shrimp and corn—team up in this quick flavor-packed skillet. While not exactly Mexican street corn, it's inspired by those punchy, bright flavors. Serve over Jenn's Steamed Rice (page 290) or grilled summer veggies, or just dive in with a spoon. Cotija is classic, but crumbled feta also gives a street-corn-like look and flavor.

SERVES 4

Prep time: 10 minutes
Cook time: 20 minutes

To make this dairy-free: Use dairy-free feta and yogurt.

GOOOD TO KNOW: This dish is also delicious with chicken! Follow the same steps, but sub in 1 pound thinly sliced chicken breast for the shrimp. Increase the cooking time by a few minutes to fully cook.

STORE IT: Refrigerate in a sealed container for up to 3 days or freeze for up to 3 months.

REHEAT IT: From the refrigerator, microwave until warm, 1 to 2 minutes, or return to a skillet over medium heat. From the freezer, thaw in the refrigerator overnight, then microwave in 30-second increments until warm or follow the same skillet instructions.

1 teaspoon chili powder
1 teaspoon kosher salt
1 teaspoon smoked paprika
½ teaspoon ground cumin
¼ teaspoon cayenne pepper (optional)
1 pound fresh or thawed frozen medium shrimp, peeled and deveined, tails removed
2 tablespoons olive oil
4 garlic cloves, minced
2½ cups fresh corn kernels (from 4 ears) or 16 ounces thawed frozen
1 cup full-fat coconut milk (from a well-shaken 13.5-ounce can)
½ cup whole-milk or low-fat Greek yogurt, plus more for topping
Juice of 1 lime
¾ cup crumbled feta (about 3 ounces)
Chopped fresh cilantro
1 lime, quartered, for serving

1. In a small bowl, stir together the chili powder, salt, smoked paprika, cumin, and cayenne (if using). Place the shrimp in a large bowl, add half of the spice mix, and toss to evenly coat.

2. Heat the oil in a large skillet over medium heat until shimmering. Working in batches if necessary, add the shrimp in a single layer with some space between them so they don't steam. Cook without moving until opaque and lightly browned, about 2 minutes, then flip and cook without moving for 2 minutes. Transfer to a large dish, leaving any remaining oil in the skillet.

3. In the same skillet, add the garlic and cook, stirring frequently, until fragrant, about 1 minute. Add the corn and the remaining spice mix and continue cooking, stirring occasionally, until lightly browned, 4 to 6 minutes.

4. Pour in the coconut milk, increase the heat to medium-high, and bring to a simmer. Let the coconut milk reduce and thicken for about 5 minutes.

Remove the skillet from heat and stir in the Greek yogurt and lime juice until evenly combined. Return the cooked shrimp to the skillet and sprinkle with the crumbled feta.

5. Serve the shrimp and corn in four bowls. Garnish with cilantro, a lime wedge, and a dollop of yogurt, if desired.

SWEET AND SPICY TOFU AND BROCCOLINI

Gluten-free, dairy-free, vegetarian, vegan, nut-free

After much trial and error, I finally nailed this ridiculously easy tofu dish. Simply toss everything together and roast until the tofu is crispy on the outside and tender on the inside. While that bakes, whip up a sweet and spicy sauce straight from your pantry. If you want to give this meal a little more heft, serve it with Jenn's Steamed Rice (page 290) and make it into a beautiful bowl.

SERVES 4

Prep time: 10 minutes
Cook time: 20 minutes

GOOOD TO KNOW: If you can't find high-protein super-firm tofu, I recommend getting firm or extra-firm tofu. Press it by wrapping it in a clean kitchen towel and placing it on a small sheet pan or in a shallow bowl. Top it with a heavy object (like a heavy-bottomed pan) and let it sit until the excess liquid is drained, 15 to 20 minutes. High-protein super-firm tofu has much less liquid, which is why it doesn't need to be pressed.

This recipe can be made in an air fryer at 400°F for 15 minutes, flipping halfway through.

FOR THE TOFU AND BROCCOLINI

16-ounce block high-protein super-firm tofu (see Goood to Know)
3 tablespoons olive oil
2 tablespoons tapioca flour or arrowroot starch (can substitute cornstarch)
½ teaspoon garlic powder
½ teaspoon kosher salt, plus more for the broccolini
½ teaspoon ground black pepper, plus more for the broccolini
16 ounces broccolini, ends trimmed and halved if thicker than ½ inch

FOR THE SWEET AND SPICY SAUCE

¼ cup coconut aminos (or reduced-sodium tamari or reduced-sodium soy sauce)
2 tablespoons rice vinegar
1 tablespoon toasted sesame oil
1 tablespoon sriracha
1 tablespoon pure maple syrup
1 teaspoon ground ginger
2 teaspoons tapioca flour or arrowroot starch (can substitute cornstarch)

1. **Make the tofu and broccolini:** Preheat the oven to 425°F. Line a sheet pan with parchment paper and set aside.

2. Slice the tofu block in half horizontally and cut each half into 4 × 4 grid to get 16 cubes (32 total).

3. In a large bowl, whisk together 2 tablespoons of the olive oil, the tapioca flour, garlic powder, salt, and black pepper. Add the tofu and gently toss to coat. Evenly space the coated cubes on the prepared sheet pan to prevent steaming in the oven. Bake until sizzling and just beginning to develop color, about 10 minutes.

4. Meanwhile, in a medium bowl, toss the broccolini with the remaining 1 tablespoon olive oil and a few pinches of salt and black pepper.

STORE IT: Refrigerate in a sealed container for up to 4 days.

REHEAT IT: Microwave until warm, 1 to 2 minutes, or return to a sheet pan and bake or air-fry at 400°F for 6 to 8 minutes.

5. **Make the sweet and spicy sauce:** In a small bowl, whisk together the coconut aminos, vinegar, sesame oil, sriracha, maple syrup, and ginger in a small bowl until smooth. Add the tapioca flour and whisk until combined.

6. When the tofu has cooked for the 10 minutes, transfer the broccolini to the sheet pan, spreading it around the tofu in a single layer. Drizzle the sauce over the tofu and broccolini. Bake until the tofu is golden brown and the broccolini is fork-tender, about 5 minutes, and toss to coat in the sauce.

7. Spoon onto four plates and serve.

DONE IN 30

ONE-POT CHICKEN SAUSAGE, SPINACH, AND RICE

Gluten-free, dairy-free, nut-free

Some recipes just connect. This one went viral for a reason—it's quick, easy, full of flavor, packed with lots of protein and veggies, and conveniently made in one pot. It may look basic, but that's why it's a weeknight hero. Everyone who makes this recipe tells me it's their go-to for a busy weeknight dinner they know their families will love. Precooked chicken sausage makes this even easier, and in the fall, I love swapping in kale, apple chicken sausage, and cubed butternut squash for a seasonal twist.

SERVES 4

Prep time: 5 minutes
Cook time: 25 minutes

GOOOD TO KNOW: See Jenn's Steamed Rice (page 290) for more rice tips.

STORE IT: Refrigerate in a sealed container for up to 4 days or freeze for up to 3 months.

REHEAT IT: From the refrigerator, microwave until warm, 1 to 2 minutes. From the freezer, thaw in the refrigerator overnight, then microwave in 30-second increments until warm.

2 teaspoons garlic powder
2 teaspoons dried oregano
1 teaspoon kosher salt
½ teaspoon ground black pepper
½ teaspoon red pepper flakes (optional)
2 tablespoons olive oil
12 ounces (5 to 6 links) fully cooked Italian-style chicken sausage, sliced into ⅛-inch-thick rounds
1½ cups uncooked jasmine rice, rinsed (see Goood to Know)
4 cups low-sodium chicken broth
3 cups roughly chopped baby spinach (about 4 ounces)
Juice of 1 lemon
1 tablespoon coconut aminos (or reduced-sodium tamari or reduced-sodium soy sauce)

1. In a small bowl, mix the garlic powder, oregano, salt, black pepper, and red pepper flakes (if using). Set aside.

2. Heat the oil in a large lidded sauté pan or Dutch oven over medium heat. Add the sausage and cook until browned and crisp, 2 to 3 minutes per side. Transfer to a plate.

3. In the same pan, add the rice, stirring occasionally, until golden brown and fragrant, about 1 minute. Stir in the spices and the broth and bring to a boil over medium-high heat. Reduce the heat to low, cover, and cook until all the liquid is absorbed and the rice is fluffy, 14 to 16 minutes, stirring halfway through to prevent sticking.

4. Add the spinach, lemon juice, and coconut aminos and stir until the spinach is wilted, about 1 minute. Turn off the heat, return the sausage to the pan, and mix well.

5. Spoon into four bowls and serve.

SPICY SAUSAGE, WHITE BEAN, AND KALE SOUP

Gluten-free, dairy-free, nut-free

Nothing says hug in a bowl like this soup. It's hearty enough, easy on the wallet, and ridiculously adaptable. As one of my top grocery series recipes, I have yet to meet anyone who doesn't love it, so of course I had to include it in the book. Want to shake things up? Swap pork sausage for chicken or vegan, go mild instead of spicy, or trade coconut milk for light cream. If you don't see ground sausage, buy links, remove the meat, and discard the casings. However you spin it, this soup's got your back and makes for perfect freezer prep.

SERVES 4

Prep time: 15 minutes
Cook time: 20 minutes

GOOOD TO KNOW: Swap for sweet Italian sausage if preferred.

STORE IT: Refrigerate in a sealed container for up to 4 days or freeze for up to to 3 months.

REHEAT IT: From the refrigerator, microwave until warm, 1 to 2 minutes, or return to a pot and bring to a simmer over medium heat. From the freezer, thaw in the refrigerator overnight, then microwave in 30-second increments or follow the same stovetop instructions.

1 tablespoon garlic powder
1 tablespoon dried oregano
Kosher salt
½ teaspoon ground black pepper
½ teaspoon red pepper flakes (optional)
2 tablespoons olive oil
½ pound ground hot Italian sausage or chicken sausage
1 large yellow onion, small-diced (about 1½ cups)
2 large carrots, small-diced (about 1 cup)
2 celery ribs, small-diced (about 1 cup)
4 cups low-sodium chicken or low-sodium vegetable broth
One 15.5-ounce can cannellini, navy, or Great Northern beans, drained and rinsed
3 cups shredded curly kale (about 4½ ounces)
¾ cup full-fat coconut milk (about half a well-shaken 13.5-ounce can)

1. In a small bowl, whisk together the garlic powder, oregano, 1 teaspoon salt, the black pepper, and red pepper flakes (if using). Set aside.

2. Heat the oil in a large lidded pot or Dutch oven over medium heat. Add the sausage and cook until browned, stirring occasionally to break into pieces, 5 to 7 minutes. Use a slotted spoon to transfer to a plate. Set aside.

3. In the same pot, over medium heat, add the onion, carrots, and celery and cook, stirring occasionally, until tender, 6 to 8 minutes.

4. Stir in the spice mixture and cook until fragrant, stirring often, 1 to 2 minutes. Stir in the broth, beans, and 1 cup water. Cover and bring to a boil. Reduce heat to low and simmer, covered, for 5 minutes.

5. Stir in the shredded kale, coconut milk, and meat, and stir until the kale wilts.

6. Season with salt to taste and divide among four bowls and serve.

HERBY CHICKPEA AND CAULIFLOWER BOWLS WITH LEMON-DILL SAUCE

Gluten-free, dairy-free option, vegetarian, vegan option, nut-free

Winner, winner, veggie dinner! Eight plants, major flavor, barely any effort—this dish delivers. Roasting the lemon takes the lemon-dill sauce from good to life-changing. No joke. Not into chickpeas or cauliflower? Swap in lentils, carrots, sweet potatoes, mushrooms, or even an animal protein. Check out page 339 for all these swaps and subs.

SERVES 4

Prep time: 10 minutes
Cook time: 20 minutes

To make this dairy-free and vegan: Use dairy-free yogurt (see Goood to Know).

GOOOD TO KNOW:
I like a plain cashew- or coconut-based yogurt best for vegan swapping!

STORE IT: Refrigerate the chickpeas and cauliflower in a sealed container for up to 4 days. Refrigerate the lemon-dill sauce in a separate sealed container for up to 1 week.

REHEAT IT: Microwave the chickpeas and cauliflower until warm, 1 to 2 minutes, or heat on a sheet pan in a 425°F oven for 10 to 12 minutes to recrisp. Assemble the bowls and top with the sauce.

FOR THE CHICKPEAS AND CAULIFLOWER
1½ tablespoons dried oregano
2 teaspoons dried basil
2 teaspoons dried parsley
2 teaspoons garlic powder
1½ teaspoons kosher salt
½ teaspoon ground black pepper
1 medium cauliflower head cut into small florets or 10-ounce bag of florets (about 4 cups)
Two 15-ounce cans chickpeas, drained and rinsed
3 tablespoons olive oil
1 lemon, halved

FOR THE LEMON-DILL SAUCE
1 cup whole-milk or low-fat Greek yogurt
¼ cup finely chopped fresh parsley
3 tablespoons finely chopped fresh dill, plus more for garnish
1 tablespoon olive oil
1 teaspoon garlic powder
½ teaspoon kosher salt

FOR THE BOWLS
Jenn's Steamed Rice (p. 290), or 3 cups cooked white rice
Chopped fresh parsley

1. Preheat the oven to 425°F. Line a sheet pan with parchment paper.

2. **Prepare the chickpeas and cauliflower:** In a large bowl, stir together the oregano, basil, parsley, garlic powder, salt, and black pepper. Add the cauliflower, chickpeas, and oil and toss until fully coated. Transfer the mixture to the prepared sheet pan and spread out in a single layer. Place the lemon halves cut side down in the center.

3. Bake until the chickpeas are crispy and the cauliflower is fork-tender, 18 to 20 minutes.

4. **Meanwhile, make the lemon-dill sauce:** In a small bowl, whisk together the yogurt, parsley, dill, oil, garlic powder, and salt until combined.

5. When the cauliflower and chickpeas are done and the roasted lemons are cool, squeeze the juice into the dill sauce. Stir to combine.

6. **Assemble the bowls:** Divide the rice among four bowls and top with the cauliflower and chickpeas. Drizzle with sauce and garnish with herbs.

STICKY BALSAMIC OYSTER MUSHROOMS

Gluten-free, dairy-free, vegetarian, vegan, nut-free

With so many mushrooms out there, oyster mushrooms speak to me the most. They hold their shape when cooked, bring the umami, and just *get it*. My favorite way to serve them? Meet my sticky balsamic sauce—glossy, punchy, smoky, and sweet from smoky paprika, maple syrup, and, yes, balsamic. This is a recipe that will convert the mushroom doubters!

SERVES 4

Prep time: 15 minutes
Cook time: 15 minutes

GOOOD TO KNOW: I love getting oyster mushrooms at my local farmers' market, where they often have different varieties, such as golden, blue, and pearl oyster mushrooms.

STORE IT: Refrigerate in a sealed container for up to 4 days.

REHEAT IT: From the refrigerator, microwave until warm, 1 to 3 minutes, or return to a skillet over medium heat with a splash of broth until lightly simmering, then serve over the reheated rice.

FOR THE SAUCE

½ cup low-sodium vegetable broth
2 tablespoons balsamic vinegar
2 tablespoons coconut aminos (or reduced-sodium tamari or reduced-sodium soy sauce)
2 tablespoons pure maple syrup
1 tablespoon tapioca flour or arrowroot starch (can substitute cornstarch)

FOR THE MUSHROOMS

2 tablespoons olive oil
12 ounces oyster or portobello mushrooms, cut into 1½-inch pieces (about 4 cups)
3 garlic cloves, minced
½ teaspoon smoked paprika
½ teaspoon kosher salt
½ teaspoon ground black pepper
¼ teaspoon chili powder

FOR SERVING

Jenn's Steamed Rice (p. 290), or 3 cups cooked white rice
Thinly sliced green onions

1. **Make the sauce:** In a small bowl, whisk together the broth, vinegar, coconut aminos, maple syrup, and tapioca flour. Set aside.

2. **Cook the mushrooms:** Heat the oil in a large skillet over medium heat until shimmering. Add the mushrooms in a single layer and cook until golden brown, 4 to 5 minutes on each side.

3. Stir in the garlic, smoked paprika, salt, black pepper, and chili powder. Reduce the heat to low, stir in the sauce, and simmer until thickened, 1 to 3 minutes.

4. **To serve:** Spoon the rice into four bowls. Top with the mushrooms, drizzle with pan sauce, and garnish with sliced green onions.

SHEET PAN BARBECUE CHICKEN AND PINEAPPLE LETTUCE CUPS

Gluten-free, dairy-free, nut-free

Pineapple and barbecue chicken on pizza? Controversial. But in these lettuce cups? Undeniably delicious. Sweet meets smoky in a quick sheet pan meal that does all the work for you. It's up to you whether you want to toss the chicken with my Tangy Maple Barbecue Sauce (page 298) or use store-bought. Don't let the lettuce limit you. Prefer a bowl situation? Pile it over rice. Feeling fancy? Toss in some cashews for crunch and protein. You may want to double the filling—leftovers are gold.

SERVES 4

Prep time: 15 minutes
Cook time: 15 minutes

GOOOD TO KNOW: Make a wrap out of your leftovers! Add the shredded lettuce, extra barbecue sauce, and the chicken mixture to a tortilla, wrap tightly, and slice in half. It makes a delicious workday lunch!

STORE IT: Refrigerate the sheet pan components and lettuce in separate sealed containers for up to 4 days. A paper towel stored with the lettuce will help keep it fresh.

REHEAT IT: From the refrigerator, microwave the sheet pan components until warm, 1 to 1½ minutes, then assemble the lettuce cups.

1½ cups small-diced fresh pineapple (about ½ small pineapple) or one 20-ounce can diced pineapple

1 medium red bell pepper, cored, seeded, and small-diced (about 1 cup)

¾ medium red onion, thinly sliced (about 1 cup)

1 tablespoon olive oil

1 teaspoon garlic powder

1 teaspoon kosher salt

½ teaspoon ground black pepper

2 pounds boneless, skinless chicken thighs, cut into 1-inch chunks

1 cup Tangy Maple Barbecue Sauce (p. 298) or barbecue sauce of your choice

16 leaves Bibb lettuce or other butter lettuce (about 1 head)

Thinly sliced green onions

1. Preheat the oven to 400°F. Line a sheet pan with parchment paper.

2. In a large bowl, toss together the pineapple, bell pepper, onion, oil, garlic powder, salt, and black pepper and mix well. Transfer to the prepared sheet pan.

3. Add the cubed chicken and ½ cup of the barbecue sauce to the same bowl. Toss to evenly coat. Transfer to the sheet pan, spreading everything out into one even layer.

4. Bake until the pineapple and bell pepper are softened and the chicken reaches an internal temperature of 165°F, 13 to 15 minutes.

5. To assemble, arrange 3 or 4 lettuce leaves on each of four plates. Divide the chicken and pineapple mixture over the lettuce leaves, drizzle with the remaining ½ cup barbecue sauce, and garnish with sliced green onions.

DONE IN 30

SAUCY BEEF AND BROCCOLI

Gluten-free, dairy-free, nut-free

When life is hectic and takeout is calling out your name, this 30-minute saucy skillet saves the day. It's also tastier, it saves money, and it's a healthier choice. Beef and broccoli are the heavenly match, but swap in chicken, shrimp, or tofu for the beef if that's your jam. Have veggies to use up? Toss them in. Skip the sriracha if your kids or crew don't want the heat! For a heartier dish, serve with Jenn's Steamed Rice (page 290).

SERVES 4

Prep time: 10 minutes
Cook time: 20 minutes

GOOOD TO KNOW: To make the steak easier to slice, freeze it for about 30 minutes before you're ready to cook. You can also swap the flank steak for skirt steak, stir-fry beef strips, or even ground beef.

STORE IT: Refrigerate in a sealed container for up to 3 days or freeze for up to 3 months.

REHEAT IT: From the refrigerator, microwave until warm, 1 to 2 minutes, or return to a skillet over medium heat with a splash of broth until gently simmering and warm. From the freezer, thaw in the refrigerator overnight, then microwave in 30-second increments until warm or follow the same skillet instructions.

FOR THE SAUCE

1 cup low-sodium beef broth
⅓ cup coconut aminos (or reduced-sodium tamari or reduced-sodium soy sauce)
1 tablespoon tapioca flour or arrowroot starch (can substitute cornstarch)
1 tablespoon sriracha (optional)
2 garlic cloves, minced
1 teaspoon ground ginger, or 1 tablespoon grated peeled fresh ginger
½ teaspoon ground black pepper

FOR THE SKILLET

2 tablespoons olive oil, plus more as needed
1 large head broccoli, cut into small florets (about 4 cups)
6 green onions, cut into 1-inch pieces
1 pound flank steak, thinly sliced
Sesame seeds (optional)

1. **Make the sauce:** In a small bowl, whisk together the broth, coconut aminos, tapioca flour, sriracha (if using), garlic, ginger, and black pepper. Set aside.

2. **For the skillet:** Heat the oil in a large skillet over medium heat. Add the broccoli and green onions and cook, stirring occasionally, until the broccoli is tender, and the green onions are lightly charred, 8 to 10 minutes. Transfer to a plate.

3. In the same pan, heat another tablespoon of oil if the pan is too dry over medium heat. Add the steak in one even layer and cook without moving until golden brown, 2 to 3 minutes. Turn the meat over and repeat to cook the other side.

4. Return the broccoli and green onions to the pan and stir to combine with the steak. Stir in the reserved sauce and simmer until thickened, 3 to 4 minutes.

5. To serve, spoon the beef and broccoli onto four plates. If desired, garnish with sesame seeds.

MARRY ME TURKEY MEATBALLS

Gluten-free, dairy-free, nut-free

If a dish could put a ring on it, this would be the one. This is my take on the creamy sun-dried tomato, basil-packed marriage of the viral Marry Me Madness—in meatball form. Bonus: It's dairy-free! Nutritional yeast brings the cheesy depth. Spoon it over rice, take a bite, and consider this your new forever favorite. I stand with the power of the classic Marry Me flavors.

SERVES 4

Prep time: 15 minutes
Cook time: 15 minutes

GOOOD TO KNOW: Sub oil from the sun-dried tomatoes for the olive oil for an easy, low-waste, flavor-boosting hack in the meatballs and/or the rice.

See Jenn's Steamed Rice (page 290) for more rice tips.

STORE IT: Refrigerate in a sealed container for up to 4 days or freeze for up to 3 months.

REHEAT IT: From the refrigerator, microwave until warm, 1 to 2 minutes. From the freezer, thaw in the refrigerator overnight, then microwave in 30-second increments until warm.

FOR THE MEATBALLS

1 pound 93% lean ground turkey
½ cup drained oil-packed sun-dried tomatoes, finely chopped
½ cup finely chopped fresh basil, plus more for garnish
1 teaspoon dried oregano
1 teaspoon kosher salt
½ teaspoon ground black pepper
½ teaspoon garlic powder
Olive oil, for rolling

FOR THE RICE

1 tablespoon olive oil
4 garlic cloves, minced
2 tablespoons nutritional yeast, plus more for garnish
2 teaspoons dried oregano
½ teaspoon kosher salt, plus more to taste
1 cup uncooked jasmine rice, rinsed (see Goood to Know)
2 cups low-sodium vegetable or low-sodium chicken broth
¾ cup full-fat coconut milk (about half a well-shaken 13.5-ounce can)
Juice of ½ lemon

1. Preheat the oven to 400°F. Line a sheet pan with parchment paper.

2. **Bake the meatballs:** In a large bowl, combine the turkey, sun-dried tomatoes, basil, oregano, salt, black pepper, and garlic powder. Mix with a rubber spatula or clean hands until evenly combined. Rub oil onto clean hands and pinch off about 1 tablespoon of the meat mixture. Roll loosely between your palms until round and smooth. Place the meatball on the prepared sheet pan. Repeat with the rest of the mixture, forming about 20 equal-size meatballs and leaving about 1 inch of space between.

3. Bake until lightly browned on the outside with an internal temperature of 160°F, 10 to 12 minutes.

4. **Meanwhile, cook the rice:** Heat the oil in a large lidded sauté pan or Dutch oven over medium heat until shimmering. Add the garlic, nutritional yeast, oregano, and salt and cook, stirring constantly, for 1 minute.

5. Stir in the rice, broth, and coconut milk and increase the heat to high. Bring the liquid to a gentle boil. Reduce the heat to medium, cover, and simmer until the rice is cooked, 10 to 13 minutes. (If you are not using a nonstick pan, I recommend stirring a couple of times as it cooks.) Turn off the heat, squeeze in the lemon juice, and, if needed, season with more salt.

6. Spoon the rice into four bowls and top each with 5 meatballs. Garnish with basil and a sprinkle of nutritional yeast.

HIGH-PROTEIN HITS

Welcome to the protein-packed corner of my kitchen—where we hit our goals, but not in an obsessive gym-rat sort of way. No plain chicken and rice here. Instead, flavor and fuel go the full round with dishes like French Onion Meatball Skillet and Slow Cooker Carnitas, packing a knockout combo of taste and protein. Think at least thirty grams of power per dish without breaking a sweat. It's about cooking smarter, eating better, and keeping the excitement high.

Jenn's Viral Baked Feta, Chicken, Quinoa, and Veggies 187

Deconstructed Turkey Lasagna Skillet 188

Greek-Style Chicken and Vegetable Skewers 191

Not-Your-Average Burrito Bowls with Sheet Pan Salsa 193

Creamy Spinach Chicken 196

French Onion Meatball Skillet 199

Sheet Pan Pesto Pizza with Asparagus and Prosciutto 201

Cauliflower Pizza Skillet 204

Mom's Game-Day Chili with Sweet Honey Bread 206

Slow Cooker Carnitas Tacos with Pineapple Salsa 209

Maple-Dijon Pork Tenderloin 212

Baked Black Bean and Poblano Tacos 215

Salmon Bites with Coconut Rice and Chilled Cucumber Salad 217

JENN'S VIRAL BAKED FETA, CHICKEN, QUINOA, AND VEGGIES

Gluten-free, nut-free

My spin on the viral baked feta pasta delivers—you guessed it—more protein and fiber. This version racked up 15 million views for good reason. I swapped pasta for quinoa, tossed in broccoli, and added tender chicken breasts for a heartier, more balanced bite. It is just as easy, has even more flavor, and is packed with good-for-you ingredients. Still a fan of the original? No shade—it's got its place too!

SERVES 4

Prep time: 15 minutes
Cook time: 30 minutes

GOOOD TO KNOW: Chicken breasts that are 1 to 1½ inches thick are ideal for this recipe. If your chicken breasts are too thick, either slice them in half horizontally or pound them to the proper thickness using a meat mallet.

STORE IT: Refrigerate the chicken and quinoa in separate sealed containers for up to 4 days or freeze for up to 3 months.

REHEAT IT: From the refrigerator, microwave until warm, 1 to 2 minutes. From the freezer, thaw in the refrigerator overnight, then microwave in 30-second increments until warm.

½ cup uncooked white or tricolor quinoa
One 8-ounce block feta cheese
1 medium head broccoli, cut into small florets (about 2 cups)
1 pint cherry tomatoes (about 1½ cups)
1½ pounds boneless, skinless chicken breasts (see Goood to Know)
2 tablespoons olive oil
2 teaspoons garlic powder
1 teaspoon kosher salt
½ teaspoon ground black pepper
½ cup chopped fresh basil, plus more for garnish

1. Preheat the oven to 400°F.

2. Bring 1 cup water to a boil in a small saucepan. Stir in the quinoa, cover, and reduce the heat to medium-low. Cook until all the liquid is absorbed and the quinoa is fluffy, 12 to 15 minutes. Remove from the heat and let steam, covered, for at least 5 minutes.

3. Place the block of feta in the center of a 9 × 13-inch baking dish. Arrange the broccoli florets and cherry tomatoes around the feta. Nestle the chicken breasts into the vegetables, spreading everything into one even layer with the feta at the center. Drizzle with the oil and sprinkle with the garlic powder, salt, and black pepper and toss to coat evenly.

4. Bake until the chicken reaches an internal temperature of 165°F, the tomatoes are jammy, and broccoli is golden brown, about 30 minutes. Transfer the cooked chicken to a cutting board and cut on a bias into ¼-inch-thick slices.

5. With a wooden spoon, mash the feta and mix to combine with the broccoli and tomatoes. Add the cooked quinoa and basil and mix well. Place the sliced chicken on top.

6. Spoon onto four plates. Garnish with more basil and serve.

DECONSTRUCTED TURKEY LASAGNA SKILLET

Gluten-free, dairy-free option, nut-free

While I love lasagna—who doesn't?—I don't love the hassle. This playful deconstructed skillet gives you all the melty, saucy goodness without the layers and labor. One pan, minimal prep, and way less time. Oh, and did I mention it's also gluten- and dairy-free? Double it and freeze for instant comfort on demand, or do as I do—keep a second batch in the fridge for cravings on cue. For the pasta, I prefer brown rice farfalle—it holds up beautifully, unlike some other gluten-free farfalle options that disintegrate mid-recipe.

SERVES 4

Prep time: 15 minutes
Cook time: 25 minutes

To make this dairy-free: Use dairy-free ricotta, omit the Parmesan, and add more salt if needed.

GOOOD TO KNOW: Any kind of ground protein will work here, including chicken, beef, or even plant-based crumbles, to make it vegetarian. To boost the protein, use chicken bone broth and swap out the ricotta for blended cottage cheese.

You can use traditional wheat farfalle, but you will need to use 1 less cup of broth, and the cooking time will vary, so keep an eye on it.

1½ teaspoons kosher salt
1 teaspoon dried basil
1 teaspoon garlic powder
1 teaspoon dried oregano
½ teaspoon ground black pepper
¼ teaspoon red pepper flakes, plus more for garnish (optional)
1 tablespoon olive oil
½ large yellow onion, finely diced (about ¾ cup)
1 pound 93% lean ground turkey
2½ cups low-sodium chicken broth
1½ cups marinara sauce
12 ounces brown rice farfalle, rice-and-corn-based farfalle, or regular farfalle
3 cups roughly chopped baby spinach (about 4 ounces)
½ cup part-skim ricotta cheese
¼ cup grated Parmesan, plus more for serving
Chopped fresh basil (optional)

1. In a small bowl, whisk together the salt, basil, garlic powder, oregano, black pepper, and red pepper flakes (if using). Set aside.

2. Heat the oil in a large lidded sauté pan or large Dutch oven over medium heat. Add the onion and cook, stirring often, until translucent, 4 to 5 minutes. Push the onion to the sides to create a hole in the middle of the pan. Add the ground turkey and cook, breaking up any large pieces with a wooden spoon or spatula, until the turkey is cooked through, 5 to 7 minutes. Stir in the herb mixture and cook until fragrant, 1 to 2 minutes. Transfer to a large bowl.

3. In the same pan, combine the broth, marinara sauce, and ½ cup water. Bring to a simmer over medium heat, then reduce the heat to medium-low.

STORE IT: Refrigerate in a sealed container for up to 4 days.

REHEAT IT: Microwave until warm, 1 to 2 minutes, or transfer back to a skillet over low heat with a splash of broth until warm.

Stir in the pasta, cover, and cook, stirring occasionally, until the pasta, is al dente, 12 to 15 minutes. (The cooking time will vary based on the brand.)

4. Remove from the heat and stir in the spinach, ricotta, and Parmesan. Add the reserved turkey mixture and stir gently to combine.

5. Spoon into four shallow bowls. Top with more grated Parmesan. Garnish with more red pepper flakes (if using) and basil (if using).

GREEK-STYLE CHICKEN AND VEGETABLE SKEWERS

Gluten-free, dairy-free option, nut-free

Take yourself to the sunny Greek islands any time of year with these vibrant veggie and chicken skewers, drizzled with my refreshing Cucumber Garlicky Sauce (page 299). Serve them over a crisp romaine and baby spinach salad, pile them onto a grain bowl, or even grab a skewer for a high-protein afternoon pick-me-up. No skewers? No problem. Check out my Goood to Know tip for an easy sheet pan swap. Got a grill? Fire it up while soaking in the sunshine. These skewers are also a party hit—prep and cook them ahead, then serve with my Tart Raspberry-Honey Lemonade (page 313).

SERVES 4

Prep time: 30 minutes
Cook time: 30 minutes

Special equipment: Eight 8-inch metal skewers

To make this dairy-free: Swap the Greek yogurt for a plain dairy-free yogurt of your choice, like a cashew- or coconut-based yogurt.

GOOOD TO KNOW: You can bake everything on the sheet pan if you don't have skewers. Line the sheet pan with parchment paper. Toss the marinated chicken and vegetables in a large bowl until combined and spread evenly on the sheet pan. Bake as directed.

I also love serving the skewers over rice for a rice bowl.

FOR THE MARINATED CHICKEN

2 teaspoons dried oregano
1 teaspoon dried basil
1 teaspoon garlic powder
1 teaspoon onion powder
1 teaspoon smoked paprika
1 teaspoon kosher salt
1 teaspoon dried thyme
½ teaspoon ground cumin
½ teaspoon ground black pepper
2 pounds boneless, skinless chicken thighs, cut into 1½-inch pieces
Grated zest and juice of ½ lemon
1 tablespoon olive oil

FOR THE SKEWERS

2 red bell peppers, cored, seeded, and cut into 1½-inch squares (about 2 cups)
1 medium red onion, cut into 1½-inch chunks
1 medium zucchini, cut into 1½-inch chunks

Cucumber Garlicky Sauce (p. 299), for serving

1. Position an oven rack 3 to 4 inches from the broiler and preheat the oven to 425°F. Line a sheet pan with aluminum foil and set aside, along with eight metal skewers.

2. **Marinate the chicken:** In a large bowl, whisk together the oregano, basil, garlic powder, onion powder, smoked paprika, salt, thyme, cumin, and black pepper until combined. Add the chicken pieces, lemon zest and lemon juice, and oil and mix with a rubber spatula or clean hands until the

(continues)

chicken is thoroughly coated in the spices. Cover with a lid or plastic wrap and marinate in the refrigerator for 20 to 25 minutes.

3. **Assemble the skewers:** Thread 2 pieces of the marinated chicken onto each skewer, followed by 2 pieces of bell pepper and 1 piece each of onion and zucchini. Continue to alternate until you are about 1 inch from the top of the skewer. You should be able to fit about 6 pieces of chicken on the skewer. Place lengthwise on the sheet pan and repeat with the remaining skewers.

4. Bake until the chicken and veggies are cooked through, turning halfway through, 22 to 25 minutes. Turn the oven to high broil and cook until lightly browned, 5 to 7 minutes.

5. **To serve:** Place the skewers on a large serving platter alongside a bowl of cucumber sauce.

STORE IT: Refrigerate the chicken and veggies in a sealed container for up to 4 days or freeze for up to 3 months.

REHEAT IT: From the refrigerator, transfer the chicken and veggies to a sheet pan and bake in a 425°F oven for 7 to 10 minutes to recrisp and warm. From the freezer, thaw in the refrigerator for at least 8 hours, then transfer to a sheet pan and bake in a 425°F oven for 9 to 12 minutes.

NOT-YOUR-AVERAGE BURRITO BOWLS WITH SHEET PAN SALSA

Gluten-free, dairy-free, vegetarian, vegan, nut-free

I'm a bit of a control freak—in the best way—which is why I refuse to settle for a burrito bowl with random ingredients and flat flavors. So I built a better one. This version levels up with tofu and mushrooms tossed in a smoky seasoning blend and roasted alongside a sheet pan salsa for deep flavor in every bite. It's 100 percent gluten-free, dairy-free, vegetarian, vegan, and yes, nut-free, all while packing 30 grams of protein per serving, and it gets even more protein with a scoop of my Chickpea Guacamole (page 128) for an extra hit of protein and flavor. *Bowl Bonus:* You'll have extra salsa to snack on with chips or to jazz up scrambled eggs the next day.

SERVES 4, WITH LEFTOVER SALSA

Prep time: 20 minutes
Cook time: 40 minutes

FOR THE SHEET PAN SALSA

3 small Roma (plum) tomatoes, quartered
½ medium red onion, peeled and quartered
4 garlic cloves
1 jalapeño pepper, halved and seeded
1 tablespoon olive oil
1 teaspoon ground cumin
Kosher salt
Juice of 1 lime

FOR THE TOFU MIXTURE

2 teaspoons smoked paprika
1 teaspoon chili powder
1 teaspoon garlic powder
1 teaspoon onion powder
1½ teaspoons kosher salt
1 teaspoon ground cumin
½ teaspoon dried oregano
One 16-ounce block high-protein super-firm tofu (see Goood to Know)
12 ounces Baby Bella mushrooms, finely diced (about 3 cups)
1 tablespoon olive oil

FOR THE BOWLS

Jenn's Steamed Rice (p. 290), or 3 cups cooked white rice
One 15-ounce can pinto beans, drained and rinsed
1 green bell pepper, cored, seeded, and medium-diced (about 1 cup)
1 lime, quartered
Chopped fresh cilantro

(continues)

GOOOD TO KNOW:

If tofu isn't your thing, you can use 1 pound lean ground beef, chicken, or turkey. Use the same amount of oil and spices, but don't toss in the mushrooms until after the meat has browned.

If you can't find high-protein super-firm tofu, I recommend getting firm or extra-firm tofu. Press it by wrapping it in a clean kitchen towel and placing it on a small sheet pan or in a shallow bowl. Top it with a heavy object (like a heavy-bottomed pan) and let it sit until the excess liquid is drained, 15 to 20 minutes. High-protein super-firm tofu has much less liquid, which is why it doesn't need to be pressed.

If you want to get fancy with it, once your steamed rice is done, mix in the juice of 1 lime, 1 teaspoon kosher salt, and ¼ cup finely chopped fresh cilantro for the most delicious and simple Cilantro-Lime Rice.

1. Position one oven rack in the middle or lower third of the oven. Position a second rack 2 to 3 inches from the broiler. Preheat the oven to 425°F. Line two sheet pans with parchment paper. Set one aside.

2. **Make the sheet pan salsa:** Combine the tomatoes, onion, garlic, jalapeño, oil, cumin, and 1 teaspoon salt on one sheet pan. Gently toss until the vegetables are evenly coated in the spices and oil. Spread the vegetables in an even layer.

3. Roast on the lower oven rack until the vegetables are very soft, 20 to 22 minutes. Let them cool on the pan for 10 to 15 minutes.

4. **Meanwhile, make the tofu mixture:** In a large bowl, whisk together the smoked paprika, chili powder, garlic powder, onion powder, salt, cumin, and oregano.

5. Crumble the block of tofu into the bowl. Add the mushrooms and oil and mix with a spatula until fully coated. Spread the mixture out on the second sheet pan and set the pan on the top oven rack.

6. Roast until the mushrooms are tender and the tofu begins to brown, about 20 minutes. Then turn the oven to a high broil and broil until the mushrooms and tofu are browned all over, 1 to 2 minutes.

7. Transfer the cooled salsa to a large food processor or blender and pulse until the salsa is mostly smooth, with a few small chunks, about eight pulses. Add the lime juice and a pinch of salt and pulse once to combine. (Makes about 1½ cups salsa.)

8. **Assemble the bowls:** Spoon the steamed rice into four bowls. Divide the pinto beans and bell pepper among the bowls on top of the rice. Top each bowl with the tofu and mushroom mixture and a few generous spoonfuls of salsa, a squeeze of lime, and cilantro.

STORE IT: Refrigerate the bowl components in separate sealed containers for up to 4 days. Refrigerate the salsa in a sealed container for up to 1 week.

REHEAT IT: Assemble a bowl without salsa and microwave until warm, 1 to 2 minutes, then top with the salsa. Alternatively, return the tofu and mushroom mix to a sheet pan and reheat in a 400°F oven for 10 to 12 minutes, warm the rice and beans in the microwave, and then assemble the bowls.

CREAMY SPINACH CHICKEN

Gluten-free, nut-free

Loaded with protein and ready in just 30 minutes, this dish is the GOAT. It's packed with bright, springy flavors and comes together in 20 minutes. Sweet peas and earthy spinach bring balance while ricotta adds a smooth, luscious texture. Plus, it rescues that sad, almost-expired bag of spinach lurking in the back of your fridge. Perfect for when you need something filling, indulgent, and fast.

SERVES 4

Prep time: 10 minutes
Cook time: 30 minutes

GOOOD TO KNOW: This recipe mixes some of my favorite dairy and dairy-free ingredients because I love the combination of lemon, ricotta, and coconut milk. If you want to choose a direction, go dairy-free by swapping the ricotta for dairy-free ricotta and the mozzarella for shredded dairy-free cheese, and omitting the Parmesan. Go all-in on the dairy by swapping the coconut milk for light cream. Want to up your protein even more? Swap the ricotta for blended 4% milkfat cottage cheese!

2 pounds boneless, skinless chicken breasts, sliced in half horizontally and pounded to a ⅛-inch thickness
Kosher salt
Ground black pepper
½ cup tapioca flour or arrowroot starch (can substitute cornstarch)
2 tablespoons olive oil
3 cups roughly chopped baby spinach (about 4 ounces)
¾ cup fresh or frozen green peas (about 6 ounces)
6 garlic cloves, minced
2 cups low-sodium chicken broth or low-sodium vegetable broth
1 cup part-skim ricotta cheese
¾ cup full-fat coconut milk (about half a well-shaken 13.5-ounce can)
Juice of 1 lemon
4 ounces mozzarella, shredded (about ¾ cup)
Grated Parmesan (optional)
Chopped fresh parsley

1. Position an oven rack at least 3 inches from the broiler and preheat the broiler to high. Line a sheet pan with parchment paper.

2. Pat the thinly sliced chicken dry with paper towels and season both sides with salt and black pepper. Add the tapioca flour to a plate or shallow bowl. Dredge each piece of chicken in the flour, shaking off any excess, and place it on the prepared sheet pan.

3. Heat the oil in a large ovenproof skillet over medium-high heat until shimmering. Working in batches if necessary to avoid overcrowding the skillet, carefully add the chicken to the pan and cook for 3 minutes, then flip and cook until the chicken is fully cooked through to an internal temperature of 165°F, about 3 minutes more.

4. Transfer the chicken to a platter or sheet pan, leaving the remaining oil behind in the skillet.

STORE IT: Refrigerate in a sealed container for up to 3 days or freeze for up to 3 months.

REHEAT IT: From the refrigerator, microwave until warm, 1 to 2 minutes. From the freezer, thaw in the refrigerator overnight, then microwave in 30-second increments until warm.

5. Add the spinach, peas, and garlic to the skillet. Cook, stirring often, until the spinach has wilted, 2 to 3 minutes. Season with a generous pinch of salt. Reduce heat to low and stir in the broth, ricotta, and coconut milk.

6. Remove the skillet from the heat and stir in the lemon juice. Return the chicken to the skillet and sprinkle the mozzarella over the top.

7. Transfer the pan to the oven and broil until the cheese is melted and golden brown, about 2 minutes.

8. Serve in the pan or spoon onto four plates. Top with grated Parmesan (if using) and chopped parsley.

FRENCH ONION MEATBALL SKILLET

Gluten-free, dairy-free option, nut-free

Ooh la la—meet the perfect mash-up of velvety, long-simmered French onion soup and a protein-packed meatball rice skillet. Traditional caramelized onions take 45 minutes *on their own*, but this clever hack gets the whole dish done in that time by simmering the rice and meatballs together, infusing every bite with deep, savory flavor. And yes, there's still that irresistible layer of bubbling, golden Gruyère, ready to be scooped straight from the skillet.

SERVES 4

Prep time: 15 minutes
Cook time: 45 minutes

To make this dairy-free: Omit the cheese.

GOOOD TO KNOW:
Add even more protein to this dish by using beef bone broth instead of regular beef broth.

Swap the ground beef for ground chicken if you're not a red-meat person!

Giving the rice a good rinse washes away excess starch, meaning less sticky cooking water and grains that stay separate and perfectly tender. Place the rice in a fine-mesh sieve and run under cold water for about 30 seconds. Let the water drain thoroughly and gently shake the sieve to remove any dripping water.

FOR THE ONIONS
2 tablespoons olive oil
2 large yellow onions, thinly sliced (about 3 cups)

FOR THE MEATBALLS
1 pound 85% lean ground beef
1 tablespoon coconut aminos (or reduced-sodium tamari or reduced-sodium soy sauce)
½ teaspoon kosher salt (omit if using tamari or soy sauce)
1 teaspoon garlic powder
1 teaspoon onion powder
½ teaspoon ground black pepper

FOR THE SKILLET
1 teaspoon olive oil, for rolling
4 garlic cloves, minced
2 tablespoons finely chopped fresh thyme, or 2 teaspoons dried
¾ teaspoon kosher salt, plus more as needed (omit if using tamari or soy sauce)
½ teaspoon ground black pepper
1 cup uncooked jasmine rice, rinsed (see Goood to Know)
3 cups low-sodium beef broth
2 tablespoons coconut aminos (or reduced-sodium tamari or reduced-sodium soy sauce)
About 6 ounces Gruyère or mozzarella, shredded (1 cup)
Chopped fresh parsley

1. Preheat the oven to 400°F. Line a sheet pan with parchment paper and set aside.

2. **Caramelize the onions:** Heat the oil in a large lidded sauté pan over medium heat until shimmering. Add the onions and cook, stirring occasionally, until very soft and beginning to caramelize, 20 to 25 minutes, taking care not to let them burn (reduce the heat to medium-low if needed). Add a splash of water if the onions brown too quickly.

(continues)

3. **Meanwhile, make the meatballs:** In a large bowl, combine the beef, coconut aminos, salt, garlic powder, onion powder, and black pepper and mix well with a rubber spatula or clean hands.

4. Rub the oil onto your clean hands and pinch off about 1 tablespoon of the meat mixture. Roll loosely between your palms until round and smooth, taking care not to overwork the mixture or the meatballs will become tough when cooked. Place the meatball on the prepared sheet pan. Repeat with the rest of the mixture, forming about 20 equal-size meatballs and leaving about 1 inch of space between each meatball.

5. Bake until lightly browned and fully cooked with an internal temperature of 165°F, 10 to 12 minutes.

6. **Finish the skillet:** Add the garlic, thyme, salt, and black pepper to the pan with the caramelized onions and cook until fragrant, 1 to 2 minutes. Add the rice and toast, stirring frequently, until golden brown, 2 to 3 minutes. Pour in the broth, coconut aminos, and ½ cup water and stir to combine. Bring the mixture to a simmer, then reduce the heat to medium-low. Cover and cook until the liquid is absorbed and the rice is fluffy, stirring halfway through to prevent any sticking, 16 to 19 minutes. If the water has been fully absorbed before the rice is done cooking, add another ½ cup water. If the liquid isn't absorbing enough, turn the heat back to medium.

7. Reduce the heat to low, uncover, and place the cooked meatballs on top of the rice. If needed, season with more salt. Sprinkle the cheese all over the top. Cover and cook until the cheese is melted, 1 to 2 minutes. (Alternatively, transfer the uncovered pan to the oven and broil on high until the cheese is melted and golden, about 2 minutes.)

8. Spoon the rice and meatballs onto four plates. Garnish with chopped parsley.

STORE IT: Refrigerate in a sealed container for up to 4 days or freeze for up to 3 months.

REHEAT IT: From the refrigerator, microwave until warm, 1 to 2 minutes. From the freezer, thaw in the refrigerator overnight, then microwave in 30-second increments until warm.

SHEET PAN PESTO PIZZA WITH ASPARAGUS AND PROSCIUTTO

Gluten-free, vegetarian option, nut-free

I had so much fun developing this pizza recipe, and it's always on repeat. It's my healthier, simpler take on pizza dough that just so happens to provide about 20 grams of protein in the crust alone. The combo of the pesto, asparagus, and peas with the savory ricotta and salty prosciutto is my all-time favorite topping, especially come spring, when all these vegetables are fully in season. The dough is crispy on the outside and tender on the inside from the addition of Greek yogurt. Feel free to swap these toppings for any other ones you crave. You could also use pancetta or even thinly sliced ham as a substitute. Please don't skip the pesto! Use my dairy-free walnut go-to pesto recipe.

SERVES 4

Prep time: 20 minutes
Cook time: 25 minutes

To make this vegetarian: Omit the prosciutto.

GOOOD TO KNOW: If you have a pizza steel or stone, roll the dough into a thin round on a lightly floured surface. Flour a pizza peel and carefully transfer the dough to a preheated steel or stone. Bake, top, and serve as directed.

Feel free to use all-purpose flour, if desired.

FOR THE PIZZA DOUGH

1¾ cups gluten-free 1:1 baking flour, plus more for shaping and rolling
2 teaspoons baking powder
1 teaspoon garlic powder
½ teaspoon kosher salt
1¼ cups whole-milk or low-fat Greek yogurt

FOR THE TOPPINGS

¾ cup Dairy-Free Walnut Pesto (p. 301) or store-bought dairy-free pesto
About 4 ounces mozzarella, shredded (¾ cup)
½ cup part-skim ricotta
½ cup fresh or frozen green peas (about 4 ounces)
2 ounces asparagus, ends trimmed, cut into 1½-inch pieces (about 8 spears)
3 ounces thinly sliced prosciutto (about 8 slices), cut into 2½-inch squares
¼ cup grated Parmesan

1. Position an oven rack in the lower third of the oven and preheat the oven to 425°F. Have a piece of parchment and a sheet pan nearby.

2. **Make the pizza dough:** In a large bowl, whisk together the flour, baking powder, garlic powder, and salt. Fold in the yogurt with a rubber spatula until just combined.

3. Lightly dust the dough and countertop with flour. Knead until the dough is soft but not sticky, 2 to 3 minutes. If the dough still feels too sticky, add more flour by the tablespoon until it feels smooth.

4. To roll the dough, place the parchment on the counter and lightly sprinkle with flour. With a lightly floured rolling pin or floured hands, roll or press the

(continues)

dough on the parchment into a thin 13 × 10-inch rectangle, adding a bit more flour if the dough is still sticky. Transfer the parchment to the sheet pan.

5. Bake until the top is lightly browned, 15 to 17 minutes. Remove from the oven, but leave the oven on.

6. **Top the pizza:** Spread the pesto evenly over the dough, leaving a ½- to 1-inch border on all sides. Top with the mozzarella and dollops of ricotta. Evenly distribute the peas, asparagus, and prosciutto over the pizza.

7. Return to the oven and bake until the cheese has melted and the edges of the prosciutto begin to crisp, 11 to 13 minutes.

8. Immediately top the pizza with the Parmesan. Let cool slightly in the pan, about 5 minutes. Slice into four even rectangles, and serve immediately.

STORE IT: Refrigerate in a sealed container for up to 4 days.

REHEAT IT: For a crispy crust, transfer slices to a sheet pan and bake in a 425°F oven until warm, 6 to 8 minutes. Alternatively, microwave until warm, 1 to 2 minutes.

CAULIFLOWER PIZZA SKILLET

Gluten-free, dairy-free option, nut-free

This is my good-for-you answer to a loaded pizza without sacrificing flavor or cheesy bliss. Ground pork, pepperoni, mushrooms, spinach, and cauliflower are tossed in sauce and a mozz blanket to make a savory, cheesy skillet with varying elements in every bite. I promise you won't miss the crust! Try it with any kind of ground meat you like, or even plant-based crumbles, and stuff it with additional veggies you might need to use up. Add extra red pepper flakes if you prefer a kick!

SERVES 4

Prep time: 10 minutes
Cook time: 30 minutes

To make this dairy-free: Use dairy-free shredded cheese.

GOOOD TO KNOW: If you have larger cauliflower florets, you may need to increase the cook time by 5 to 7 minutes.

STORE IT: Refrigerate in a sealed container for up to 4 days.

REHEAT IT: Transfer back to a skillet and bake in a 425°F oven until warm, 8 to 10 minutes. Alternatively, transfer to a microwave-safe dish and microwave until warm, 1 to 2 minutes.

2 teaspoons dried basil
2 teaspoons dried oregano
2 teaspoons kosher salt
1 teaspoon garlic powder
½ teaspoon ground black pepper
¼ teaspoon red pepper flakes, plus more as needed (optional)
1 tablespoon olive oil
1 pound 90% lean ground pork
1 medium head cauliflower, cut into 1-inch florets (about 4 cups)
8 ounces Baby Bella mushrooms, thinly sliced (about 2 cups)
1½ cups baby spinach (about 2 ounces)
2 cups marinara sauce
About 4 ounces mozzarella, shredded (¾ cup)
4 ounces sliced uncured pork and beef pepperoni

1. Position an oven rack at least 3 inches from the broiler and preheat the oven to 425°F.

2. In a small bowl, stir together the basil, oregano, salt, garlic powder, black pepper, and red pepper flakes (if using). Set aside.

3. Heat the oil in a 12-inch cast-iron skillet over medium-high heat until shimmering. Add the ground pork and cook, breaking up into small pieces and stirring often until no pink remains, 5 to 7 minutes.

4. Stir in the reserved herb-spice mixture and cook until fragrant, 30 to 60 seconds. Add the cauliflower, mushrooms, and spinach and stir until evenly combined. Pour the marinara sauce into the pan and stir to evenly combine with the pork and vegetables. Sprinkle the mozzarella over the sauce and arrange the pepperoni in a single layer over the top.

5. Bake until the sauce bubbles and the cheese fully melts, 18 to 20 minutes (see Goood to Know). Turn the broiler on high and broil until the cheese is melted and golden and the pepperoni is browned, about 2 minutes.

6. Serve from the skillet or spoon onto four plates or into bowls.

MOM'S GAME-DAY CHILI WITH SWEET HONEY BREAD

Gluten-free, dairy-free, nut-free

My mom's famous chili was one of the first recipes I ever learned to cook. I can still picture myself as a kid, standing beside her in the kitchen, eagerly soaking in each step—the moment that first sparked my love for cooking. Since then, I've made this chili more times than I can count, and every time, the rich, simmering aroma takes me right back to slow Sundays with my family, a pot bubbling on the stove, and the Patriots playing at full volume. This protein-packed, freezer-friendly comfort is a staple in my home—and I hope it becomes one in yours too.

SERVES 4

Prep time: 10 minutes
Cook time: 35 minutes

GOOOD TO KNOW: Swap the beef for 93% lean ground turkey if you'd prefer. The spice mix is the star and will flavor whatever protein you want to add in!

STORE IT: Refrigerate in a sealed container for up to 4 days or freeze for up to 3 months.

REHEAT IT: From the refrigerator, microwave until warm, 1 to 2 minutes, or return to a pot over medium-low heat and cook until warm. From the freezer, thaw in the refrigerator overnight, then microwave in 30-second increments until warm or follow the same stovetop instructions.

2 teaspoons ground cumin
1 teaspoon dried oregano
1 teaspoon smoked paprika
1 teaspoon kosher salt, plus more to taste
½ teaspoon ground black pepper
½ teaspoon chili powder
1 tablespoon olive oil
2 green bell peppers, cored, seeded, and small-diced (about 2 cups)
½ large yellow onion, small-diced (about ¾ cup)
3 garlic cloves, finely minced
1 pound 85% lean ground beef
One 28-ounce can crushed tomatoes
One 15-ounce can kidney beans, drained and rinsed
Optional toppings: shredded cheese, sour cream, thinly sliced green onions (omit the cheese and sour cream if dairy-free)
Sweet Honey Bread (recipe follows)

1. In a small bowl, stir together the cumin, oregano, smoked paprika, salt, black pepper, and chili powder. Set aside.

2. Heat the oil in a lidded pot or Dutch oven over medium heat. Add the bell peppers and onion and cook until slightly softened, 6 to 7 minutes. Add the garlic and cook, stirring often, until fragrant, 1 to 2 minutes.

3. Push the vegetables to the sides of the pan to make a hole in the center of the pot. Add the ground beef and cook, stirring to break up the large chunks, until browned, 6 to 7 minutes.

4. Add the spice mixture and stir to combine. Add the tomatoes and kidney beans and bring to a boil over high heat. Add up to 1 cup water if the chili

looks too thick. Reduce the heat to medium-low and simmer for about 15 minutes. If needed, season with more salt.

5. Spoon the chili into four bowls. If desired, top with shredded cheese, sour cream, and sliced green onions. Serve with sweet honey bread on the side.

SWEET HONEY BREAD

Gluten-free, dairy-free option, vegetarian

MAKES 12 PIECES

Prep time: 10 minutes

Cook time: 25 minutes

To make this dairy-free: Use unsalted vegan butter.

STORE IT: Keep the bread in a sealed container in a cool, dry place for up to 4 days or freeze for up to 3 months.

REHEAT IT: Enjoy at room temperature or microwave for 30 to 45 seconds to warm. From the freezer, thaw in the refrigerator overnight.

4 large eggs, at room temperature

6 tablespoons unsalted butter or unsalted vegan butter, melted

½ cup raw honey

1½ cups blanched almond flour

½ cup tapioca flour or arrowroot starch (can substitute cornstarch)

1 teaspoon baking powder

1 teaspoon baking soda

1 teaspoon kosher salt

1. Preheat the oven to 350°F. Line a 9 × 9-inch baking dish with parchment paper cut to hang over all four sides for easy removal.

2. In a large bowl, whisk together the eggs, melted butter, and honey until smooth. Add the almond flour, tapioca flour, baking powder, baking soda, and salt and mix with a rubber spatula until the dry ingredients are fully incorporated into the wet ingredients. Do not overmix. Transfer to the prepared baking dish and spread evenly into all corners.

3. Bake until the bread is golden on top and a toothpick inserted into the middle comes out clean, 20 to 24 minutes. Let the bread cool for 10 minutes.

4. Lift the parchment paper edges to remove the bread. Slice into 12 even rectangles.

SLOW COOKER CARNITAS TACOS WITH PINEAPPLE SALSA

Gluten-free, dairy-free

The secret to crispy yet tender carnitas? A long, slow braise in lime, orange, and warm spices. Nestled into corn tortillas and topped with a sweet, slightly spicy pineapple salsa, they're the ultimate refresh on a scorching summer night. I let the slow cooker do the work, keeping the kitchen cooler and giving me a head start on dinner. If you don't have a slow cooker, these carnitas can be made in a Dutch oven (see Goood to Know). The real magic happens with a quick flash under the broiler for that signature crispy edge. It's one of the easiest ways to feed a crowd—just set up a self-serve taco bar and let everyone build their perfect bite!

SERVES 4 TO 6

Prep time: 15 minutes
Cook time: 5 to 8 hours

GOOOD TO KNOW: To make carnitas in a Dutch oven or large, heavy pot with a lid, preheat the oven to 325°F. Season and prepare the pork as directed. Add 2 to 3 cups water, cover the pot, and roast in the oven until the meat is tender enough to shred with a fork, 4 to 4½ hours. Shred and broil as directed.

FOR THE PINEAPPLE SALSA

1½ cups small-diced fresh pineapple (about ½ small pineapple), or one 20-ounce can diced pineapple

½ large yellow onion, finely diced (about ½ cup)

1 jalapeño, seeded and finely diced

⅓ cup chopped fresh cilantro

Juice of 1 lime

1 tablespoon raw honey

1 garlic clove, minced

1½ teaspoons kosher salt

FOR THE CARNITAS

2 teaspoons chili powder

2 teaspoons ground cumin

2 teaspoons dried oregano

2 teaspoons kosher salt

1 teaspoon ground black pepper

One 2- to 2½-pound boneless pork shoulder or pork butt

Juice of 2 medium oranges (about ½ cup)

Juice of 2 limes (about ¼ cup)

½ large yellow onion, diced (about ¾ cup)

4 garlic cloves, minced

FOR THE TACOS

Twelve 6-inch corn, almond flour, or chickpea flour tortillas

Lime wedges, for serving

(continues)

1. **Make the pineapple salsa:** In a medium bowl, combine the pineapple, onion, jalapeño, cilantro, lime juice, honey, garlic, and salt and mix well. Cover and refrigerate until serving.

2. **Make the carnitas:** In a small bowl, whisk together the chili powder, cumin, oregano, salt, and black pepper.

3. Place the pork shoulder in a 6-quart slow cooker and cover with the spice mixture. Pour the orange and lime juices to either side of the pork shoulder so you don't rinse the spices off the top of the pork. Add the onion and garlic to the liquid surrounding the pork. Cover and cook on low for 8 hours or high for 5 hours. (Alternatively, use a Dutch oven; see Goood to Know.)

4. **When you're ready to make tacos:** Position an oven rack 3 to 4 inches from the broiler and heat the broiler to high. Line a sheet pan with aluminum foil.

5. Using two forks, shred the meat directly in the slow cooker. Transfer the shredded pork to the prepared sheet pan, spread it in an even layer, and drizzle 2 to 3 tablespoons of the slow cooker juices over the top. Broil until the pork is browned on the edges, 5 to 10 minutes.

6. To serve, arrange 2 to 3 warmed tortillas on each plate. Top each tortilla with ¼ cup of the carnitas and 3 to 4 tablespoons of pineapple salsa. Serve with lime wedges for squeezing.

STORE IT: Refrigerate the carnitas and pineapple salsa in separate sealed containers, up to 4 days for the carnitas and up to 7 days for the salsa. Freeze the carnitas in a sealed container for up to 3 months (broil after reheating). I don't recommend freezing the pineapple salsa.

REHEAT IT: From the refrigerator, microwave the carnitas until warm, 1 to 2 minutes, or return to a sheet pan to broil for 3 to 5 minutes to recrisp. From the freezer, thaw in the refrigerator overnight, then microwave in 30-second increments until warm.

MAPLE-DIJON PORK TENDERLOIN

Gluten-free, dairy-free, nut-free

A mustard and maple sauce is the essence of fall, turning an affordable pork tenderloin into a dinner worthy of the weekend—or even date night. This lean cut gets a bad rap for being dry, but trust me, this method delivers a juicy, flavor-packed roast. The secret? A good sear to lock in moisture, then finishing it right in the sauce for maximum tenderness. I always serve this with my Roasted Garlic Mashed Potatoes (page 280)—because every drop of that sauce deserves to be soaked up and savored.

SERVES 4

Prep time: 10 minutes
Cook time: 35 minutes

GOOOD TO KNOW: The silver skin becomes chewy when cooked. To remove it, carefully insert a knife under that skin and cut away from the tenderloin, then turn the knife, lift, and cut down the length of the tenderloin to separate it.

STORE IT: Refrigerate in a sealed container for up to 4 days or freeze the pork and pan sauce separately for up to 3 months.

REHEAT IT: From the refrigerator, microwave the pork with the sauce until warm, 1 to 2 minutes. From the freezer, thaw in the refrigerator overnight, then microwave in 30-second increments until warm.

FOR THE MAPLE-DIJON SAUCE

1½ cups low-sodium chicken broth
¼ cup pure maple syrup
2 tablespoons coconut aminos (or reduced-sodium tamari or reduced-sodium soy sauce)
2 tablespoons Dijon mustard
4 garlic cloves, minced
1 tablespoon apple cider vinegar
2 teaspoons tapioca flour or arrowroot starch (can substitute cornstarch)

FOR THE PORK

1 teaspoon garlic powder
1 teaspoon smoked paprika
1 teaspoon dried rosemary
1 teaspoon kosher salt
½ teaspoon ground black pepper
1½ pounds pork tenderloin, silver skin removed (see Goood to Know)
2 tablespoons olive oil

1. Preheat the oven to 400°F.

2. **Make the maple-Dijon sauce:** In a medium bowl, whisk together the broth, syrup, coconut aminos, mustard, garlic, vinegar, and tapioca flour. Set aside.

3. **Cook the pork:** In a small bowl, stir together the garlic powder, smoked paprika, rosemary, salt, and black pepper. Pat the pork tenderloin dry with paper towels and coat all sides with the spice mixture.

4. Heat the oil in a large cast-iron or ovenproof skillet over medium heat until shimmering. Add the pork and sear until browned and a crust forms, 2 to 3 minutes per side. Transfer to a plate and set aside.

5. Reduce the heat under the skillet to medium-low, add the sauce, and stir with a wooden spoon to release any browned bits from the bottom of the pan. Bring to a simmer and cook, stirring often, until the sauce thickens,

about 3 minutes. Return the seared pork to the skillet and turn it with tongs to evenly coat with the sauce. Transfer to the oven.

6. Roast the pork until golden brown on the outside and it reaches an internal temperature of 140°F, 15 to 18 minutes.

7. Remove the pork from the skillet, cover loosely with aluminum foil, and rest on a cutting board for about 5 minutes, then cut it into ½-inch slices.

8. To serve, divide among four plates and drizzle with the pan sauce.

BAKED BLACK BEAN AND POBLANO TACOS

Gluten-free, dairy-free option, vegetarian, vegan option, nut-free

When I was growing up in a traditional Irish American household, plant-based meals weren't exactly the norm. Shepherd's pie, corned beef and cabbage, and hearty stews? Absolutely. Meat-free dishes? Not so much. But these crispy baked tacos changed the game for me. Stuffed with smoky, slightly sweet poblanos and baked to golden perfection, they prove that vegetarian meals can be just as bold and satisfying. Plus, my sheet pan hack makes them effortless—use it for any taco filling you love!

SERVES 4

Prep time: 15 minutes
Cook time: 30 minutes

To make this dairy-free and vegan: Use dairy-free cheese and dairy-free yogurt for the sauce.

GOOOD TO KNOW: If needed, use a press or weighted object, like a can or plate, to hold the tortillas closed while finishing the batch.

FOR THE BEAN AND POBLANO FILLING

2 tablespoons olive oil
2 teaspoons chili powder
2 teaspoons ground cumin
1 teaspoon garlic powder
1 teaspoon smoked paprika
1 teaspoon kosher salt
½ large yellow onion, small-diced (about ¾ cup)
2 medium poblano peppers, seeded and small-diced (about 2 cups)
Two 15-ounce cans black beans, drained and rinsed

FOR THE TACOS

Twelve 6-inch corn, almond flour, or chickpea flour tortillas
About 6 ounces Cheddar cheese, shredded (1½ cups)
Creamy Cilantro Sauce (p. 294)
1 lime, quartered

1. Position oven racks in the upper and lower thirds of the oven and preheat the oven to 425°F. Brush 1 tablespoon of the oil on two sheet pans.

2. **Make the bean and poblano filling:** In a small bowl, combine the chili powder, cumin, garlic powder, smoked paprika, and salt. Set aside.

3. Heat the remaining 1 tablespoon oil in a large skillet or Dutch oven over medium heat. Add the onion and poblanos and cook until the onion is translucent and the peppers are softened, 6 to 8 minutes.

4. Add the black beans and reserved spice mixture and cook, stirring occasionally, until fragrant and the beans are softened, about 5 minutes. Mash the black beans gently with a potato masher or the back of a large spoon. Remove from the heat.

(continues)

5. **Assemble and bake the tacos:** Wrap the stack of tortillas in one or two damp paper towels and microwave until softened and pliable, about 1 minute. Remove the tortillas from the towel and place them on the prepared sheet pans, flipping to lightly coat each side. Add 2 heaping tablespoons of the bean mixture to the center of each tortilla and spread with the back of a spoon, leaving a ½-inch border. Top the tortillas with 2 tablespoons of the Cheddar. Fold each tortilla in half, gently pressing down with a spatula to seal.

6. Bake until the cheese is melted and the tortillas are golden brown and crispy on one side, about 8 minutes. Carefully flip. Return to the oven, switching racks and rotating the sheet pans front to back, and bake until golden brown and crispy on the other side, about 5 minutes more. Let the tortillas cool on the pans for at least 5 minutes.

7. Set 3 tacos on each plate, drizzle with the sauce, and serve with a lime wedge for squeezing.

STORE IT: Refrigerate in a sealed container for up to 4 days or freeze for up to 3 months. For best results, store the stuffed but unbaked tacos and wait to bake until you're ready to enjoy them.

REHEAT IT: From the refrigerator, sear for 2 to 3 minutes per side on an oiled skillet over medium heat or microwave until warm, 1 to 2 minutes. From the freezer, thaw in the refrigerator overnight, then sear or microwave until warm.

SALMON BITES WITH COCONUT RICE AND CHILLED CUCUMBER SALAD

Gluten-free, dairy-free, nut-free

This was one of the first recipes I wrote because what's a cookbook without a killer salmon bowl? It's quick, versatile, and my go-to for a low-effort, high-reward date-night dinner with my husband. This is a total trifecta: perfectly marinated salmon, fragrant coconut rice, and crisp cucumbers—harmony in every bite. I broke out the rice and cuke so you can prep them in advance or multitask while the salmon marinates (see Store It). Stylish, simple, and seriously good!

SERVES 4

Prep time: 40 minutes
Cook time: 25 minutes

GOOOD TO KNOW: Use the same weight of skinless, boneless chicken thighs cut into 1-inch pieces instead of salmon. Cook for 14 to 16 minutes, or until the internal temperature is 165°F. For plant-based, try pressed tofu cut into 1-inch cubes and roasted for 20 to 22 minutes.

STORE IT: Refrigerate the salmon, rice, and salad in separate sealed containers for up to 3 days.

REHEAT IT: Reheat the rice in a microwave-safe container until warm, 1 to 2 minutes, stirring halfway through. Microwave the salmon until warm, 1 to 2 minutes, and plate with chilled cucumber salad and rice.

FOR THE SALMON

⅓ cup coconut aminos (or reduced-sodium tamari or reduced-sodium soy sauce)
1 tablespoon pure maple syrup
1 tablespoon minced peeled fresh ginger
1 tablespoon sriracha
1 tablespoon toasted sesame oil
1½ pounds skinless salmon fillets, cut into 1-inch cubes
Olive oil for the baking dish

FOR SERVING

Coconut Rice (recipe follows)
Chilled Cucumber Salad (recipe follows)
Sesame seeds

1. **Prepare the salmon:** In a large bowl, combine the coconut aminos, maple syrup, ginger, sriracha, and sesame oil and mix well. Add the salmon cubes and gently toss to cover with the marinade. Cover the bowl and marinate in the refrigerator while you make the salad and rice (for no longer than 1 hour).

2. Preheat the oven to 400°F. Lightly coat a 9 × 13-inch baking dish with oil.

3. Transfer the salmon and marinade to the baking dish. Separate the cubes so they are at least ½ inch apart.

4. Bake until the centers of the salmon cubes are light pink and opaque or until internal temperature of 145°F, 8 to 10 minutes.

5. **To serve:** Divide the rice among four plates. Top the rice with salad and the salmon and drizzle with the remaining sauce. Garnish with sesame seeds.

(continues)

CHILLED CUCUMBER SALAD

Gluten-free, dairy-free, vegetarian, vegan, nut-free

SERVES 4

Prep time: 10 minutes, plus 10 to 15 minutes marinating

Cook time: none

1 English cucumber, unpeeled, halved, and thinly sliced into half-moons

6 green onions, thinly sliced

2 tablespoons coconut aminos (or reduced-sodium tamari or reduced-sodium soy sauce)

2 tablespoons rice vinegar

1 tablespoon toasted sesame oil

1 teaspoon minced peeled fresh ginger

In a medium bowl, combine the cucumber, green onions, coconut aminos, vinegar, sesame oil, and ginger and mix well. Cover and refrigerate for 10 to 15 minutes to marinate. Serve chilled.

COCONUT RICE

Gluten-free, dairy-free, vegetarian, vegan, nut-free

SERVES 4

Prep time: 10 minutes

Cook time: 15 minutes

One 13.5-ounce can light coconut milk

½ teaspoon kosher salt

1 cup uncooked jasmine rice, rinsed (see Goood to Know)

Juice of 1 lime

In a small saucepan, combine the coconut milk, salt, and ⅔ cup water. Bring to a boil over high heat. Stir in the rinsed rice, reduce the heat to low, cover, and cook for 14 minutes, stirring once halfway through. Fluff with a fork and mix in the lime juice. Cover until serving.

> **GOOOD TO KNOW:** Giving the rice a good rinse washes away excess starch, meaning less sticky cooking water and grains that stay separate and perfectly tender. Place the rice in a fine-mesh sieve and run under cold water for about 30 seconds. Let the water drain thoroughly and gently shake the sieve to remove any dripping water.
>
> This rice is delicious served with Blackened Swordfish with Mango Salsa (page 268), Miso Salmon with Acorn Squash (page 270), Sticky Sesame Tofu (page 238), and Sweet and Spicy Tofu and Broccolini (page 168).

PLANT-POWERED

I don't follow a strictly plant-based diet myself, but I get a serious thrill from creating (and eating) plant-forward dishes. If you're not all-in on vegan but are plant-curious—or just looking to mix things up—this chapter's for you. These dozen recipes are 100 percent vegan, but don't expect bland or boring. They're rich in texture, layered with flavor, and satisfying in a way that feels complete. Tofu, beans, and cashews bring the protein and the personality with textures and flavors that'll surprise you. You might not even notice what's missing—and that's the point.

Creamy Wild Rice and Mushroom Soup   222

Coconut Curry Soup with Tofu and Rice Noodles   224

Pantry Staples Spicy Black Bean Soup   226

Creamy Lemon Pesto Pasta with Walnut Crumbs   228

Sheet Pan Gnocchi with Sun-Dried Tomato Cashew Cream   230

Sheet Pan Butternut Squash Mac and "Cheese"   233

Spiced Sweet Potato Tacos with Avocado Slaw   235

Sticky Sesame Tofu   238

Sweet and Spicy Tempeh with Sesame Noodles   240

Tomato-Basil Saucy Butter Bean Skillet   243

Mashed Chipotle Chickpea Quesadillas   244

Crusted Buffalo Tempeh Strips   246

CREAMY WILD RICE AND MUSHROOM SOUP

Gluten-free, dairy-free, vegetarian, vegan, nut-free

There's nothing better than the smell of this satisfying soup simmering away on the stove on a chilly afternoon. Don't let the rich flavor fool you; it's vegan! The nutritional yeast provides a cheesy umami taste, and the wild rice adds a nutty, earthy flavor with a bit more bite than the usual white, helping this soup to feel both rustic yet elevated. Wild rice needs to cook longer than white (or you can soak it overnight to speed things up). Either way, this fall favorite is well worth the extra time—it's a fan favorite for a reason!

SERVES 4

Prep time: 10 minutes
Cook time: 1 hour 30 minutes

GOOOD TO KNOW: Add the unsoaked rice to a fine-mesh sieve and run under cold water for about 30 seconds. Let the water drain thoroughly and gently shake the sieve to remove any dripping water.

STORE IT: Refrigerate in a sealed container for up to 4 days or freeze for up to 3 months.

REHEAT IT: From the refrigerator, microwave until warm, 1 to 2 minutes, or simmer over medium heat until warm. From the freezer, thaw in the refrigerator overnight, and rewarm as above.

2 tablespoons olive oil
3 large carrots, small-diced (about 1½ cups)
1 large yellow onion, small-diced (about 1½ cups)
10 ounces white mushrooms, thinly sliced (about 3 cups)
4 garlic cloves, minced
1 teaspoon dried thyme
1 teaspoon kosher salt
½ teaspoon ground black pepper
2 tablespoons tapioca flour or arrowroot starch (can substitute cornstarch)
½ cup nutritional yeast
3½ cups low-sodium vegetable broth
1 cup wild rice blend or wild rice, rinsed (see Goood to Know)
2 tablespoons coconut aminos (or reduced-sodium tamari or reduced-sodium soy sauce)
2 cups shredded curly kale (about 3 ounces)
One 13.5-ounce can full-fat coconut milk
Chopped fresh parsley (optional)

1. Heat the oil in a large pot over medium heat. Add the carrots and onion and cook, stirring occasionally, until softened, about 10 minutes. Add the mushrooms and garlic and continue to cook, stirring occasionally, for about 10 more minutes to let the flavors meld.

2. Add the thyme, salt, and black pepper and cook, stirring occasionally, about 3 minutes. Stir in the tapioca flour and nutritional yeast. Add the broth, ½ cup water, the wild rice, and coconut aminos. Bring to a boil.

3. Reduce to medium-low and cook, covered, stirring occasionally, until the rice is tender, 45 to 50 minutes or 20 to 25 minutes more if unsoaked.

4. Add the kale and coconut milk and stir frequently until the kale wilts, 1 to 2 minutes. Garnish with parsley (if using) and serve immediately.

COCONUT CURRY SOUP WITH TOFU AND RICE NOODLES

Gluten-free, dairy-free, vegetarian, vegan, nut-free

When I'm feeling under the weather, I crave this filling soup. It uses two of my best flavor-bomb ingredients that I always keep on hand—Thai red curry paste and coconut milk—and provides easy protein with cubed tofu. Its healing qualities come from a bit of spiciness, plus antioxidant-rich ginger and a mix of nutrient-dense veggies. If you're looking for even more heat, add minced serrano or Fresno chile pepper. Fresh herbs on top really make a difference in this double-digit-plant-count recipe.

SERVES 4

Prep time: 15 minutes
Cook time: 30 minutes

GOOOD TO KNOW:
To make ahead, prepare the soup without the rice noodles and tofu and freeze until needed. When ready for a cozy meal, warm the frozen soup, add the noodles, and cook until softened. Add the tofu and simmer until warm.

I love tofu in here, but if it's not your thing, you can add another type of protein—try cooked shrimp, chicken, or pork.

1 tablespoon olive oil
1 large yellow onion, medium-diced (about 1½ cups)
10 ounces white mushrooms, thinly sliced (about 3 cups)
1 red bell pepper, cored, seeded, and thinly sliced (about 1 cup)
3 garlic cloves, minced
2 teaspoons ground ginger
½ teaspoon kosher salt, plus more to taste
½ teaspoon ground black pepper
½ to 1 tablespoon Thai red curry paste (depending on your spice preference)
4 cups low-sodium vegetable broth
¾ cup full-fat coconut milk (half a well-shaken 13.5-ounce can)
2 tablespoons coconut aminos (or reduced-sodium tamari or reduced-sodium soy sauce)
6 ounces stir-fry rice noodles, such as pad Thai noodles
One 14-ounce block firm tofu, cut into ½-inch cubes
Thinly sliced green onions
Chopped fresh cilantro

1. Heat the oil in a large lidded pot or Dutch oven over medium heat until shimmering. Add the onion and cook, stirring occasionally, until translucent, 3 to 5 minutes. Stir in the mushrooms and bell pepper and cook until softened, 4 to 6 minutes.

2. Add the garlic, ginger, salt, and black pepper and cook, stirring frequently, until fragrant, 2 to 3 minutes. Stir in the red curry paste to evenly coat the vegetables and cook, stirring occasionally, until fragrant, 1 to 2 minutes.

3. Pour in the broth, coconut milk, and coconut aminos and stir until combined. Cover the pot and bring to a boil over high heat. Stir in the rice noodles and cook until softened, 4 to 7 minutes. (The time varies by brand.)

STORE IT: Refrigerate in a sealed container for up to 4 days (for best results, store the rice noodles separately or wait to cook them until reheating). Freeze the soup without noodles in a sealed container for up to 3 months.

4. Carefully add the tofu cubes. Add up to 1 cup water to the broth depending on your preference for a thicker or thinner soup. Simmer until the tofu is warmed through, 3 to 5 minutes. If needed, season with more salt.

5. Spoon into four bowls and garnish with green onions and cilantro.

REHEAT IT: From the refrigerator, microwave until warm, 1 to 2 minutes, or return a pot to medium heat, bring to a boil, add the uncooked rice noodles, and cook until al dente, 4 to 7 minutes. From the freezer, thaw the soup in the refrigerator overnight, then follow the same stovetop instructions.

PANTRY STAPLES SPICY BLACK BEAN SOUP

Gluten-free, dairy-free, vegetarian, vegan, nut-free

This soup always makes me think of my dad. When I was a kid, he would take me to Panera, where he would always order their spicy black bean soup. Feeling nostalgic, I decided to develop my own version for the book and for him. I'm happy to report that he was floored! A little bit spicy, this soup is full of different textures and is even creamy despite no cream in sight (thanks to partially blended beans). Best of all, these basic, budget-friendly ingredients can most likely already be found in your pantry!

SERVES 4

Prep time: 15 minutes
Cook time: 25 minutes

GOOOD TO KNOW: I love packing all the veggies I typically have on hand, like carrots, celery, and bell peppers, but don't feel like you have to use all of them to make this soup. Use what's in your fridge!

STORE IT: Refrigerate in a sealed container for up to 4 days or freeze for up to 3 months.

REHEAT IT: From the refrigerator, microwave until warm, 1 to 2 minutes, or return to a pot over medium heat with a splash of broth until warm. From the freezer, thaw in the refrigerator overnight, then microwave in 30-second increments until warm, or follow stovetop instructions.

2 tablespoons olive oil
4 celery ribs, finely diced (about 2 cups)
2 large carrots, finely diced (about 1 cup)
1 large yellow onion, finely diced (about 1½ cups)
1 green bell pepper, cored, seeded, and finely diced (about 1 cup)
4 garlic cloves, minced
1 to 3 canned chipotle peppers in adobo sauce (depending on your spice preference), finely chopped into a paste
2 teaspoons ground cumin
1 teaspoon smoked paprika
1 teaspoon kosher salt
½ teaspoon ground black pepper
Two 15-ounce cans black beans, undrained
2 cups low-sodium vegetable broth
Chopped fresh cilantro
1 lime, quartered

1. Heat the oil in a large lidded pot or Dutch oven over medium heat until shimmering. Add the celery, carrots, and onion and cook, stirring occasionally, until the onions are translucent, 5 to 7 minutes.

2. Add the bell pepper and garlic and cook, stirring frequently, until fragrant, 2 to 3 minutes. Add the chipotle peppers, cumin, smoked paprika, salt, and black pepper and continue to cook, stirring, until fragrant, 2 to 3 minutes.

3. Add the black beans and their liquid and the broth, cover, and bring to a boil over high heat. Reduce the heat to medium and simmer, covered, stirring occasionally to prevent the beans from sticking to the bottom of the pot, until thickened, 7 to 9 minutes.

4. Let cool, uncovered, for about 5 minutes. Transfer half of the soup to a blender and blend (with the steam vent open on the blender top) until the mixture is almost smooth and still has small pieces of beans. If you have a

smaller blender, blend the soup in batches. Return the blended soup to the pot and mix well.

5. Spoon the soup into four bowls and garnish with the cilantro and a squeeze of lime.

CREAMY LEMON PESTO PASTA WITH WALNUT CRUMBS

Gluten-free, dairy-free, vegetarian, vegan

This is one of the best ways to enjoy walnuts other than eating out of hand or tossed in a salad! They make the most mind-blowing walnut crumbs—so simple but with so much flavor and texture, not to mention extra omega-3 fatty acids and protein. This is a plant-based recipe that sent even my meat-loving friends back for seconds. Use my Dairy-Free Walnut Pesto (page 301) or any store-bought pesto if you're short on time.

SERVES 4

Prep time: 15 minutes
Cook time: 20 minutes

GOOOD TO KNOW: Enjoy immediately for best results. It's almost as delish the next day, although the pesto needs to be remixed and the walnut crumbs will soften. Sometimes I prep the pesto and pasta in advance and make the walnut crumbs on the day of serving. If you do prep the crumbs ahead, toasting for a few minutes in a skillet helps bring them back to life.

FOR THE WALNUT CRUMBS

½ cup roughly chopped unsalted raw walnuts
⅓ cup packed fresh parsley
1 garlic clove
1 teaspoon kosher salt

FOR THE PESTO PASTA

Kosher salt
12 ounces brown rice spaghetti, rice-and-corn-based spaghetti, or regular spaghetti
1 tablespoon olive oil, plus more for drizzling
1 medium shallot, minced
4 garlic cloves, minced
½ teaspoon ground black pepper
¾ cup full-fat coconut milk (about half a well-shaken 13.5-ounce can)
¾ cup low-sodium vegetable broth or low-sodium chicken broth (use vegetable for vegan or vegetarian)
¾ cup Dairy-Free Walnut Pesto (p. 301) or store-bought dairy-free pesto
Grated zest of ½ lemon

1. **Make the walnut crumbs:** In a food processor or blender, combine the walnuts, parsley, garlic, and salt and pulse until coarse crumbs form, about 10 seconds. Set aside.

2. **Make the pesto pasta:** Bring a large pot of salted water to a boil. Add the spaghetti and cook until al dente according to the package directions. Reserve ½ cup of the pasta water. Drain the pasta into a colander and toss with a drizzle of oil to prevent the noodles from sticking together. Return the pasta to the pot and set aside.

3. While the pasta cooks, heat the 1 tablespoon of oil over medium heat in a large skillet. Add the shallot and cook, stirring frequently, until translucent,

STORE IT: Refrigerate the pasta and walnut crumbs in separate sealed containers for up to 4 days.

REHEAT IT: Microwave until warm, 1 to 2 minutes, with crumbs on top. Or for extra crispy crumbs, cook the crumbs in a dry skillet over medium heat, stirring frequently until warm and crisp, 1 to 2 minutes.

2 to 3 minutes. Add the garlic and cook, stirring frequently, until fragrant, 1 to 2 minutes. Add 1 teaspoon salt, the black pepper, coconut milk, and broth and mix well. Bring to a boil, reduce the heat to low, and simmer until the mixture is warm, about 3 minutes.

4. Add the drained pasta, pesto, and lemon zest and stir until the pasta is evenly coated. Add the reserved pasta water, 1 tablespoon at a time, to thin the sauce slightly, up to 5 tablespoons, if needed.

5. Spoon the pasta onto four plates or into shallow bowls and top with the walnut crumbs.

PLANT-POWERED

SHEET PAN GNOCCHI WITH SUN-DRIED TOMATO CASHEW CREAM

Gluten-free, dairy-free, vegetarian, vegan

This recipe partners pillowy textured gnocchi with a creamy, nut-based, dairy-free sun-dried tomato spread for a luxurious plant-based dish. It's a go-to when I want to make an entrée for all types of eaters—gluten-free, dairy-free, vegetarian, or vegan. While many recipes call for gnocchi to be boiled, this oven-baked version makes it a snap to prepare and clean up.

SERVES 4

Prep time: 30 minutes
Cook time: 25 minutes

GOOOD TO KNOW: Swap in cauliflower gnocchi for yet another veggie in this plant-powered meal, or if you'd like to add an animal protein, try Italian-style chicken sausage.

STORE IT: Refrigerate the sheet pan components and cashew cream in separate sealed containers for up to 4 days.

REHEAT IT: Microwave the sheet pan components and cashew cream separately until warm, 1 to 2 minutes. Alternatively, microwave the cashew cream, but return the sheet pan components to a 350°F oven for 9 to 12 minutes to recrisp.

FOR THE SUN-DRIED TOMATO CASHEW CREAM

⅔ cup unsalted raw cashews
Boiling water
½ cup drained oil-packed sun-dried tomatoes
1 teaspoon kosher salt, plus more to taste

FOR THE SHEET PAN

12 ounces gluten-free frozen or shelf-stable gnocchi
1 medium eggplant, peeled and large-diced
1 medium zucchini, large-diced
1 pint cherry tomatoes, halved (about 1½ cups)
2 garlic cloves
3 tablespoons olive oil, plus more as needed
1 teaspoon dried basil
1 teaspoon dried oregano
1 teaspoon kosher salt
½ teaspoon ground black pepper
¼ teaspoon red pepper flakes (optional)

1. **For the sun-dried tomato cashew cream:** Place the cashews in a large heat-proof glass jar or medium bowl and cover with boiling water. Soak until the cashews are softened, 25 to 30 minutes, or let cool and soak overnight in the fridge. (A longer soak creates a smoother blend.)

2. **For the sheet pan:** When ready to cook, preheat the oven to 375°F. Line a sheet pan with parchment paper.

3. In a large bowl, combine the gnocchi, eggplant, zucchini, cherry tomatoes, and garlic cloves. Add the oil, basil, oregano, salt, black pepper, and red pepper flakes (if using) and toss to coat evenly. Transfer to the prepared sheet pan and spread out in an even layer.

4. Bake until the vegetables are softened and slightly browned around the edges, 22 to 25 minutes. Set aside the roasted garlic cloves.

5. **Finish the sun-dried tomato cashew cream:** Drain the cashews in a colander and transfer them to a blender or food processor, along with the garlic, sun-dried tomatoes, salt, and ¾ cup water. Blend on high speed until smooth, about 60 seconds. Add more water if needed for a pourable consistency. If needed, season with more salt.

6. To serve, spread the cashew cream onto the surface of four plates. Top with the gnocchi and vegetables.

SHEET PAN BUTTERNUT SQUASH MAC AND "CHEESE"

Gluten-free, dairy-free, vegetarian, vegan

When I first started developing recipes, I quickly discovered the beauty that is soaked and blended cashews as a dairy-free cheese replacement. In fact, I was such a fan of cashews that I named my dog after them! When combined with my other favorite cheesy replacement, nutritional yeast, you get a flavorful sauce that is honestly mind-blowing. If you have picky eaters in your home who need to get their veggies in, this is the answer. Make sure you do an allergy check with your friends because they won't believe this healthy, great-tasting pasta is made with cashews—the nut, not my dog!

SERVES 4

Prep time: 30 minutes
Cook time: 30 minutes

- ½ cup unsalted raw cashews
- Boiling water
- 2 cups peeled and ½-inch-cubed butternut squash (about half a large squash, or 10 ounces precut squash)
- 1 medium shallot, finely diced
- 4 garlic cloves, minced
- 2 tablespoons olive oil, plus more for drizzling
- Kosher salt
- ½ teaspoon ground black pepper
- ½ teaspoon ground sage
- 12 ounces brown rice elbow macaroni, rice-and-corn-based macaroni, or regular macaroni
- ½ cup low-sodium vegetable broth
- 2 tablespoons nutritional yeast
- 1 tablespoon white miso paste (optional)

1. Preheat the oven to 400°F. Line a sheet pan with parchment paper and set aside.

2. Place the cashews in a large heatproof glass jar or bowl and cover with boiling water. Set aside to soak and soften for at least 20 minutes. Soak until the cashews are softened, 25 to 30 minutes, or let cool and soak overnight in the fridge. (A longer soak creates a smoother blend.)

3. Meanwhile, in a large bowl, combine the butternut squash, shallot, garlic, oil, 1½ teaspoons kosher salt, the black pepper, and sage and mix well. Transfer to the prepared sheet pan and spread in an even layer.

4. Bake until the squash is fork-tender, 20 to 25 minutes. Let cool in the pan for about 5 minutes.

(continues)

GOOOD TO KNOW: Here's the easiest way to cut squash if you're not using store-bought precut squash: Prick the skin all over with a knife or fork. Microwave for 2 to 3 minutes to soften the squash. Let cool and cut off ½ inch of the top and bottom. Using a sharp peeler (I prefer a Y-peeler), remove the skin. Slice the squash in half crosswise, then cut each piece in half down the middle. Scoop and discard the seeds (or save them to roast!). Lay the cut side down and cut into ½-inch cubes.

5. Meanwhile, bring a pot of salted water to a boil over high heat. Add the macaroni and cook until al dente according to the package directions. Drain the pasta into a colander and toss with a drizzle of oil to prevent the noodles from sticking together. Return the pasta to the pot and set aside.

6. Drain the cashews in a colander. In a blender or food processor, combine the cashews, cooled vegetables, broth, nutritional yeast, miso paste (if using), and ½ cup water and blend on high speed until completely smooth, about 2 minutes. If the sauce is too thick, add warm water, 2 tablespoons at a time, until smooth and pourable. Salt to taste. Pour the sauce over the cooked pasta and mix until evenly coated.

7. Spoon the mac and "cheese" into four bowls and serve.

STORE IT: Refrigerate in a sealed container for up to 4 days. For freezing, make the sauce ahead of time but not the noodles. Freeze the blended sauce in a sealed container for up to 3 months.

REHEAT IT: From the refrigerator, microwave until warm, 1 to 2 minutes. From the freezer, thaw the sauce in the refrigerator overnight, then microwave in 30-second increments until warm. Mix with the cooked noodles.

SPICED SWEET POTATO TACOS WITH AVOCADO SLAW

Gluten-free, dairy-free, vegetarian, vegan, nut-free

These deliciously simple throw-together tacos aren't just for Tuesdays! Tossed with a smoky spice mix and roasted until crisp, the sweet potatoes really take on the flavor of the seasonings. The avocado slaw is creamy yet crunchy and contrasts with the crispy sweet potatoes for the most balanced, flavor-packed bite with every mouthful. If you have extra slaw at the end, I'll never say no to finishing the leftovers with tortilla chips. As a side dish, Avocado, Corn, and Black Bean Dip (page 133) completes the spread.

SERVES 4

Prep time: 15 minutes
Cook time: 30 minutes

GOOOD TO KNOW: Make this recipe with chicken breast or thighs instead of sweet potatoes, if you prefer; simply reduce the cooking time accordingly. The key is the spice mix and the slaw! You can even try this with lettuce wraps instead of tortillas.

FOR THE SWEET POTATOES

4 medium sweet potatoes, peeled and cut into ½-inch cubes (about 6 cups)
3 tablespoons olive oil
2 teaspoons chili powder
2 teaspoons garlic powder
2 teaspoons smoked paprika
1½ teaspoons ground cumin
1½ teaspoons kosher salt

FOR THE SLAW

One 10-ounce bag coleslaw mix or shredded cabbage
1 ripe avocado, halved and pitted
½ cup chopped fresh cilantro
Juice of 1 lime
1 tablespoon olive oil
1 garlic clove
1 teaspoon kosher salt, plus more to taste

FOR THE TACOS

Twelve 6-inch corn flour, almond flour, or chickpea flour tortillas
Olive oil, as needed
Chopped fresh cilantro

1. Preheat the oven to 425°F. Line a sheet pan with parchment paper.

2. **Roast the sweet potatoes:** In a large bowl, combine the sweet potatoes, oil, chili powder, garlic powder, smoked paprika, cumin, and salt and toss until the sweet potatoes are fully coated. Spread the sweet potatoes into an even layer on the prepared sheet pan.

(continues)

3. Bake, tossing halfway through, until fork-tender and crispy on the outside, 25 to 30 minutes.

4. **Meanwhile, make the slaw:** Place the coleslaw mix in a large bowl. Scoop out the avocado into a food processor or blender. Add the cilantro, lime juice, oil, garlic, and salt and blend on high speed until smooth and pourable, about 60 seconds. If it's too thick, add water, 2 tablespoons at a time and up to ½ cup, until you reach a pourable consistency. If needed, season with more salt. Add half of the avocado sauce, or more if desired, to the slaw, and toss until the cabbage is fully coated.

5. **For the tacos:** To warm the tortillas, stack them, wrap them in one or two damp paper towels, and microwave until softened and pliable, about 1 minute.

6. To assemble the tacos, set 3 tortillas on each of four plates and top with the sweet potatoes. Spoon the avocado slaw over the potatoes and garnish with chopped cilantro.

STORE IT: Refrigerate the sweet potatoes and slaw in separate sealed containers for up to 4 days. If prepping ahead, wait to dress the slaw until just before serving.

REHEAT IT: For optimal results, return the sweet potatoes to a sheet pan in a 425°F oven for 8 to 10 minutes to recrisp, then assemble tacos with the chilled slaw. Alternatively, microwave the sweet potatoes until warm, 1 to 2 minutes.

STICKY SESAME TOFU

Gluten-free, dairy-free, vegetarian, vegan, nut-free

One of my most satisfying accomplishments has been getting tons of DMs saying, "You finally got me to try tofu, and I love it." I'm always inspired to find new ways to prepare it myself at home and I would definitely recommend this dish to someone dipping their toes into the world of tofu for the first time. Each crispy cube is coated with a delicious sticky sauce that might change your life. Try them with Sesame-Crisped Brussels Sprouts (page 285) or Coconut Rice (page 219) to level up the dish.

SERVES 4

Prep time: 25 minutes
Cook time: 20 minutes

GOOOD TO KNOW: While I absolutely love this dish with tofu, this sticky sesame sauce complements many proteins.

STORE IT: Refrigerate in a sealed container for up to 4 days. To freeze, leave the tofu and sauce unmixed and freeze in separate sealed containers for up to 3 months.

REHEAT IT: From the refrigerator, microwave until warm, 1 to 2 minutes, or return to a skillet over medium heat with a splash of broth. From the freezer, thaw in the refrigerator overnight, then return the tofu to a sheet pan in a 400°F oven for 10 to 12 minutes to recrisp. Microwave the sauce for 1 to 2 minutes to warm and toss in a bowl with the tofu.

FOR THE TOFU
One 14-ounce block firm tofu
2 tablespoons coconut aminos (or reduced-sodium tamari or reduced-sodium soy sauce)
2 tablespoons tapioca flour or arrowroot starch (can substitute cornstarch)
1 tablespoon toasted sesame oil

FOR THE SAUCE
2 teaspoons tapioca flour or arrowroot starch (can substitute cornstarch)
⅓ cup coconut aminos (or reduced-sodium tamari or reduced-sodium soy sauce)
2 tablespoons rice vinegar
1½ tablespoons pure maple syrup
1 tablespoon toasted sesame oil
4 garlic cloves, minced

FOR SERVING
1 batch Jenn's Steamed Rice (p. 290), or 3 cups cooked white rice
Thinly sliced green onions
Sesame seeds

1. **Prepare the tofu:** Press the tofu block with a tofu press or wrap it in a clean kitchen towel or paper towels. Place the block on a plate and top with a heavy object, like a cast-iron pan or large can of tomatoes. Let sit until the excess liquid has drained, 15 to 20 minutes.

2. Preheat the oven to 400°F. Line a sheet pan with parchment paper.

3. In a medium bowl, whisk together the coconut aminos, tapioca flour, and sesame oil. Slice the pressed tofu block horizontally in half. Cut each half in a 4 × 4-inch grid into 16 cubes (32 cubes total). Add them to the coconut amino mixture and toss until evenly coated. Evenly space the coated cubes on the prepared sheet pan to prevent steaming in the oven. Discard any liquid remaining in the bowl. Bake until the outsides are browned and crispy, 20 to 25 minutes.

4. **Meanwhile, make the sauce:** In a small bowl, whisk together the tapioca flour and ¼ cup cold water until you have a smooth slurry. Set aside. Heat a large skillet over medium heat. Add the coconut aminos, rice vinegar, maple syrup, sesame oil, and garlic and cook, stirring often, until the sauce begins to bubble and thicken, about 2 minutes. Whisk in the tapioca mixture and cook until the sauce is sticky and thick, about 30 seconds. Add the crispy tofu to the skillet and gently mix to coat evenly with the sauce.

5. Spoon the rice into four bowls and top each bowl with about 8 pieces of the tofu. Garnish with green onions and sesame seeds.

SWEET AND SPICY TEMPEH WITH SESAME NOODLES

Gluten-free, dairy-free, vegetarian, vegan, nut-free

Tempeh, a fiber-packed plant protein, is a favorite of mine because it cooks quickly and has such a unique texture. A fermented ingredient, it's known for being beneficial for gut health, so you can feel good about adding it into the rotation. The lightly sauced sesame noodles balance this dish and make it a simple take-out replacement! For another option, you can make this with tofu instead of tempeh. Or try cooking some shrimp in the olive oil until opaque, then follow the rest of the recipe.

SERVES 4

Prep time: 10 minutes
Cook time: 25 minutes

GOOOD TO KNOW: I love eating this meal as cold leftovers. The chilled sesame noodles make for a leisurely next-day lunch that requires no prep!

STORE IT: Refrigerate in a sealed container for up to 4 days.

REHEAT IT: Enjoy chilled right out of the refrigerator or microwave until warm, 1 to 2 minutes. Alternatively, return to a skillet over medium heat with a splash of broth.

FOR THE SWEET AND SPICY TEMPEH
Two 8-ounce blocks tempeh, medium-diced
1 tablespoon olive oil
1 tablespoon toasted sesame oil
1 tablespoon minced peeled fresh ginger, or 1 teaspoon ground ginger
2 garlic cloves, minced
½ teaspoon kosher salt
½ cup coconut aminos (or reduced-sodium tamari or reduced-sodium soy sauce)
1 tablespoon pure maple syrup
1 tablespoon rice vinegar
1 tablespoon sriracha
3 ounces preshredded carrots, or 2 large carrots, coarsely shredded (about 1 cup)
Sesame seeds

FOR THE SESAME NOODLES
8 ounces dried stir-fry rice noodles, such as pad Thai noodles
2 tablespoons coconut aminos (or reduced-sodium tamari or reduced-sodium soy sauce)
2 tablespoons toasted sesame oil
Juice of 1 lime
1 tablespoon rice vinegar
3 green onions, finely chopped

1. **Start the tempeh:** Bring 1 cup water to a simmer in a large, deep, lidded skillet over medium heat. Add the tempeh and olive oil and spread the tempeh into one even layer. Cover and steam until the tempeh is softened and the water is absorbed, about 10 minutes.

2. **Meanwhile, prepare the sesame noodles:** Bring a 5-quart pot of water to a boil over high heat. Add the rice noodles and cook, stirring occasionally, until softened, 5 to 6 minutes. Drain in a colander and rinse under cold water. Return the noodles to the pot and add the coconut aminos, sesame oil, lime juice, and rice vinegar and toss to combine. Stir in the green onions and set aside.

3. **Finish the tempeh:** Uncover the tempeh and stir in the sesame oil, ginger, garlic, and salt until evenly combined. Cook, stirring often, until the tempeh is aromatic and lightly browned, 2 to 3 minutes. Stir in the coconut aminos, maple syrup, rice vinegar, and sriracha and bring the sauce to a simmer. Reduce the heat to medium-low and stir in the shredded carrots. Cook until the tempeh is golden brown and glazed in the sauce, 2 to 3 minutes.

4. Divide the sesame noodles among four plates, top with the tempeh and carrot mixture, and garnish with sesame seeds.

TOMATO-BASIL SAUCY BUTTER BEAN SKILLET

Gluten-free, dairy-free, vegetarian, vegan, nut-free

Bean skillets are so versatile, while providing major amounts of fiber and protein. Not only are they affordable and nutrient dense, they're also incredibly easy to put together when you use canned beans. Eat this saucy bean skillet in bowls with a spoon, use it as a dip for bread, or even make it stretch and use it as a textured pasta sauce. You're getting vodka sauce vibes from ingredients that can mostly be found in your pantry. I use butter beans, but you can also use cannellini, navy, or Great Northern beans for a similar taste. Just use what you have on hand or what is accessible!

SERVES 4

Prep time: 10 minutes
Cook time: 15 minutes

GOOOD TO KNOW: Adding plant-based crumbles (or sweet or spicy Italian sausage for non-vegan friends) to the skillet makes it heartier and extra savory. If you don't have (or don't love) kale, an equal amount of baby spinach makes a great sub.

2 tablespoons olive oil
1 medium shallot, minced
4 garlic cloves, minced
¼ cup nutritional yeast
1 teaspoon dried oregano
1 teaspoon kosher salt, plus more to taste
½ teaspoon ground black pepper
One 28-ounce can crushed tomatoes
Two 15-ounce cans butter beans, drained and rinsed
3 cups shredded curly kale (about 4½ ounces)
1 cup packed chopped fresh basil, plus more for garnish
¾ cup full-fat coconut milk (about half a well-shaken 13.5-ounce can)

1. Heat the oil in a large lidded skillet over medium heat until shimmering. Add the shallot and cook, stirring occasionally, until translucent, 3 to 5 minutes. Stir in the garlic, nutritional yeast, oregano, salt, and black pepper and continue to cook, stirring occasionally, until fragrant, 2 to 3 minutes.

2. Add the tomatoes and beans, cover, and cook for 5 minutes, stirring halfway through to prevent sticking. Add the kale and basil and cook, stirring constantly, until wilted, 1 to 2 minutes. Stir in the coconut milk and, if needed, season with more salt. Garnish with chopped basil and serve.

STORE IT: Refrigerate in a sealed container for up to 4 days or freeze for up to 3 months.

REHEAT IT: From the refrigerator, microwave until warm, 1 to 2 minutes, or reheat in a skillet over medium heat with a splash of broth. From the freezer, thaw in the refrigerator overnight, then microwave in 30-second increments until warm or follow the same skillet instructions.

MASHED CHIPOTLE CHICKPEA QUESADILLAS

Gluten-free, dairy-free, vegetarian, vegan

These quesadillas are what's on tap when I have no energy to make dinner. They are incredibly quick to assemble since you don't need to precook anything—just make your protein-based mashed chickpea mixture, fill your tortillas, and sear! Feel free to adjust the spice from the chipotle in adobo to your preference, keeping it mild at 2 or 3 chiles, or really spice it up with 6 or 7. If you want to make them kid-friendly swap the chipotle peppers for 3 to 4 tablespoons of Tangy Maple Barbecue Sauce (page 298). Pair with Chickpea Guacamole (page 128) for a powerful plant-forward dinner.

SERVES 4

Prep time: 15 minutes
Cook time: 15 minutes

GOOOD TO KNOW: The quesadilla filling is a simple protein-packed mix with many uses. Add it to a wrap, smash it on a piece of toast, or serve as a dip with tortilla chips. With two ingredients that you likely have in the pantry, it couldn't be easier!

STORE IT: Wrap uncooked quesadillas tightly in foil and refrigerate for up to 4 days or freeze, tightly wrapped and in a plastic or silicone bag, for up to 3 months.

REHEAT IT: From the refrigerator, unwrap and cook in the skillet as directed. From the freezer, thaw in the refrigerator overnight, then unwrap and cook as directed.

Two 15-ounce cans chickpeas, drained and rinsed

2 to 7 canned chipotle peppers in adobo sauce (depending on your spice preference), finely diced into a paste

1 teaspoon garlic powder

Kosher salt

Eight 6-inch almond flour or flour tortillas

6 ounces shredded dairy-free cheese (about 1½ cups; can substitute shredded Cheddar cheese, not vegan)

Avocado oil

1. Microwave the chickpeas in a large microwave-safe bowl to soften, about 1 minute. (This will make it easier to mash the chickpeas.) Use a fork or potato masher to mash until almost completely smooth. Add the chipotle peppers, garlic powder, and 1 teaspoon salt and mix well.

2. Wrap the tortillas in one or two damp paper towels and microwave until softened and pliable, about 1 minute. Place the tortillas on the prepared sheet pan. Scoop about ¼ cup of the chickpea mixture over half the tortilla. Dividing evenly, top the chickpea mixture with the shredded cheese. Fold the plain side of the tortilla in half over the chickpea mash and press so the tortilla sticks together.

3. Heat the oil in a large nonstick or stainless steel skillet over medium heat. Working in batches of 2 or 3 quesadillas, carefully add the folded tortillas to the pan and cook until crispy, 2 to 3 minutes per side. (Alternatively, if you have a griddle, work in batches of 4 or 5.) Transfer the quesadillas to a large plate. Repeat with the remaining quesadillas. Sprinkle a pinch of salt over each cooked quesadilla while hot.

4. Slice the quesadillas in half. Set 2 halved quesadillas on each of four plates.

CRUSTED BUFFALO TEMPEH STRIPS

Gluten-free, dairy-free, vegetarian, vegan, nut-free

Why should the spicy, tangy goodness of Buffalo flavor be just for chicken wings? Here I swap in tempeh, an earthy, fermented, plant-based option loaded with protein and excellent for promoting gut health. This recipe works for everything from Sunday football to dinner-party apps that even meat eaters will love. Chop and add them to my Goes-with-Anything Kale Salad (page 283) to mimic crispy chicken on a salad (my fave!). Just use your favorite dairy-free yogurt to keep it plant-based.

SERVES 4

Prep time: 20 minutes
Cook time: 20 minutes

GOOOD TO KNOW: These savory bites could also be made with firm tofu, but you'll need to remove the excess moisture. Press the block with a tofu press or wrap in kitchen or paper towels. Place on a plate and top with a heavy object, like a cast-iron pan or large can of tomatoes. Let sit until the liquid has drained, 15 to 20 minutes, and slice in half horizontally. Cut each half in a 4 × 4 grid into 16 cubes (32 cubes total). Be careful, as tofu breaks more easily than tempeh.

STORE IT: Refrigerate in a sealed container for up to 4 days.

REHEAT IT: Return to a sheet pan and bake at 400°F for 8 to 10 minutes on a sheet pan, or air-fry on 400°F for 3 to 5 minutes.

⅓ cup tapioca flour or arrowroot starch (can substitute cornstarch)
1½ cups Buffalo hot sauce
1 teaspoon garlic powder
1 teaspoon onion powder
½ teaspoon ground black pepper
½ teaspoon kosher salt
3 cups gluten-free panko bread crumbs (about 12 ounces)
Two 8-ounce blocks tempeh, cut crosswise into ¼-inch-wide strips (about 40 strips total)
8 tablespoons (1 stick) unsalted vegan butter or unsalted butter, melted
Herby Yogurt Ranch Dressing (p. 302), made with dairy-free yogurt

1. Preheat the oven to 375°F. Line a large sheet pan with parchment paper.

2. Set up a dredging station with three medium shallow bowls: Add the tapioca flour to one bowl. In the second bowl, whisk together ¾ cup of the Buffalo sauce, the garlic powder, onion powder, black pepper, and salt. Place the panko in the third bowl.

3. Add the tempeh to the tapioca flour using tongs and toss to coat thoroughly. Shake off any excess flour, then transfer the tempeh to the Buffalo sauce mixture and toss gently to evenly coat. Place 3 to 4 pieces of tempeh in the panko and thoroughly coat all sides, pressing the crumbs into the tempeh if necessary. Place the tempeh in a single layer on the prepared sheet pan. Repeat with the remaining tempeh.

4. Bake until golden brown and crispy, 18 to 20 minutes. Let cool on the sheet pan for at least 5 minutes.

5. Meanwhile, in a medium bowl, whisk together the remaining ¾ cup Buffalo sauce and the melted butter until combined.

6. Add the cooled tempeh to the sauce and toss gently until coated. Transfer the tempeh to a large plate or platter and serve with a bowl of ranch dressing alongside.

A LITTLE FANCIER

The difference between basic and fancy can be less than you think. Finding elegance in food doesn't have to mean using expensive specialty ingredients or spending hours in the kitchen laboring over tiny details. Sometimes it's just using a protein you don't often cook with, combined with unexpected flavors or prepared in a unique way. These recipes will have you covered for a variety of occasions, from date night to family dinner and everything in between. Perfect for those times when you want things to feel a little fancier.

Garlic and Herb Spatchcock Chicken 251

Slow Cooker Short Ribs 253

Garlicky Mushroom and Sage Risotto 256

Skirt Steak with Chimichurri 259

Brian's Favorite Lamb Bolognese 260

Seared Pork Chops with Apple Fennel Pan Sauce 262

Mediterranean-Inspired Smashed Tacos 264

Lemon-Caper Shrimp and Linguine 266

Blackened Swordfish with Mango Salsa 268

Miso Salmon with Acorn Squash 270

Hidden Veggie Spaghetti with Crispy Kale and Sausage 273

Grain-Free Chicken Parmesan 275

GARLIC AND HERB SPATCHCOCK CHICKEN

Gluten-free, dairy-free, nut-free

If you were to ask me to pick one meal from this book to really wow someone with for an at-home date, dinner with the in-laws, or even a holiday main, I'd tell you to make this one. While it might sound intimidating to "spatchcock"—remove the backbone from the chicken and splay it flat in the pan to cook—doing so allows for reduced cooking time, crispier skin, optimized seasoning coverage, and easier carving of a moister chicken. Once you try it, you'll see that this fancier meal is actually easier than a lot of the basics you already prepare. Not to mention, it's a one-pan meal that cooks your chicken and veggies all-in-one for streamlined prep.

SERVES 4

Prep time: 20 minutes
Cook time: 45 minutes

GOOOD TO KNOW: If you have the time, remove the chicken from the refrigerator 30 minutes prior to preparing it to ensure even cooking. The cooking time may vary depending on the weight of the chicken; a meat thermometer is always a reliable way to tell doneness.

For a low-waste hack, freeze the backbone and use it to make homemade broth.

2 teaspoons dried rosemary
2 teaspoons dried thyme
1 teaspoon ground sage
2 teaspoons kosher salt
½ teaspoon ground black pepper
3 tablespoons olive oil
6 garlic cloves, minced
One 3- to 4-pound whole chicken (see Goood to Know)
4 medium Yukon Gold potatoes, peeled and cut into ½-inch cubes (about 4 cups)
1 large yellow onion, thinly sliced (about 1½ cups)
1 lemon, quartered

1. Preheat the oven to 400°F. Line a sheet pan with parchment paper and set aside.

2. In a small bowl, combine the rosemary, thyme, sage, salt, and black pepper. Add the oil and garlic and mix until a paste forms. Set aside.

3. To spatchcock the chicken, place it on a large cutting board breast side down and pat dry with paper towels. With kitchen scissors or poultry shears, carefully cut along both sides of the backbone and remove it (see Goood to Know). Flip the chicken over so the breast side is up. Press down firmly in the center of the breast with the heels of your hands until you hear a small crack, breaking the breastbone. This will help the chicken lie flatter. Pat dry again with a paper towel and place the chicken on the prepared sheet pan.

4. In a large bowl, combine the potatoes, onion, and half of the garlic-herb paste. Toss until evenly coated. Spread the vegetables around the chicken.

(continues)

A LITTLE FANCIER

Place 1 lemon quarter in each corner of the sheet pan. Use a pastry brush or clean hands to coat both sides of the chicken with the remaining garlic-herb paste. Place the chicken skin side up, then pull the wings forward toward the neck cavity and tuck them firmly under the body to secure and prevent burning.

5. Roast until the chicken is golden brown on the outside and a meat thermometer inserted through the thickest part of the breast reads 165°F, 45 to 55 minutes. If the chicken is fully browned outside but not done cooking internally, place a piece of aluminum foil on top to prevent burning and continue roasting until it reaches the proper temperature, checking every 5 minutes or so. The potatoes should be tender, with browned edges.

6. Transfer the chicken to a clean cutting board to rest for at least 10 minutes.

7. Cut the chicken into serving pieces (see Cutting Chicken into Serving Pieces, below) and transfer to a serving platter along with the roasted lemon wedges.

STORE IT: Refrigerate the chicken and vegetables in separate sealed containers for up to 4 days. If I'm meal-prepping, I find it easier to cut up the chicken and discard the bones ahead of time. Freeze the cut-up chicken for up to 3 months.

REHEAT IT: From the refrigerator, microwave the chicken and vegetables until warm, 1 to 2 minutes. From the freezer, thaw the chicken in the refrigerator for at least 8 hours, then microwave in 30-second increments until warm. Alternatively, place on a sheet pan in a 400°F oven for 6 to 10 minutes to reheat.

CUTTING CHICKEN INTO SERVING PIECES

1. Lay the chicken breast side up on a cutting board—preferably one with grooves to catch the juices. If you don't have one with grooves, use a sheet pan under the board to catch the juices.

2. Gently pull the leg away from the body and use a sharp knife to cut through the skin between the thigh and the body, then through the joint. Repeat on the other side.

3. Place each leg skin side down and cut through the joint to separate the drumsticks from the thigh. You can slice the thigh meat off the bone crosswise or serve it whole.

4. Using the breastbone as your guide, carve against the ribs and remove each breast, keeping the wing attached. Cut off the wings at the joint, then slice each breast crosswise into 2 pieces.

SLOW COOKER SHORT RIBS

Gluten-free, dairy-free, nut-free

Short ribs are a cozy-night-in kind of meal. While they may not be an everyday dish, they cook up quickly in a slow cooker, and this version is the ideal introduction. After a bit of prep to get the meat nice and crispy on the outsides, place everything in the slow cooker and let it do the work for the rest of the day. When dinnertime rolls around, you'll have a homemade meal that tastes like it's from a restaurant! Serve with my "Cheesy" Polenta (page 282) so the delicious broth is soaked up, and you'll have a recipe that can be served for all occasions, from weeknight meals to holiday dinners. If you don't have a slow cooker, see Cooking Short Ribs in a Dutch Oven (page 254) or Cooking Short Ribs in a Pressure Cooker (page 254).

SERVES 4

Prep time: 20 minutes
Cook time: 5 to 8 hours

GOOOD TO KNOW: Short ribs are a very fatty cut of beef—if you want to remove some of the excess fat from the liquid after they're done cooking, refrigerate the finished dish in a sealed container overnight, scrape off the hardened layer of fat that rises to the top, reheat, and enjoy. Cooking the short ribs the day before will also improve the tenderness of the meat.

3 pounds bone-in beef short ribs (about 4 large ribs)
Kosher salt and ground black pepper
2 tablespoons olive oil
3 tablespoons tomato paste
3 cups low-sodium beef broth
3 tablespoons coconut aminos (or reduced-sodium tamari or reduced-sodium soy sauce)
3 large carrots, cut into 1-inch chunks (about 2½ cups)
3 celery ribs, cut into 1-inch pieces (about 1½ cups)
½ large yellow onion, thinly sliced (about ¾ cup)
4 garlic cloves, minced
3 fresh thyme sprigs
2 fresh rosemary sprigs
"Cheesy" Polenta (p. 282)

1. Pat the short ribs dry with paper towels and season them generously on all sides with salt and black pepper. Set aside on a plate.

2. Heat the oil in a large skillet over medium heat until shimmering. Working in batches to avoid overcrowding, carefully add the short ribs to the pan. (The ribs will steam rather than caramelize if you crowd the pan.) Cook until golden brown and crispy, 3 to 5 minutes per side. Transfer to a large plate.

3. Reduce the heat to low, add the tomato paste, and cook, stirring frequently, until caramelized and deep red, 1 to 2 minutes.

4. Transfer the tomato paste to a 6-quart slow cooker. Add the broth and coconut aminos and mix well. Add the carrots, celery, onion, garlic, and a few pinches of salt and stir. Add the short ribs and arrange the thyme and rosemary sprigs on top of the meat.

(continues)

5. Cover and cook on low for 8 hours or high for 5 hours, until the meat is tender and falls off the bone.

6. Discard the thyme and rosemary sprigs. Remove the short ribs from the slow cooker and separate the meat from the bones. Discard the bones.

7. To serve, spoon the polenta into four bowls. Top with the meat and vegetables and add a few spoonfuls of the broth to each bowl.

STORE IT: Refrigerate in a sealed container for up to 4 days or freeze for up to 3 months. (You'll have extra sauce.)

REHEAT IT: From the refrigerator, place the short ribs and vegetables in a Dutch oven, covered, over low heat, stirring occasionally until heated through, about 15 minutes, or microwave until warm for 1 to 2 minutes. From the freezer, thaw in the refrigerator overnight and follow the same directions.

COOKING SHORT RIBS IN A DUTCH OVEN

Preheat the oven to 325°F. Pat the short ribs with paper towels until completely dry and season generously on all sides with salt and black pepper. Set aside on a plate.

1. Heat the oil in a 6-quart Dutch oven or large, heavy ovenproof pot with a lid over medium heat until shimmering. Carefully add the short ribs, working in batches if necessary so as not to overcrowd the pan. (The ribs will steam rather than caramelize if you crowd the pan.) Transfer to a large plate.

2. Add the carrots, celery, and onion and cook, stirring often, until the onions are translucent and begin to caramelize, 7 to 9 minutes. Add the garlic and cook, stirring frequently, for 1 to 2 minutes. Stir in the tomato paste and cook, stirring until deep red, 1 to 2 minutes. Add the broth and coconut aminos and mix well. Season with a few pinches of salt, add the short ribs, arrange the thyme and rosemary on top of the meat, and cover.

3. Bake until the meat is tender and falling off the bone, 2½ to 3 hours.

4. Serve as directed.

COOKING SHORT RIBS IN A PRESSURE COOKER

Follow the same directions as for the slow cooker: Lock the lid and cook at high pressure for 45 minutes. Follow the manufacturer's steam release directions and let sit for 10 additional minutes before serving.

GARLICKY MUSHROOM AND SAGE RISOTTO

Gluten-free, dairy-free option, vegetarian, vegan option, nut-free

A creamy, savory risotto is one of the first things I think of when coming up with a fancy dinner with minimal ingredients. I like to use a blend of wild mushrooms for this creamy risotto made from short-grain Arborio rice from northern Italy. Although it calls for only a few ingredients, including a staple of mine—balsamic vinegar—for punchy flavor, it's restaurant quality for sure. The secret is patience; you'll need to wait for each cup of warm broth to be stirred in and absorbed by the rice for that creamy texture, but the end result is worth it.

SERVES 4

Prep time: 5 minutes
Cook time: 45 minutes

To make this dairy-free and vegan: Swap in ⅓ cup nutritional yeast for the traditional Parm.

GOOOD TO KNOW: If you want to add meat to this recipe, cook chicken, salmon, shrimp, or steak separately and add it on top at the end.

STORE IT: Refrigerate in a sealed container for up to 4 days or freeze for up to 3 months.

REHEAT IT: From the refrigerator, microwave until warm, 1 to 2 minutes. From the freezer, thaw in the refrigerator overnight, then microwave in 30-second increments until warm.

2 tablespoons olive oil

12 ounces mushrooms (a blend of wild or Baby Bella, shiitake, oyster mushrooms, or whatever you can find!), roughly torn or chopped (about 4 cups)

4 garlic cloves, minced

1½ teaspoons ground sage

1 teaspoon dried thyme

1 teaspoon kosher salt

½ teaspoon ground black pepper

2 cups Arborio rice

¼ cup balsamic vinegar

4 cups low-sodium vegetable broth, warmed

2 cups hot water

1 cup grated Parmesan, plus more for topping

1. Heat the oil in a large sauté pan or Dutch oven over medium heat until shimmering. Add the mushrooms, garlic, sage, thyme, salt, and black pepper and cook, stirring often, until the mushrooms release their liquid and are softened, 5 to 7 minutes. Increase the heat to high and cook until the mushrooms are browned and caramelized and the liquid is evaporated, 2 to 3 minutes. Transfer the mushrooms to a plate with a slotted spoon and set aside.

2. Reduce the heat to medium, add the rice, and toast until golden brown, 1 to 2 minutes. Add the vinegar and stir constantly, scraping up any browned bits from the bottom of the pan, about 30 seconds.

3. Add 1 cup of broth at a time, stirring constantly to prevent the rice from sticking. Allow each cup to be fully absorbed into the rice before stirring in the next cup. Repeat until all 4 cups of broth are added to the rice. Add the hot water, 1 cup at a time, as above.

4. If the rice is not fully cooked, add more water, 2 tablespoons at a time and up to 1 cup, until fully absorbed. If the rice sticks to the skillet, reduce the heat to low. If the broth is not absorbed, increase the heat to medium-high. This process will take about 30 minutes of active pouring and stirring.

5. When all the broth is absorbed and the rice is tender, gently fold in the mushrooms and stir in the Parmesan. If needed, season with more salt.

6. Spoon the risotto onto four plates and top with more grated Parmesan.

SKIRT STEAK WITH CHIMICHURRI

Gluten-free, dairy-free, nut-free

The puckery, garlicky, herby deliciousness that is chimichurri sauce transforms this lean cut of meat into something truly next level. A classic Argentinian salsa designed for grilled meats, it's also endlessly adaptable—one spoonful instantly punches up roasted or grilled vegetables, chicken, or fish. In this dish, it's paired with my favorite cut of steak—skirt steak. When Brian and I want to prepare a fancy yet simple date-night meal, it's almost always this. On the off chance you're left with extras, leftovers make for iron-rich, savory protein to top off a grain bowl or salad. I especially love this seared skirt steak on top of the Goes-with-Anything Kale Salad (page 283).

SERVES 4

Prep time: 20 minutes
Cook time: 10 minutes

GOOOD TO KNOW: If you're new to cooking with steak and want to make things easier, I highly recommend getting an instant-read meat thermometer to build confidence. (You'll have extra sauce.)

STORE IT: Refrigerate the steak and chimichurri in separate sealed containers, up to 4 days for the steak and up to 7 days for the sauce. (You'll have extra sauce.)

REHEAT IT: Microwave the steak until warm, 1 to 2 minutes, then top with chilled chimichurri. Alternatively, sear the pieces in a skillet over medium heat with a drizzle of avocado oil for about 1 minute per side, then top with chimichurri.

1½ pounds skirt steak or flank steak
1 cup finely chopped fresh parsley
½ cup olive oil
¼ cup red wine vinegar
4 garlic cloves, minced
2 teaspoons dried oregano
2 teaspoons kosher salt, plus more for seasoning the steak
1 teaspoon ground black pepper, plus more for seasoning the steak
½ teaspoon red pepper flakes (optional)
2 tablespoons avocado oil

1. Remove the skirt steak from the refrigerator and let come to room temperature for about 30 minutes before cooking.

2. To make the chimichurri sauce, in a small bowl, whisk together the parsley, olive oil, vinegar, garlic, oregano, salt, black pepper, and red pepper flakes (if using). Cover and refrigerate until ready to serve.

3. Slice the steak with the grain into four even 6- to 8-inch-long pieces. Pat the meat dry with a paper towel and generously season with salt and black pepper on both sides.

4. Heat the avocado oil in a large stainless steel or cast-iron skillet over medium heat until shimmering. Carefully add the steak to the pan, leaving space between the pieces of meat. (If your pan is smaller than 12 inches, you may need to work in batches.) Cook until the steak is golden brown around the edges and can easily be flipped without sticking to the pan, 4 to 5 minutes per side for medium-rare. Transfer to a wooden cutting board to rest for at least 10 minutes before slicing.

5. To serve, cut the steaks against the grain into ¼-inch slices and divide among four plates. Top each with 3 or 4 generous spoonfuls of chimichurri.

A LITTLE FANCIER

BRIAN'S FAVORITE LAMB BOLOGNESE

Gluten-free, dairy-free, nut-free

My husband, Brian, and I have always bonded over cooking. On Friday nights you'll often find us in the kitchen cooking up a new dish. If this Bolognese happens to be on our menu, you know it's a special occasion. The ground lamb in the pasta sauce infuses it with a deep, rich flavor. While lamb is not traditionally in Bolognese, the twist is a favorite. The sauce makes generous servings, so you can easily freeze leftovers or go super saucy!

SERVES 4 GENEROUSLY

Prep time: 15 minutes
Cook time: 90 minutes

GOOOD TO KNOW: Traditionally, Bolognese is made with a mix of ground beef and pork. If that's more up your alley, feel free to use it instead of the ground lamb.

STORE IT: Refrigerate the sauce in a sealed container for up to 4 days or freeze for up to 3 months.

REHEAT IT: From the refrigerator, microwave the sauce until warm, 2 to 3 minutes, then serve over cooked pasta. Or return the sauce to a pot over medium heat and bring to a simmer until warm. From the freezer, thaw the sauce in the refrigerator overnight, then microwave in 30-second increments until warm or return to a pot over medium heat until warm.

1 tablespoon dried oregano
1½ teaspoons kosher salt, plus more to taste
½ teaspoon ground black pepper
¼ teaspoon red pepper flakes (optional)
1 tablespoon olive oil
1 pound 85% lean ground lamb
1 large yellow onion, finely chopped (about 1½ cups)
2 large carrots, finely chopped (about 1 cup)
2 celery ribs, finely chopped (about 1 cup)
4 garlic cloves, minced
¼ cup tomato paste
1 cup low-sodium beef broth or dry red wine
One 28-ounce can crushed tomatoes
5 fresh thyme sprigs, tied together with kitchen twine
¾ cup full-fat coconut milk (about half a well-shaken 13.5-ounce can)
12 ounces brown rice tagliatelle, rice-and-corn-based tagliatelle, or regular tagliatelle
Finely chopped fresh parsley

1. In a small bowl, mix together the oregano, salt, black pepper, and red pepper flakes (if using). Set aside.

2. Heat the oil in a large lidded pot or Dutch oven over medium heat until shimmering. Add the ground lamb and cook, breaking up the large chunks with a spatula, until browned, about 8 minutes.

3. Add the onion, carrots, and celery and cook, stirring occasionally, until the vegetables are softened, about 10 minutes. Add the garlic and cook, stirring frequently, until fragrant, 1 to 2 minutes. Stir in the spice mixture and cook until fragrant, about 2 minutes. Add the tomato paste and cook, stirring occasionally, until caramelized and deep red, about 5 minutes.

4. Pour in the broth and crushed tomatoes and mix well. Submerge the thyme sprigs in the sauce. Reduce the heat to low, cover, and simmer for about 45 minutes, until thickened, stirring every 15 minutes to prevent scorching.

5. Reduce the heat to low, discard the thyme sprigs, and stir in the coconut milk. Simmer until the sauce is slightly thickened, about 10 minutes.

6. Meanwhile, bring a large pot of salted water to a boil. Add the tagliatelle and cook until al dente according to package directions and drain.

7. To serve, spoon the pasta into four shallow bowls. Top with sauce and garnish with chopped parsley.

SEARED PORK CHOPS WITH APPLE FENNEL PAN SAUCE

Gluten-free, dairy-free option, nut-free

Apples and pork go together, at least according to my ten-year-old self, who always loved pork chops with applesauce. This is my elevated adult version. The chops are crispy on the outside and moist on the inside and paired with a bright, seasonal sauce. I love pork chops as a protein because they feel fancy and they're budget-friendly. It's a restaurant-level dish, yet making it is so simple. Serve with Cauliflower and Parsnip Puree (page 288) to soak up the sweet and creamy pan sauce.

SERVES 4

Prep time: 15 minutes
Cook time: 30 minutes

To make this dairy-free: Use plant milk.

GOOOD TO KNOW: If you have the time, remove the pork chops from the refrigerator 30 minutes before seasoning and cooking. This ensures that the pork will cook evenly.

STORE IT: Refrigerate in a sealed container for up to 4 days or freeze for up to 3 months.

REHEAT IT: From the refrigerator, microwave until warm, 2 to 3 minutes. From the freezer, thaw in the refrigerator overnight, then microwave in 30-second increments until warm.

Four 3-ounce boneless pork chops
Kosher salt and ground black pepper
2 tablespoons olive oil, plus more as needed
1 medium fennel bulb, thinly sliced
1 red apple, such as Fuji or Honeycrisp, unpeeled and thinly sliced (about 1 cup)
4 garlic cloves, minced
1 teaspoon dried thyme
½ cup milk of your choice, preferably whole milk
½ cup low-sodium vegetable broth
Juice of ½ lemon
Finely chopped fresh parsley

1. Pat the pork chops dry with a paper towel and season generously on both sides with salt and black pepper.

2. Heat the oil in a large lidded skillet over medium heat until shimmering. Carefully add the pork chops, leaving ½ to 1 inch of space between them. Cook without disturbing until golden brown, 2 to 3 minutes per side.

3. Reduce the heat to low, cover, and cook until the pork chops reach an internal temperature of 145°F, 8 to 12 minutes, depending on the thickness of the pork chops. Transfer the pork chops to a large plate, cover with aluminum foil, and set aside to rest.

4. Heat the same skillet over medium heat, adding another drizzle of oil if needed. Add the fennel and apple and cook, stirring often, until golden brown and softened, 5 to 7 minutes. Stir in the garlic, thyme, 1 teaspoon salt, and ½ teaspoon black pepper and cook, stirring often, until the garlic is soft and fragrant, 1 to 2 minutes.

5. Stir in the milk, broth, and lemon juice. Bring the mixture to a simmer and cook, stirring occasionally, until thickened, about 5 minutes.

6. Return the pork chops to the pan, nestling them into the fennel and apple mixture. Heat for 2 minutes to warm the pork chops.

7. Set a pork chop on each of four plates and spoon the fennel and apple pan sauce over the top. Garnish with chopped parsley.

MEDITERRANEAN-INSPIRED SMASHED TACOS

Gluten-free, dairy-free option, nut-free

Inspired by the flavors of a few favorites—gyros, tacos, and smash burgers—I created something that mashed them all up into one unique dish. Think tender lamb, crumbled feta, and fresh herbs nestled in a crisp tortilla—a Mediterranean twist on taco night. Just the thing for when you want dinner to feel stylish yet effortless, these tacos are at their best with my creamy Cucumber Garlicky Sauce (see page 299). Fresh herbs tie it all together, making this a nontraditional recipe that feels both adventurous and familiar. While it might be a bit fancier than usual, it comes together quickly since you cook the lamb directly in the tortilla. That's where the smash burger inspo comes in!

SERVES 4

Prep time: 20 minutes
Cook time: 30 minutes

To make this dairy-free: Omit the feta or use vegan feta.

GOOOD TO KNOW: I love using lamb in these tacos to bring out those Greek-inspired flavors, but if lamb isn't your thing, swap it for a pound of lean ground beef or ground chicken.

STORE IT: Wrap each taco tightly in foil and refrigerate in a sealed bag or container for up to 3 days (but these are best eaten immediately). Refrigerate the cucumber sauce and Mediterranean salsa in separate sealed containers up to 7 days for the sauce and up to 4 days for the salsa.

FOR THE MEDITERRANEAN SALSA

1 small cucumber, unpeeled, small-diced (about 1 cup)
2 small Roma (plum) tomatoes, small-diced (about 1 cup)
¾ cup crumbled feta (about 3 ounces)
Juice of 1 lemon
2 tablespoons finely chopped fresh dill
2 tablespoons finely chopped fresh mint
½ teaspoon kosher salt

FOR THE SMASHED TACOS

1 pound 85% lean ground lamb
1 garlic clove, grated
1 teaspoon ground cumin
1 teaspoon dried oregano
1 teaspoon kosher salt
½ teaspoon smoked paprika
½ teaspoon ground black pepper
Eight 6-inch corn tortillas, almond flour tortillas, or flour tortillas
Cucumber Garlicky Sauce (p. 299)
Optional garnishes: finely chopped fresh mint, finely chopped fresh dill

1. **Make the Mediterranean salsa:** In a medium bowl, combine all the ingredients. Cover and refrigerate until serving.

2. **Make the smashed tacos:** In a large bowl, combine the lamb, garlic, cumin, oregano, salt, smoked paprika, and black pepper and mix well. Form the mixture into eight 2-ounce balls. Place one meatball in the center of each tortilla and use clean hands to spread the meat thinly across the entire tortilla.

REHEAT IT: The tacos are best eaten immediately, but leftover tacos can be reheated in an oiled skillet over low heat for 2 to 3 minutes per side and topped with the chilled sauce and salsa.

3. Heat a large cast-iron skillet over medium heat. Place the tortilla meat side down directly on the skillet, then use a burger press or a flat heavy object to keep it completely flat against the skillet. (If your grill pan or griddle doesn't have ridges, you can cook multiple tacos at a time.) Cook, without moving, until the lamb is cooked through and crispy, 2 to 3 minutes. Flip the tortilla and continue to cook until crisp, about 1 minute. Transfer to a platter and cover loosely with aluminum foil to keep warm. Repeat with the remaining tacos.

4. **To serve:** Place 2 tacos on each of four plates and top each with about 2 tablespoons of the cucumber garlicky sauce and a generous spoonful of salsa. Garnish with chopped mint and dill, if desired.

A LITTLE FANCIER

LEMON-CAPER SHRIMP AND LINGUINE

Gluten-free, dairy-free option, nut-free

While this snappy little recipe could happily sit in the "Done in 30" chapter, I purposely put it in this chapter to remind you that even if a dish is a bit more elevated, it doesn't have to take more time and effort. Salty! Acidic! Smooth! This shrimp scampi-y, chicken piccata-ish skillet hits all the right notes. It's also quite light but feels very decadent. You could swap out the shrimp for a quick-cooking fish—like cod or haddock—or even chicken, and pair with rice if that's more your vibe—many options!

SERVES 4

Prep time: 10 minutes
Cook time: 20 minutes

To make this dairy-free: Omit the Parmesan.

GOOOD TO KNOW: You can swap the linguine for another shape of pasta if you'd like—spaghetti or even orzo would be delicious here!

STORE IT: Refrigerate in a sealed container for up to 3 days.

REHEAT IT: Microwave until warm, 1 to 2 minutes, or return to a skillet over medium heat and bring to a simmer to warm.

Kosher salt

12 ounces brown rice linguine or regular linguine

1 pound fresh or thawed frozen medium shrimp, peeled and deveined, tails off, if preferred

½ teaspoon ground black pepper

2 tablespoons olive oil

10 ounces asparagus, trimmed and cut into 1-inch pieces (about 2 cups)

1 medium shallot, minced

3 garlic cloves, minced

2 cups low-sodium chicken broth or low-sodium vegetable broth

Juice of 1 lemon

¼ cup capers, drained

¼ cup grated Parmesan

Finely chopped fresh parsley

1. Bring a large pot of salted water to a boil over high heat. Add the linguine and cook until al dente, according to the package directions. Drain and set aside.

2. Meanwhile, in a medium bowl, toss the shrimp with 1 teaspoon salt and the black pepper. Heat 1 tablespoon of the oil in a large skillet over medium heat. Add the shrimp to the pan in one layer. Cook without disturbing until lightly browned and opaque, 2 to 3 minutes, flip, and cook another 2 to 3 minutes. Transfer the shrimp to a large plate.

3. Heat the remaining 1 tablespoon oil in the same skillet over medium heat. Add the asparagus and shallot and cook, stirring occasionally, until softened, about 3 minutes. Stir the garlic and continue to cook until fragrant, 1 to 2 minutes more. Stir in the broth, lemon juice, and capers. Bring to a simmer, reduce to medium-low, and simmer until the sauce is slightly reduced, about 5 minutes.

4. Add the linguine and the shrimp to the pan and toss until combined. Season to taste with salt.

5. Spoon into four shallow bowls. Garnish with the Parmesan and parsley.

BLACKENED SWORDFISH WITH MANGO SALSA

Gluten-free, dairy-free, nut-free

During warmer months, I like to make this swordfish outside on the grill. But when the weather gets cooler, I head back indoors and either sear the fish in a cast-iron skillet or on a grill pan. With its bright, sweet, and refreshing notes, the mango salsa is the star of this dish, perfectly complementing the slight spiciness of the blackened fish. When I want to switch (and bulk) things up, I'll serve the blackened swordfish and salsa on top of a rice bowl or use it as a filling for fish tacos. This is equally delicious with salmon, cod, halibut, or shrimp, and you can dress it up with my Coconut Rice (page 219).

SERVES 4

Prep time: 20 minutes
Cook time: 10 minutes

GOOOD TO KNOW: To swap the swordfish for a different protein like salmon, cod, halibut, or shrimp, season with the same spice mix and sear on each side until cooked. If you're not a seafood person, swap for chicken breast or boneless, skinless chicken thighs and increase the cooking time until fully cooked through, 5 to 7 minutes per side.

FOR THE MANGO SALSA

1 ripe avocado, small-diced (about 1¼ cups)
1 mango, small-diced (about 1½ cups)
¼ medium red onion, finely diced (about ⅓ cup)
¼ cup finely chopped fresh cilantro
Juice of 1 lime
1 teaspoon kosher salt

FOR THE SWORDFISH

2 teaspoons smoked paprika
1 teaspoon garlic powder
1 teaspoon kosher salt
½ teaspoon ground black pepper
½ teaspoon cayenne pepper
½ teaspoon dried oregano
Four 6-ounce swordfish steaks, skin removed
Olive oil for the pan

1. **Make the mango salsa:** In a medium bowl, combine the avocado, mango, onion, cilantro, lime juice, and salt and mix well. Cover with plastic wrap and refrigerate until ready to serve.

2. **Cook the swordfish:** In a small bowl, whisk together the smoked paprika, garlic powder, salt, black pepper, cayenne, and oregano.

3. Pat the swordfish steaks dry with a paper towel and place them on a large plate or sheet pan. Evenly sprinkle the spice mixture on both sides of the steaks and gently press down with your fingers to completely coat.

4. Lightly coat a large cast-iron grill pan or cast-iron skillet with oil and set the pan over medium heat. (You can also cook the swordfish directly on a grill if

you have one, following the cook times below.) Working in batches if necessary, place the swordfish in the pan, leaving about ½ inch of space between the steaks, and cook until the center is opaque, 3 to 4 minutes per side.

5. Set a swordfish steak on each of four plates and top each with the salsa.

STORE IT: Refrigerate the swordfish and salsa in separate sealed containers, up to 3 days for the swordfish and up to 4 days for the salsa.

REHEAT IT: Microwave the swordfish until warm, 1 to 2 minutes, or return to a skillet to sear for about 2 minutes per side and top with the chilled salsa.

MISO SALMON WITH ACORN SQUASH

Gluten-free, dairy-free, nut-free option

I'm a big fan of acorn squash because it becomes super tender when baked, fully absorbing any sauce or seasonings you pair it with. Plus, you can eat the roasted skin for an extra fiber boost. But the real hero here is white miso paste, which is excellent for a hit of umami and for optimal gut health (another great fermented food!). This sauce alone is one of my favorites, so even if you don't make the salmon, at least make the sauce and drizzle it on any cooked protein and veggies that need some extra love. I recommend pairing this saucy salmon with Coconut Rice (page 219) for a hearty plate. Other delicious pairings include Fluffy Does-It-All Quinoa (page 291), Sesame-Crisped Brussels Sprouts (page 285), or Chilled Cucumber Salad (page 219).

SERVES 4

Prep time: 15 minutes
Cook time: 40 minutes

To make this nut-free: Omit the cashews.

GOOOD TO KNOW: If salmon isn't your thing, swap in a white fish, such as cod, haddock, or swordfish. Even cubed tofu tossed with a couple of tablespoons of tapioca flour makes a delicious plant-based sub!

STORE IT: Refrigerate the salmon and squash in separate sealed containers for up to 4 days.

REHEAT IT: Microwave the salmon and squash until warm, 1 to 2 minutes, or return to a sheet pan in a 400°F oven for 6 to 8 minutes.

3 tablespoons coconut aminos (or reduced-sodium tamari or reduced-sodium soy sauce)
3 tablespoons white miso
2 tablespoons olive oil, plus more for brushing
1 tablespoon toasted sesame oil
1 tablespoon raw honey or light brown sugar
2 teaspoons ground ginger
1 teaspoon garlic powder
Kosher salt
1 medium acorn squash
Four 4-ounce salmon fillets, skin removed, if desired
Thinly sliced green onions
Sesame seeds (optional)
½ cup unsalted raw cashews, chopped

1. Position an oven rack at least 3 inches from the broiler and preheat the oven to 400°F. Line a sheet pan with parchment paper and set aside.

2. In a medium bowl, whisk together the coconut aminos, miso, olive oil, sesame oil, honey, ginger, and garlic powder. Season to taste with salt. Set aside ¼ cup of the miso sauce for drizzling.

3. Place the acorn squash on a cutting board and slice off the top and bottom so it will sit flat. Cut the squash in half from top to bottom. Scoop out the seeds with a spoon and discard. Slice each half into 1-inch-thick half-circles. Transfer the squash pieces to the prepared sheet pan, then brush each side with olive oil and sprinkle with salt.

4. Bake until fork-tender and golden, flipping halfway through, about 25 minutes.

5. Push the squash to the sides of the sheet pan, leaving a space in the middle. Place the salmon fillets in the center. Generously brush each fillet with the miso sauce and lightly brush the squash with any remaining sauce.

6. Bake until the salmon is opaque, 10 to 13 minutes. Turn the broiler to high and broil until the tops are caramelized, 2 to 3 minutes.

7. Divide the salmon fillets and squash among four plates. Drizzle the reserved miso sauce over the top and garnish with green onions. Add a sprinkling of sesame seeds (if using) and cashews.

HIDDEN VEGGIE SPAGHETTI WITH CRISPY KALE AND SAUSAGE

Gluten-free, dairy-free, vegetarian option, vegan option, nut-free

I call this recipe Hidden Veggie because the pasta sauce is loaded with different vegetables, and you would never know it once it's blended up. With its multiple components, this one takes a bit more effort (which is why it landed in this chapter), but I promise it's worth it. Skip the sausage to make it vegetarian/vegan, but don't skip the crispy kale to top the pasta—that extra step is what "fancy" is all about! Bonus round: The sauce freezes beautifully. You'll likely have extra sauce left over from this recipe (I like a *lot* of sauce), so be sure to save any extras in the freezer for another day.

SERVES 4

Prep time: 20 minutes
Cook time: 45 minutes

To make this vegetarian and vegan: Omit the Italian sausage.

GOOOD TO KNOW: Rinsing gluten-free pasta in cold water after cooking helps it from sticking. You can skip this step with regular pasta and add a drizzle of oil if you're not adding the pasta to the sauce immediately.

FOR THE CRISPY KALE

3 cups shredded curly kale (about 4½ ounces)
2 tablespoons olive oil
Kosher salt

FOR THE SPAGHETTI AND SAUCE

1 teaspoon garlic powder
1 teaspoon dried oregano
Kosher salt
½ teaspoon ground black pepper
¼ teaspoon red pepper flakes (optional)
2 tablespoons olive oil, plus more as needed
½ pound ground hot or sweet Italian sausage or chicken sausage, removed from links, casings discarded if necessary
2 large carrots, small-diced (about 1 cup)
½ large yellow onion, small-diced (about ¾ cup)
1 celery rib, small-diced (about ½ cup)
One 28-ounce can crushed tomatoes
¾ cup full-fat coconut milk (about half a well-shaken 13.5-ounce can)
14 ounces brown rice spaghetti, rice-and-corn-based spaghetti, or regular spaghetti, cooked and kept warm

1. **Make the crispy kale:** Preheat the oven to 325°F. Line a sheet pan with parchment paper.

2. In a large bowl, combine the kale, oil, and a few pinches of salt and toss with tongs or your clean hands until the kale is evenly coated. Transfer the kale to the prepared sheet pan.

3. Bake until dry and crispy, 25 to 30 minutes. Set aside.

(continues)

A LITTLE FANCIER

4. **Meanwhile, make the spaghetti and sauce:** In a small bowl, combine the garlic powder, oregano, 1 teaspoon salt, the black pepper, and red pepper flakes (if using) and set aside.

5. Line a plate with paper towels and set it near the stove. Heat the oil in a large, deep, lidded skillet or Dutch oven over medium heat until shimmering. Add the sausage and cook, stirring occasionally to break up any large pieces, until browned, 5 to 6 minutes. Use a slotted spoon to transfer the sausage to the paper towels to drain. Set aside.

6. Heat the same skillet over medium heat, adding a drizzle of oil if the pan is too dry. Add the carrots, onion, and celery and cook, stirring occasionally, until very soft, 8 to 10 minutes. Add the spice mixture and cook, continuing to stir occasionally, until fragrant, 3 to 4 minutes. Stir in the crushed tomatoes. Bring to a simmer and cook until slightly reduced and warm, about 5 minutes. Stir in the coconut milk and cook until heated through, about 1 minute. Cover and set aside.

7. Transfer the cooked vegetables to a blender or food processor and, working in batches if needed, blend (with the steam vent open on the blender top) on high speed until completely smooth, about 1 minute.

8. Mix half of the sauce with the cooked pasta until fully coated. Add more sauce if desired. Stir in the cooked sausage until evenly combined.

9. Spoon the pasta into four bowls and top with the crispy kale.

STORE IT: Refrigerate the spaghetti and crispy kale in separate sealed containers for up to 4 days (or wait to cook the spaghetti until serving and store the sauce separately). Freeze the sauce without pasta in a sealed container for up to 3 months. I don't recommend freezing the crispy kale.

REHEAT IT: From the refrigerator, microwave the sauce until warm, 1 to 2 minutes, or return to a pot or skillet over medium heat until simmering, then toss with cooked spaghetti. To recrisp the kale, place it on a parchment-lined sheet pan and bake it at 325°F until crispy, about 5 minutes. From the freezer, thaw the sauce in the refrigerator overnight, then microwave in 30-second increments until warm or return to a pot or skillet over medium heat until simmering, then toss with cooked spaghetti.

GRAIN-FREE CHICKEN PARMESAN

Gluten-free, dairy-free option

These grain-free breaded chicken cutlets are a favorite for kids and adults too! It's a breading method I've been using for years in various recipes (crispy chicken salads, chicken nuggets, and so on), but my all-time favorite is in this chicken Parm. Serve alone over the pillowy whipped ricotta or pair with cooked pasta or steamed or roasted vegetables. If you want to get ahead of things, prep the chicken in advance and store it in the fridge until ready to serve, then sear as directed. Whipped ricotta is not essential, but it's part of what makes this recipe a little fancier! (I've also been known to slather it on garlic-rubbed toast.)

SERVES 4

Prep time: 15 minutes
Cook time: 30 minutes

To make this dairy-free: Use dairy-free mozzarella (or omit the mozzarella) and dairy-free ricotta.

GOOOD TO KNOW: If you have the time, freeze the breaded chicken for about 20 minutes before frying to help the coating stick to the cutlet while frying. This will keep your oil cleaner and prevent any burning.

Thinly sliced cutlets tend to be pricier than regular chicken breasts. To save money, simply slice each breast in half horizontally and pound it thin with a meat mallet.

FOR THE CHICKEN

½ cup tapioca flour or arrowroot starch (can substitute cornstarch)
1 large egg
1½ cups blanched almond flour
1 teaspoon dried oregano
½ teaspoon garlic powder
Kosher salt and ground black pepper
2 pounds boneless, skinless chicken breasts, sliced in half horizontally and pounded to a ⅛-inch thickness
Avocado oil, for frying

FOR ASSEMBLY

3 cups marinara sauce
About 6 ounces mozzarella, shredded (1 cup)
Chopped fresh basil
Grated Parmesan (optional)

FOR THE WHIPPED RICOTTA

1 cup part-skim ricotta
Juice of ½ lemon, plus more to taste
1 tablespoon olive oil
½ teaspoon kosher salt, plus more to taste
½ teaspoon ground black pepper, plus more to taste

1. Preheat the oven to 400°F.

2. **Coat the chicken:** Set up a dredging station with three large shallow bowls: Place the tapioca flour in one bowl. Whisk the egg with 2 tablespoons of water in the second bowl. In the third bowl, whisk together the almond flour, oregano, garlic powder, and ½ teaspoon salt.

(continues)

3. Pat the chicken dry with a paper towel and season all over with salt and black pepper.

4. Line a sheet pan or large platter with parchment paper. Working with one piece at a time, add the chicken to the tapioca flour, coating both sides of the chicken and tapping off any excess flour. Next, dip it in the beaten egg evenly to coat. Then dredge in the almond flour mixture, thoroughly and evenly coating the chicken on both sides. Place on the prepared sheet pan. Repeat with the remaining chicken.

5. **Fry the chicken:** Line a second sheet pan with paper towels and have near the stove. Heat about ½ inch of avocado oil in a large skillet and heat over medium heat until shimmering. Working in batches to make sure the chicken browns rather than steams, carefully add a few pieces of the chicken to the pan and fry until the chicken is golden brown, about 4 minutes. Carefully flip and cook about 3 minutes, reducing the heat as needed to avoid burning. Transfer the chicken to the prepared sheet pan.

6. **To assemble the dish:** Spread half of the marinara on the bottom of a 9 × 13-inch baking dish and place the cutlets over the sauce. Spread the rest of the sauce over the chicken and sprinkle evenly with the shredded mozzarella.

7. Bake until the cheese is melted with golden brown spots, 8 to 10 minutes.

8. **Meanwhile, make the whipped ricotta:** In a food processor or blender, combine the ricotta, lemon juice, olive oil, salt, and black pepper and process until completely smooth and light, 1 to 1½ minutes. If needed, add more lemon juice, salt, and/or black pepper.

9. To serve, spoon the whipped ricotta across four plates and top with 2 cutlets per plate. Garnish with chopped basil and grated Parmesan (if using).

STORE IT: Refrigerate the chicken and whipped ricotta in separate sealed containers for up to 4 days or freeze the chicken for up to 3 months. I don't recommend freezing the whipped ricotta.

REHEAT IT: From the refrigerator, microwave the chicken until warm, 2 to 3 minutes, or place on a sheet pan or skillet in a 350°F oven for 8 to 10 minutes to warm. Serve over the chilled whipped ricotta. From the freezer, thaw in the refrigerator overnight, then microwave in 30-second increments until warm or place on a sheet pan or skillet in a 350°F oven for 11 to 14 minutes to warm.

STANDOUT SIDES & BASICS

A great side dish isn't just an afterthought—it's the supporting act that can steal the show. Sides add a pop of flavor to a simple main, balance out a bold dish, and bring personality to your plate. The best part? They're low on effort but *big* on flexibility. I've included my favorite pairings, but you can mix and match to your heart's content. And because a solid foundation is key, you'll also find my failproof methods for perfect rice and quinoa—and when your basics are on point, everything else falls into place.

Roasted Garlic Mashed Potatoes 280

"Cheesy" Polenta 282

Goes-with-Anything Kale Salad 283

Sesame-Crisped Brussels Sprouts 285

Crispy Japanese Sweet Potato Wedges 286

Roasted Lemon Broccoli with Feta 287

Cauliflower and Parsnip Puree 288

Jenn's Steamed Rice 290

Fluffy Does-It-All Quinoa 291

ROASTED GARLIC MASHED POTATOES

Gluten-free, dairy-free option, vegetarian, vegan option, nut-free option

There are plenty of ways to make mashed potatoes, but if you want the *best* garlic mashed potatoes, I'm going to let you in on a little secret: Roast the whole head of garlic. Yes, the *entire* head—don't hold back. Roasting brings out this deep, nutty sweetness that turns good mashed potatoes into the kind you sneak extra spoonfuls of straight from the pot. Just make sure to get the garlic in the oven first (or prep it ahead if you're a planner). These are the kind of mashed potatoes that play well with anything, but they really shine next to Maple-Dijon Pork Tenderloin (page 212)—trust me on that one.

SERVES 4

Prep time: 15 minutes
Cook time: 45 minutes

To make this dairy-free and vegan: Use plant milk and unsalted vegan butter.

GOOOD TO KNOW:

If making ahead of your main dish, keep the mashed potatoes warm by setting up a double boiler: Boil a pot of water and place the mashed potatoes in a glass bowl on top.

If the garlic is still too hot to the touch, wait until cooled down enough to handle, then squeeze out the cloves.

1 garlic bulb
1 teaspoon olive oil
2 pounds russet potatoes, peeled and cut into 2-inch cubes (about 4 medium potatoes)
2 teaspoons kosher salt, plus more to taste
1 cup milk, preferably whole milk
6 tablespoons unsalted butter or unsalted vegan butter
½ teaspoon ground black pepper

1. Position an oven rack in the middle of the oven. Preheat the oven to 400°F.

2. Slice off the top third of the garlic bulb, discard, and drizzle the remaining head with the oil. Wrap the garlic loosely in aluminum foil and place it seam side up on the oven rack. Roast until soft and browned on the edges, 35 to 40 minutes.

3. After the garlic has been in the oven for 15 to 20 minutes, start the potatoes. In a large pot, combine the potatoes, 1 teaspoon of the salt, and water to cover by 3 inches and bring to a boil over high heat. Reduce the heat to medium-low and simmer, uncovered, until the potatoes are fork-tender, about 15 minutes. Drain in a colander and return the potatoes to the pot. Mash the potatoes with a potato masher, ricer, or fork until no large pieces remain.

4. Carefully squeeze the roasted garlic cloves into the pot and mash until fully combined. Add the milk, butter, the remaining 1 teaspoon salt, and the black pepper and stir constantly until the butter has melted and the potatoes are creamy.

STORE IT: Refrigerate in a sealed container for up to 4 days or freeze for up to 3 months.

REHEAT IT: From the refrigerator, microwave until warm, 1 to 2 minutes. From the freezer, thaw in the refrigerator overnight, then microwave in 30-second increments until warm. Alternatively, return the potatoes to a pot over low heat with a generous splash of milk, stirring occasionally, until heated.

"CHEESY" POLENTA

Gluten-free, dairy-free, vegetarian, vegan, nut-free option

Rice, quinoa, pasta—yeah, yeah, they get all the love. But poor polenta? Totally underrated. This creamy, dreamy side is just waiting for its moment, and honestly, it deserves a standing ovation. This version? It's got umami magic from nutritional yeast and a silky, rich texture thanks to the cornmeal and nut milk combo. Of course, if you're feeling more classic, regular milk and Parmesan work too—but even my most devoted dairy-loving friends have been converted. Pair this with Slow Cooker Short Ribs (page 253), and boom: comfort food jackpot.

SERVES 4

Prep time: 5 minutes
Cook time: 20 minutes

To make this nut-free: Use soy, oat, or whole milk.

GOOOD TO KNOW: For fried polenta, spread the warm polenta evenly into a 9 × 9-inch parchment-lined baking dish and refrigerate overnight. Cut into wedges and fry them in about 1 inch of avocado oil for a delicious treat. This is also a great trick for your leftover polenta. If you're not a fan of nutritional yeast, swap in ½ cup grated Parm (although of course it will no longer be dairy-free).

2 cups milk of your choice, preferably unsweetened nut milk
1 cup stone-ground yellow-corn instant polenta
¼ cup nutritional yeast
1 tablespoon olive oil
½ teaspoon kosher salt, plus more to taste
¼ teaspoon red pepper flakes (optional)

1. In a medium lidded saucepan, combine the milk and 1½ cups water and bring to a gentle boil over medium heat. Slowly whisk in the polenta until incorporated. Cook, whisking often, until the polenta thickens, 3 to 5 minutes (or according to package directions). If the polenta is too thick to whisk, gradually add up to ½ cup water to thin it out.

2. Whisk in the nutritional yeast, oil, salt, and red pepper flakes (if using) until incorporated. Cover, remove from the heat, and let steam until thickened, 5 to 7 minutes. If needed, season with more salt.

STORE IT: Refrigerate in a sealed container for up to 4 days or freeze for up to 3 months.

REHEAT IT: From the refrigerator, microwave until warm, 1 to 2 minutes. From the freezer, thaw in the refrigerator overnight, then microwave in 30-second increments until warm. Alternatively, return the polenta to a pot over low heat with a splash of milk, stirring often, until heated.

GOES-WITH-ANYTHING KALE SALAD

Gluten-free, dairy-free, vegetarian, vegan, nut-free

No joke—this salad goes with *everything*. It's creamy, nutty, and just the right amount of lemony, making it the perfect nutrient-packed base for whatever you're in the mood for. Keep it simple, or go wild with add-ins like sliced almonds, crushed walnuts, toasted pine nuts, sunflower seeds, or even some crispy panko for extra crunch. My personal favorite move? Pairing it with my Crusted Buffalo Tempeh Strips (page 246)—just chop them up, toss them in, and enjoy one of the most satisfying plant-based salads ever. And whatever you do, don't sleep on the tahini dressing. Keep a jar in the fridge for drizzling over roasted veggies, chicken, greens—honestly, anything that could use a little creamy, tangy upgrade.

SERVES 4

Prep time: 10 minutes, plus 15 minutes marinating

Cook time: none

GOOOD TO KNOW: If you have bunches of kale, remove the stems and mid-ribs and roughly chop the leaves.

If you're not a fan of nutritional yeast, swap in ½ cup grated Parm (although of course it will no longer be dairy-free).

FOR THE DRESSING

3 tablespoons olive oil
3 tablespoons tahini
Juice of 1 lemon
1 tablespoon apple cider vinegar
1 tablespoon pure maple syrup
¾ teaspoon kosher salt
½ teaspoon garlic powder

FOR THE SALAD

5 cups shredded curly kale (about 7 ounces)
2 tablespoons nutritional yeast

1. **Make the dressing:** In a small bowl, whisk together all the ingredients until smooth. (You can also shake everything in a jar.)

2. **Assemble the salad:** In a large bowl, combine the shredded kale and dressing. Massage the dressing into the kale using clean hands or tongs. (Massaging the kale helps fully coat the salad and tenderize the leaves.) Let the salad marinate for 10 to 15 minutes at room temperature.

3. Add the nutritional yeast, mix well, and serve.

STORE IT: Refrigerate in a sealed container for up to 4 days. Stored separately, the dressing will last up to 7 days.

STANDOUT SIDES & BASICS

"Cheesy" Polenta (p. 282)

Goes-with-Anything Kale Salad (p. 283)

Sesame-Crisped Brussels Sprouts (opposite)

Crispy Japanese Sweet Potato Wedges (p. 286)

SESAME-CRISPED BRUSSELS SPROUTS

Gluten-free, dairy-free, vegetarian, vegan, nut-free

I went *years* without a single Brussels sprout passing my lips—then college happened, and suddenly I was a full-blown Brussels fangirl. (Seriously, where had they been all my life?) Now, I'm all about getting them as crispy as possible, and this version delivers in just 30 minutes. They're the perfect sidekick to my Sticky Sesame Tofu (page 238) or Miso Salmon with Acorn Squash (page 270), but don't stop there—toss them into leftover fried rice, pair them with my Sticky Balsamic Oyster Mushrooms (page 176), or even sneak them into a skillet, like the Weeknight Honey-Garlic Turkey Skillet (page 155). Brussels sprouts are never *just* a side—they share top billing.

SERVES 4

Prep time: 10 minutes
Cook time: 20 minutes

GOOOD TO KNOW: If you have an air fryer, you can make these even faster and crispier. Instead of transferring to a sheet pan, add the Brussels sprouts to the basket in a single layer and air-fry at 425°F until deep brown and crispy, 5 to 7 minutes.

1 pound Brussels sprouts, trimmed and halved (about 4 cups)
2 tablespoons coconut aminos (or reduced-sodium tamari or reduced-sodium soy sauce)
1 tablespoon pure maple syrup
2 tablespoons toasted sesame oil
1 teaspoon garlic powder
½ teaspoon ground black pepper
Sesame seeds

1. Preheat the oven to 425°F. Line a sheet pan with parchment paper.
2. Combine the Brussels sprouts, coconut aminos, maple syrup, sesame oil, garlic powder, and black pepper in a large bowl and mix well. Transfer the sprouts to the sheet pan and spread them out evenly.
3. Bake until deep brown in color and crispy, 15 to 20 minutes.
4. Serve garnished with sesame seeds.

STORE IT: Refrigerate in a sealed container for up to 4 days.

REHEAT IT: For the best results, place the Brussels sprouts on a sheet pan and bake them in a 425°F oven for 6 to 8 minutes to recrisp. Alternatively, air-fry them at 425°F for 3 to 4 minutes or microwave until warm, 1 to 2 minutes.

CRISPY JAPANESE SWEET POTATO WEDGES

Gluten-free, dairy-free, vegetarian, vegan, nut-free

Japanese sweet potatoes—aka my "ride-or-die" spuds—are in a league of their own. With their deep purple-red skin and golden, nutty insides, they're fluffier and sweeter than your standard sweet potato. Think of them as the cool, slightly mysterious cousin in the potato family. That said, if you can't track them down, regular sweet potatoes or even trusty russets will still do the job. But if you *do* find them? Get ready for something special. Pair them with Skirt Steak with Chimichurri (page 259) or Spinach, Goat Cheese, and Sun-Dried Tomato Stuffed Chicken (page 140). And if you somehow have leftovers, reheat them in the morning and serve alongside scrambled eggs—breakfast upgrade unlocked.

SERVES 4

Prep time: 25 minutes
Cook time: 30 minutes

GOOOD TO KNOW: Why soak the fries? This removes excess starch from the potatoes and helps get those perfectly crispy oven-roasted edges. Try to plan ahead for the soak, but skip it if you're in a time crunch—I don't want you to miss out on these!

STORE IT: Refrigerate in a sealed container for up to 4 days.

REHEAT IT: Place the wedges on a sheet pan and cook at 425°F for 9 to 11 minutes for the crispiest results. Alternatively, microwave until warm, 1 to 2 minutes.

2 large or 3 medium Japanese sweet potatoes (about 1 pound)
1 teaspoon garlic powder
1 teaspoon onion powder
1 teaspoon dried oregano
1 teaspoon smoked paprika
1 teaspoon kosher salt, plus more for topping
½ teaspoon ground black pepper
2 tablespoons avocado oil

1. Fill a large bowl with 3 to 4 cups ice and add about 4 cups water, leaving about 3 inches of space from the top of the bowl. Set aside.

2. Cut each sweet potato crosswise and slice each half into wedges 3 inches long and ½ inch thick. Place the sweet potato wedges in the ice water to submerge them. Soak until the starch has washed off, about 20 minutes. For extra-crispy sweet potato wedges, let soak for 2 to 3 hours.

3. Drain the potatoes in a colander. Dry the bowl. Briefly rinse the potatoes with cold water, pat them completely dry with a kitchen towel or paper towel, and return them to the bowl.

4. Preheat the oven to 425°F.

5. In a small bowl, whisk together the garlic powder, onion powder, oregano, smoked paprika, salt, and black pepper. Sprinkle the mixture over the sweet potatoes. Add the oil and toss to coat evenly. Spread the potatoes on a sheet pan in a single layer to prevent them from steaming.

6. Bake until golden brown and crispy, 30 to 40 minutes. Sprinkle with a little salt, then let cool on the sheet pan for 5 to 10 minutes before serving.

ROASTED LEMON BROCCOLI WITH FETA

Gluten-free, dairy-free option, vegetarian, vegan option, nut-free

This crispy, crave-worthy side is proof that veggies can be just as exciting as the main event. It's packed with fiber, totally addicting, and guaranteed to win over kids and adults alike. The real magic? That hit of lemon zest—*do not* skip it!—and the salty, tangy feta that makes eating your greens feel downright luxurious. Want to mix things up? Throw in some cauliflower and Brussels sprouts and turn it into a full-on cruciferous party. Serve it up with my Greek-Style Chicken and Vegetable Skewers (page 191) or Spiced Lamb Meatballs (page 164). Because yes, broccoli *can* be *this* good!

SERVES 4

Prep time: 5 minutes
Cook time: 25 minutes

To make this dairy-free and vegan: Use a dairy-free feta or simply omit the feta.

GOOOD TO KNOW: This roasted broccoli is a Sunday ingredient prep repeat of mine. Having a delicious, fiber-rich vegetable in the fridge makes for easy protein pairings through the week.

2 large heads broccoli, cut into small florets (about 8 cups)
3 tablespoons olive oil
1 teaspoon garlic powder
1 teaspoon dried oregano
1 teaspoon kosher salt
¾ cup crumbled feta (about 3 ounces)
Grated zest and juice of ½ lemon

1. Preheat the oven to 400°F. Line a sheet pan with parchment paper.

2. In a large bowl, combine the broccoli florets, oil, garlic powder, oregano, and salt and toss until fully coated. Transfer the broccoli to the sheet pan in a single layer to prevent steaming.

3. Bake until the tops of the florets are browned, 15 to 20 minutes.

4. Remove from the oven and sprinkle the crumbled feta and lemon zest and juice over the broccoli. Toss with a spatula to evenly distribute the cheese. Spread the broccoli back into one layer.

5. Return to the oven and bake until the florets are crispy and the feta is soft, 5 to 7 minutes.

STORE IT: Refrigerate in a sealed container for up to 4 days.

REHEAT IT: For best results, place the broccoli on a sheet pan and bake in a 400°F oven for 6 to 8 minutes to recrisp. Alternatively, microwave for 1 to 2 minutes to warm.

CAULIFLOWER AND PARSNIP PUREE

Gluten-free, dairy-free option, vegetarian, vegan option, nut-free

As someone *truly* obsessed with vegetables, making them taste ridiculously good is my favorite kind of challenge. Funny enough, I was a *super*-picky eater as a kid, and if you had tried to serve me a cauliflower and parsnip puree back then? No chance. Fast-forward to today and I'm basically licking the bowl while jotting down recipe notes for this one. This is my nutrient-packed twist on classic whipped potatoes—light, silky, and totally addictive. No parsnips? Swap in the same amount of peeled, diced Yukon Gold or russet potatoes. I especially love this alongside Seared Pork Chops with Apple Fennel Pan Sauce (page 262), but honestly, I'd eat it straight from the pot with a spoon.

SERVES 4

Prep time: 10 minutes
Cook time: 20 minutes

To make this dairy-free and vegan: Use plant milk and unsalted vegan butter.

GOOOD TO KNOW: If you don't have a blender or food processor, use a potato masher or even a fork to mash up the vegetables. If needed, add a few extra splashes of milk to help mash.

- 1½ teaspoons kosher salt, plus more for boiling
- 1 pound parsnips (about 4 parsnips), peeled and cut into 1-inch cubes (about 2 cups)
- 1 medium head cauliflower, cut into florets, or 10-ounce bag cauliflower florets (about 4 cups)
- ½ cup milk, preferably whole milk, plus more as needed
- 4 tablespoons (½ stick) unsalted butter or unsalted vegan butter
- 1 teaspoon garlic powder
- ½ teaspoon ground black pepper

1. Bring a large pot of salted water to a boil over high heat. Add the parsnips and cook until they begin to soften, 6 to 7 minutes. Add the cauliflower florets and continue boiling until both the parsnips and the cauliflower are fork-tender, 9 to 11 minutes more. If the water starts boiling over, reduce the heat to medium.

2. Drain the cauliflower and parsnips in a colander. Let cool slightly, about 3 minutes, then transfer the vegetables to a blender or food processor. Add the milk, butter, garlic powder, the 1½ teaspoons salt, and the black pepper and blend (with the steam vent open on the blender top) on high speed until completely smooth, 45 to 60 seconds. If the puree is too thick, add more milk by the tablespoon to thin. Season to taste with salt.

3. Transfer the puree to a shallow bowl and serve.

STORE IT: Refrigerate in a sealed container for up to 4 days or freeze for up to 3 months.

REHEAT IT: From the refrigerator, microwave until warm, 1 to 2 minutes. From the freezer, thaw in the refrigerator overnight, then microwave in 30-second increments until warm. Alternatively, return the puree to a pot over low heat with a splash of milk, stirring often, until heated.

Roasted Lemon Broccoli with Feta (p. 287)

Cauliflower and Parsnip Puree (opposite)

Jenn's Steamed Rice (p. 290)

Fluffy Does-It-All Quinoa (p. 291)

JENN'S STEAMED RICE

Gluten-free, dairy-free, vegetarian, vegan, nut-free

Steamed rice is a total staple in my kitchen, and this foolproof method guarantees it turns out light, fluffy, and never sticky. The secret is all in the prep. Giving the rice a good rinse washes away excess starch, meaning less sticky cooking water and grains that stay separate and perfectly tender. Once you've got your fluffy rice, the possibilities are endless—serve it with Herby Chickpea and Cauliflower Bowls (page 174), Not-Your-Average Burrito Bowls (page 193), Sticky Sesame Tofu (page 238), or literally *any* protein and veggie combo to round out a meal.

MAKES 3 CUPS

Prep time: 5 minutes
Cook time: 20 minutes

GOOOD TO KNOW: To prevent foodborne bacteria from growing, it's important to not leave cooked rice out at room temperature for more than a couple of hours. Refrigerate it in a sealed container as soon as it has cooled down.

1 cup uncooked jasmine rice
Kosher salt

1. Place the rice in a fine-mesh sieve and run under cold water for about 30 seconds. Let the water drain thoroughly and gently shake the sieve to remove any dripping water.

2. Bring 2 cups water to a boil in a 1½-quart pot. Add the rice, cover, reduce the heat to low, and cook until the rice is fluffy, 15 to 18 minutes. Season to taste with salt.

STORE IT: Refrigerate in a sealed container for up to 4 days or freeze for up to 3 months (freeze in individual-size portions for easy reheating).

REHEAT IT: From the refrigerator, microwave until warm, 1 to 2 minutes. From the freezer, thaw in the refrigerator overnight, then microwave in 30-second increments until warm. It is not recommended to reheat rice more than once (that bacteria!), so only reheat the portion you're planning on eating.

FLUFFY DOES-IT-ALL QUINOA

Gluten-free, dairy-free, vegetarian, vegan, nut-free

Fun fact: Quinoa isn't actually a grain—it's a seed! But don't let its tiny size fool you; it's packed with fiber, magnesium, and enough protein to make it a total kitchen workhorse. You can serve it hot, chilled, or anywhere in between. With its mild, nutty flavor (kind of like brown rice, but a little *fancier*), it's an easy swap in salads, bowls, and sides. Try it in my Golden Turmeric Herby Quinoa Salad (page 99), Greek-Style Crispy Chickpea Bowls (page 118), or Spicy Tofu Crunch Bowls (page 111). Here's my go-to method for perfectly steamed quinoa—because once you have it ready to go, the possibilities are endless!

MAKES 3 CUPS

Prep time: 5 minutes
Cook time: 20 minutes

GOOOD TO KNOW: Try swapping low-sodium chicken broth for the water to boost flavor. Or level up even more and swap in chicken bone broth for additional protein.

½ teaspoon kosher salt
1 cup uncooked white or tricolor quinoa

Bring 2 cups water with the salt to a boil in a saucepan over high heat. Stir in the quinoa, reduce the heat to medium-low, cover, and cook until the quinoa is fluffy, 15 to 18 minutes, stirring halfway through to prevent sticking. Remove from the heat and let steam, covered, for at least 5 minutes before serving.

STORE IT: Refrigerate in a sealed container for up to 4 days or freeze for up to 3 months.

REHEAT IT: From the refrigerator, microwave until warm, 1 to 2 minutes. From the freezer, thaw in the refrigerator overnight, then microwave in 30-second increments until warm.

EVERYDAY ELEVATED SAUCES

Some sauces are just built different—they're the all-stars of the fridge, ready to turn any meal into something special. I call them "anything" sauces because, well, I'd happily put them on *anything*. They bring instant excitement to whatever they touch, whether it's a quick weeknight dinner or a snack that needs a little love. Keep them on hand for drizzling, dressing, marinating, or spreading on whatever inspires you. And if you want to see them in action, you'll find them in recipes throughout the book—because trust me, once you taste them, you'll want to use them everywhere.

Creamy Cilantro Sauce 294

Lick-the-Bowl Peanut Sauce 295

Smoky Chipotle Sauce 296

Tangy Maple Barbecue Sauce 298

Cucumber Garlicky Sauce 299

Dairy-Free Walnut Pesto 301

Herby Yogurt Ranch Dressing 302

Lemony Red Wine Vinaigrette 303

CREAMY CILANTRO SAUCE

Gluten-free, dairy-free option, vegetarian, vegan option, nut-free

With its big herbaceous kick, this cilantro-packed sauce is the fresh boost your fridge needs. Cilantro's slightly peppery citrus notes meet tangy lime juice and creamy Greek yogurt, creating a dreamy, sharp, and smooth spoon-worthy blend that will actually up your protein too. It's a natural match for tacos—like my Baked Black Bean and Poblano Tacos (page 215)—but don't stop there. Spoon it over quesadillas, grilled chicken, or veggies, and watch everything become instantly more exciting as you reach for it again and again.

MAKES 1½ CUPS

Prep time: 5 minutes
Cook time: none

To make this dairy-free and vegan: Swap the Greek yogurt for a plain dairy-free yogurt of your choice, like a cashew- or coconut-based yogurt.

GOOOD TO KNOW: Bonus! The thickness of this sauce works well as a dip served with chopped veggies or crackers. It's an instant appetizer for guests.

1 cup chopped fresh cilantro
1 garlic clove, roughly chopped
1 cup whole-milk or low-fat Greek yogurt
Juice of 1 lime
1 teaspoon kosher salt, plus more to taste

In a food processor or blender, combine the cilantro and garlic and blend on high speed until finely chopped, about 30 seconds, scraping down the sides as needed. Add the yogurt, lime juice, and salt and blend on high speed until smooth, about 60 seconds. If needed, season with more salt.

STORE IT: Refrigerate in a sealed container for up to 7 days.

LICK-THE-BOWL PEANUT SAUCE

Gluten-free, dairy-free, vegetarian, vegan

This peanut sauce is a fan favorite for a reason. Ever since it made its debut in my viral Crispy Quinoa, Peanut, and Edamame Salad (page 105), it's been showing up in rice bowls, salads, stir-fries, and beyond. It's got that perfect balance of sweet, salty, and nutty warmth that makes you want to lick the spoon (or the bowl, no shame). Make a batch of this aptly named sauce and see how long it actually lasts in your fridge—spoiler: not long.

MAKES ¾ CUP

Prep time: 5 minutes
Cook time: none

GOOOD TO KNOW:
Peanut sauces tend to thicken after sitting or being stored in the fridge. To thin the sauce into a pourable consistency, whisk in 2 to 3 tablespoons of warm water to loosen the sauce.

¼ cup creamy natural peanut butter
3 tablespoons toasted sesame oil
2 tablespoons coconut aminos (or reduced-sodium tamari or reduced-sodium soy sauce)
1 tablespoon pure maple syrup
1 tablespoon rice vinegar
1½ teaspoons ground ginger
1 teaspoon garlic powder
Kosher salt and ground black pepper

In a medium bowl, combine the peanut butter, sesame oil, coconut aminos, maple syrup, vinegar, ground ginger, garlic powder, and 3 tablespoons warm water and whisk until smooth. If the sauce is too thick, add 2 to 3 tablespoons of warm water to thin it to a pourable consistency. Season to taste with salt and black pepper and whisk again to combine.

STORE IT: Refrigerate in a sealed container for up to 7 days.

SMOKY CHIPOTLE SAUCE

Gluten-free, dairy-free, vegetarian, vegan, nut-free

This four-ingredient chipotle sauce is like a magic trick in a blender—smoky, creamy, and just spicy enough to keep things exciting. It doesn't require a lot of time, energy, or ingredients. Chipotle peppers in adobo are my go-to for instant flavor, and when blended with coconut milk and lime juice they transform into a velvety sauce that's just begging to be drizzled, dipped, or slathered on whatever's on your plate. You'll spot it making a fiery cameo in my Chipotle Sweet Potato Breakfast Hash (page 84) and Chipotle Sweet Potato and Black Bean Bowls (page 113), but don't stop there—try it on eggs, tacos, burgers, or just straight off the spoon.

MAKES ABOUT ¾ CUP

Prep time: 5 minutes
Cook time: none

GOOOD TO KNOW: If you're not using the rest of the coconut milk in the can (although there are a lot of uses in here!), refrigerate it in a sealed jar for up to 1 week and add to your smoothies or lattes.

¾ cup full-fat coconut milk (about half a well-shaken 13.5-ounce can)

2 to 4 canned chipotle peppers in adobo sauce (depending on spice preference)

Juice of 1 lime

½ teaspoon kosher salt

In a food processor or blender, combine the coconut milk, chipotle peppers, lime juice, and salt, and pulse until you have a smooth sauce, about 1 minute.

STORE IT: Refrigerate in a sealed container for up to 7 days.

Creamy Cilantro Sauce (p. 294)

Lick-the-Bowl Peanut Sauce (p. 295)

Smoky Chipotle Sauce (opposite)

Tangy Maple Barbecue Sauce (p. 298)

TANGY MAPLE BARBECUE SAUCE

Gluten-free, dairy-free, vegetarian, vegan, nut-free

Most store-bought barbecue sauces are either loaded with mystery ingredients or way too pricey for what they are. Enter my tangy maple BBQ sauce. With just a few pantry staples, you get all the smoky-sweet magic without the additives. It's the heart and soul of my Barbecue Chicken Chopped Salad (page 117) and Sheet Pan Barbecue Chicken and Pineapple Lettuce Cups (page 179), but you can also swap it in for Buffalo hot sauce in my Buffalo Chickpea Stuffed Sweet Potatoes (page 151). Make a batch, slather it on everything, and feel good about a BBQ sauce you can rely on.

MAKES 1 CUP

Prep time: 10 minutes
Cook time: none

GOOOD TO KNOW: If you prefer raw honey to maple, swap away! Since raw honey is stickier, you may need to add up to 2 tablespoons warm water to thin the sauce. (Although it will no longer be vegan.)

- ½ teaspoon chili powder
- ½ teaspoon garlic powder
- ½ teaspoon smoked paprika
- ½ teaspoon onion powder
- ½ teaspoon ground black pepper
- ¼ cup coconut aminos (or reduced-sodium tamari or reduced-sodium soy sauce)
- ¼ cup tomato paste
- 2 tablespoons apple cider vinegar
- 2 tablespoons pure maple syrup
- 2 tablespoons olive oil

In a medium bowl, combine the chili powder, garlic powder, smoked paprika, onion powder, and black pepper. Add the coconut aminos, tomato paste, vinegar, maple syrup, and oil and whisk rapidly until smooth, about 35 seconds.

STORE IT: Refrigerate in a sealed container for up to 7 days.

CUCUMBER GARLICKY SAUCE

Gluten-free, dairy-free option, vegetarian, vegan option, nut-free

This riff on Greek tzatziki is like a tiny edible symphony: The lemon brings the high notes; the yogurt and olive oil lay down a smooth, creamy baseline (and a protein boost); and the grated cucumber adds a fresh, crunchy rhythm. It's the perfect way to add a bright, cooling contrast to rich dishes. Try it with my Greek-Style Chicken and Vegetable Skewers (page 191), Mediterranean-Inspired Smashed Tacos (page 264), or Greek-Style Crispy Chickpea Bowls (page 118). Or just keep a jar in the fridge and spread it on anything that needs a little extra protein and flavor.

MAKES 1½ CUPS

Prep time: 10 minutes
Cook time: none

To make this dairy-free and vegan: Swap the Greek yogurt for a plain dairy-free yogurt of your choice, like a cashew- or coconut-based yogurt.

GOOOD TO KNOW: I always use a bowl because I love to drink the squeezed cuke water or add it to a mocktail!

If using an English cucumber, you'll only need to use half since they are bigger.

- 1 small cucumber, unpeeled
- 1 cup whole-milk or low-fat Greek yogurt
- Juice of 1 lemon
- 1 tablespoon olive oil
- ½ teaspoon garlic powder
- ½ teaspoon kosher salt

1. Finely grate the cucumber on the fine holes of a box grater into a clean kitchen towel. Gather the ends of the towel and squeeze as much liquid from the cucumber as possible into a bowl (see Goood to Know) or the sink.

2. In a medium bowl, combine the cucumber, yogurt, lemon juice, oil, garlic powder, and salt and mix well. Refrigerate until ready to serve.

STORE IT: Refrigerate in a sealed container for up to 7 days.

Cucumber Garlicky Sauce (p. 299)

Dairy-Free Walnut Pesto (opposite)

Herby Yogurt Ranch Dressing (p. 302)

Lemony Red Wine Vinaigrette (p. 303)

DAIRY-FREE WALNUT PESTO

Gluten-free, dairy-free, vegetarian, vegan

This has been my go-to pesto for years, because let's be real—nothing else compares. It takes center stage in my Creamy Lemon Pesto Pasta with Walnut Crumbs (page 228), plays a supporting role in the Pesto and Roasted Red Pepper Egg Casserole (page 83), and steals the show in the Sheet Pan Pesto Pizza with Asparagus and Prosciutto (page 201). It's also an excellent team player as a sandwich spread, a quick dip, or a finishing touch for grilled fish, chicken, or veggies. Packed with vitamins from the basil and protein-rich walnuts, it's as nutritious as it is delicious.

MAKES ¾ CUP

Prep time: 5 minutes
Cook time: none

GOOOD TO KNOW: I use walnuts in this recipe because they're a cheaper option than pine nuts, but if you'd prefer the traditional pine nuts, feel free to sub. Both nuts have the perfect texture for pesto. If you don't mind the dairy, you can also opt for ½ cup grated Parmesan instead of nutritional yeast.

2 cups packed fresh basil
¼ cup nutritional yeast
2 tablespoons roughly chopped unsalted raw walnuts
1 garlic clove
Juice of ½ lemon
¾ teaspoon kosher salt
½ teaspoon ground black pepper
⅓ cup olive oil

In a food processor, combine the basil, nutritional yeast, walnuts, garlic, lemon juice, salt, and black pepper and pulse until a sand-like texture forms, about 30 seconds. With the machine running on low speed, slowly stream in the oil until a smooth and uniform sauce forms, about 1 minute.

STORE IT: Refrigerate in a sealed container for up to 7 days or freeze for up to 3 months (thaw in the refrigerator overnight and bring to room temperature for 1 hour before use); oil separation and slight discoloration are normal. Mix the pesto well before use.

HERBY YOGURT RANCH DRESSING

Gluten-free, dairy-free option, vegetarian, vegan option, nut-free

Store-bought dressings can be so convenient, but to be honest, bottled ranch doesn't do it for me. Since I'm picky about it, I made my own—a fresh, herby ranch dressing that's leagues ahead of the store-bought stuff. Bright lemon juice, fresh herbs, and Greek yogurt come together in a creamy dream that works as both a dressing and a dip. Use it on my Barbecue Chicken Chopped Salad (page 117) or dunk Crusted Buffalo Tempeh Strips (page 246) in it. It's a back-pocket recipe!

MAKES 1 CUP

Prep time: 5 minutes
Cook time: none

To make this dairy-free and vegan: Swap the Greek yogurt for a plain dairy-free yogurt of your choice, like a cashew- or coconut-based yogurt.

GOOOD TO KNOW: If you prefer a completely smooth ranch, blend everything in a food processor or blender.

⅔ cup whole-milk or low-fat Greek yogurt
1 tablespoon finely chopped fresh chives
1 tablespoon finely chopped fresh dill
1 tablespoon finely chopped fresh parsley
Juice of 1 lemon
1 teaspoon garlic powder
1 teaspoon onion powder
½ teaspoon kosher salt

In a small bowl, whisk together the yogurt, chives, dill, parsley, lemon juice, garlic powder, onion powder, and salt until well combined, 30 to 45 seconds.

STORE IT: Refrigerate in a sealed container for up to 7 days.

LEMONY RED WINE VINAIGRETTE

Gluten-free, dairy-free, vegetarian, vegan, nut-free

Everyone needs a trusty vinaigrette, ready to whisk up at the last minute. This tangy dressing is my everything vinaigrette, brightening up greens, from peppery arugula to tender butter lettuce. It ties together the Mediterranean-Inspired Chickpea Chopped Salad (page 95) and the Farmers' Market Lentil Salad (page 96), but really, it's just as at home on roasted veggies and bowls or as a quick chicken marinade for the grill.

MAKES ⅔ CUP

Prep time: 5 minutes
Cook time: none

GOOOD TO KNOW: Separation is expected after the dressing sits, so use a whisk or fork to mix it up before pouring, or shake well in a sealed jar.

¼ cup olive oil
¼ cup red wine vinegar
Juice of 1 lemon
1 teaspoon garlic powder
1 teaspoon dried oregano
1 teaspoon kosher salt
½ teaspoon ground black pepper

In a small bowl, whisk the oil, vinegar, lemon juice, garlic powder, oregano, salt, and black pepper until thoroughly combined.

STORE IT: Refrigerate in a sealed container for up to 7 days. Let the dressing come to room temperature for 5 to 10 minutes and whisk before using.

FUNCTIONAL SIPS

If you follow me on social media, you *already* know how much I love sharing my morning drinks. They're my little daily kickoff—a cozy, refreshing, or downright energizing moment to set the tone for the day. So, of course, I had to include some of my favorites in this book! The best part? These drinks aren't just pretty or delicious (though they *definitely* are)—each one has a functional twist, whether it's reducing inflammation, supporting sleep, or even boosting overall wellness. So why not turn "fun drink o'clock" into a chance to sip on something that actually does some good?

From left to right: Salted Tahini-Maple Latte (page 307), Golden Milk Latte (page 308), My Everyday Matcha Latte (page 306), Dreamy Blueberry Matcha Latte (page 309)

My Everyday Matcha Latte 306

Salted Tahini-Maple Latte 307

Golden Milk Latte 308

Dreamy Blueberry Matcha Latte 309

Rich and Creamy Vegan Hot Chocolate 310

Tart Raspberry-Honey Lemonade 313

Sleepytime Cherry Tonic 314

MY EVERYDAY MATCHA LATTE

Gluten-free, dairy-free option, vegetarian, vegan option, nut-free

I became a full-blown matcha girl in college—back when getting my hands on a matcha latte felt like a rare, luxe treat (especially on a college budget). Pretty quickly, I realized the only way to keep up my obsession was to learn how to make them myself, so that's exactly what I did! Matcha is made from finely ground green tea leaves, meaning you're getting *way* more antioxidants than from a regular cup of steeped tea. (Think of it as green tea's cooler, more powerful cousin.) I personally love using unsweetened cashew milk for the creamiest lattes, but honestly, anything goes—almond, soy, flax, oat, even skim. Just grab your favorite milk, whisk up that vibrant green goodness, and start your day *right*.

MAKES TWO 10-OUNCE ICED LATTES

Prep time: 10 minutes
Cook time: none

To make this dairy-free and vegan: Use plant milk.

GOOOD TO KNOW: The quality of matcha can vary; I look for ceremonial-grade sourced from Japan for the best quality and taste. Make it a hot matcha by leaving out the ice and heating the milk in a saucepan over medium-low heat.

2 teaspoons matcha powder (see Goood to Know)
¾ cup hot water (170°F, or almost boiling)
1 tablespoon pure maple syrup, plus more to taste
1 teaspoon pure vanilla extract
Ice
1½ cups milk of your choice

1. Sift the matcha into a glass measuring cup. Pour the hot water over the matcha and whisk vigorously until frothy, 30 to 45 seconds. Add the maple syrup and vanilla and whisk until combined.

2. Fill two 12-ounce glasses with ice. Evenly divide the milk between the glasses. Carefully pour half of the matcha mixture into each glass. Stir the matcha and milk until the liquid becomes a uniform light-green color. Taste and, if desired, add more maple syrup for sweetness.

STORE IT: The matcha mixture can be refrigerated in a sealed container (without the ice) for up to 2 days. It will separate, so you'll need to whisk or blend it.

SALTED TAHINI-MAPLE LATTE

Gluten-free, dairy-free option, vegetarian, vegan option, nut-free

Believe it or not, one of the *most* common questions I get on Instagram is: "How do you make your lattes?" I share my morning latte routine a *lot*—it's kind of my thing now—but I have to admit, my usual answer feels a little anticlimactic: just some nut milk and a double shot of espresso. That's it! But for those days when I want something a little extra (without dropping $$$ at an expensive coffee bar), I turn to this salted tahini-maple concoction. It's just the right mix of sweet and salty—aka, *way* more exciting than my usual. If you're looking to up your at-home latte game, this one's for you!

MAKES TWO 10-OUNCE ICED LATTES

Prep time: 10 minutes
Cook time: none

To make this dairy-free, and vegan: Use plant milk.

GOOOD TO KNOW: Make this hot! Just mix your tahini, maple, cinnamon, vanilla, and salt with the hot brewed espresso and top with steamed milk.

2 cups milk of your choice
1 tablespoon pure maple syrup
1 tablespoon tahini
1 teaspoon ground cinnamon, plus more for garnish
1 teaspoon pure vanilla extract
½ teaspoon kosher salt
Ice
2 double shots brewed or instant espresso

1. In a blender, combine the milk, maple syrup, tahini, cinnamon, vanilla, and salt and blend on high speed until frothy, 20 to 30 seconds.

2. Fill two 12-ounce cups with ice. Evenly divide the tahini milk between the glasses. Carefully pour 1 double shot of espresso into each glass and stir until combined. Sprinkle a little cinnamon on top.

STORE IT: This latte is best enjoyed right after brewing the espresso, but the tahini milk can be made beforehand. Refrigerate it in a sealed container for up to 4 days, shake well, pour over ice, and top it with your brewed espresso.

FUNCTIONAL SIPS

GOLDEN MILK LATTE

Gluten-free, dairy-free option, vegetarian, vegan option, nut-free

I had my first turmeric latte years ago while working at a vegetarian café, and it was a total *game changer*. I knew turmeric was great for cooking, but I had no idea it could shine in a drink too. Turns out, this golden spice has been used for centuries in Ayurvedic medicine for its anti-inflammatory, antibacterial, and antioxidant properties—basically, it's been a wellness MVP long before it was trendy. To get the most out of turmeric's benefits, you need the ultimate *absorption power trio*—turmeric, black pepper, and fat. This latte nails all three, making it as functional as it is flavorful. It's a little sweet, a little spicy, and has just the right amount of warmth. Plus, that vibrant golden color? Absolutely stunning. One sip and you'll get why I can't stop making it!

MAKES TWO 10-OUNCE ICED LATTES

Prep time: 5 minutes
Cook time: none

To make this dairy-free and vegan: Use plant milk.

GOOOD TO KNOW: Add a scoop of collagen or vanilla vegetarian protein powder before blending for a boost.

2½ cups milk of your choice
1 tablespoon pure maple syrup, plus more to taste
1 teaspoon coconut oil
1 teaspoon ground turmeric
¼ teaspoon ground cinnamon
¼ teaspoon ground ginger
Pinch of ground black pepper
Ice

1. In a blender, combine the milk, maple syrup, coconut oil, turmeric, cinnamon, ginger, and black pepper and blend on high speed until well combined, 20 to 30 seconds.

2. Fill two 12-ounce glasses with ice. Evenly divide the mixture between the glasses. Taste and, if desired, add more maple syrup for sweetness.

STORE IT: Refrigerate in a sealed container (without the ice) for up to 4 days. Shake well and pour over ice.

DREAMY BLUEBERRY MATCHA LATTE

Gluten-free, dairy-free option, vegetarian, vegan option, nut-free

Homemade syrup might *sound* fancy, but it's way easier than you'd think—and it can totally upgrade your matcha or spritz, especially when fruit is involved. This blueberry matcha takes me straight back to summer days, when I'd make batch after batch to use up the endless supply of blueberries from my CSA boxes. It's just the right amount of sweet, extra refreshing, and packed with antioxidants—perfect for switching up your usual iced matcha routine. But don't stop there! This blueberry syrup is a multitasker—use it in other drinks, drizzle it over ice cream, or swirl it into Lemon-Blueberry Overnight Oats (page 62) for an extra fruity boost.

MAKES TWO 10-OUNCE ICED LATTES

Prep time: 5 minutes, plus 5 minutes resting

Cook time: 15 minutes

To make this dairy-free and vegan: Use plant milk.

STORE IT: Double or triple the syrup recipe, as it can be refrigerated in a sealed container or jar for to 2 weeks. Drinks for days!

The matcha mixture and syrup can be refrigerated and stored in separate sealed containers (without the ice) for up to 2 days. It will separate, so you'll need to whisk or blend it again before combining and pouring over ice-filled glasses.

FOR THE BLUEBERRY SYRUP

1 heaping cup frozen blueberries
2 tablespoons pure maple syrup
1 teaspoon pure vanilla extract

FOR THE MATCHA LATTE

2 teaspoons matcha powder
Ice
⅔ cup hot water (170°F, or almost boiling)
1½ cups milk of your choice

1. **Make the blueberry syrup:** In a saucepan, combine the blueberries, maple syrup, and ¼ cup water. Bring to a boil over medium heat. Reduce the heat to low and simmer until the blueberries are softened and juicy, 12 to 14 minutes. Remove from the heat and stir in the vanilla extract. Let cool for at least 5 minutes.

2. Strain the syrup through a fine-mesh sieve set over a small jar or measuring cup. You should have just under ¼ cup.

3. Divide the syrup between two 12-ounce glasses.

4. **Make the matcha latte:** Sift the matcha into a glass measuring cup. Pour the hot water over the matcha and whisk thoroughly until frothy, 30 to 45 seconds.

5. Fill the glasses with ice. Divide the milk between the glasses. Carefully pour the matcha mixture into each glass. Use a spoon to stir until the syrup, milk, and matcha are incorporated (but don't forget to snap a pic before stirring!).

FUNCTIONAL SIPS

RICH AND CREAMY VEGAN HOT CHOCOLATE

Gluten-free, dairy-free, vegetarian, vegan, nut-free

Thick, creamy, and totally indulgent—without a drop of dairy—this is my ultimate cozy-up-on-a-chilly-day drink. It's officially my favorite hot chocolate, and it's become a tradition in our house. Every December 1, Brian and I whip up a couple of mugs, queue up a Christmas movie, and let the holiday season *officially* begin. It comes together in no time and just so happens to be the perfect match for Mocha Brownie Cream Pie Sandwiches (page 323)—because sometimes, a *full-blown* chocolate party is the only way to go. Feeling festive? Top it off with whipped cream, a sprinkle of shaved dark chocolate, or whatever makes you happiest.

MAKES TWO 10-OUNCE HOT CHOCOLATES

Prep time: 5 minutes
Cook time: 15 minutes

GOOOD TO KNOW:
End up with extra? Reheat with a shot of espresso for a morning drink!

Add a scoop of vanilla protein powder before blending for a protein boost.

One 13.5-ounce can light coconut milk
2 tablespoons cacao powder or unsweetened cocoa powder
2 tablespoons pure maple syrup
2 teaspoons pure vanilla extract
½ teaspoon ground cinnamon
½ teaspoon kosher salt
Optional toppings: Coconut whipped cream, shaved dark vegan chocolate

1. In a blender, combine 1 cup water, the coconut milk, cacao powder, maple syrup, vanilla, cinnamon, and salt. Blend on high speed until smooth, 45 to 60 seconds.

2. Transfer to a saucepan and bring to a simmer over medium heat. Reduce the heat to low and continue simmering, stirring occasionally, about 5 minutes.

3. Remove from the heat, pour into mugs, and add coconut whipped cream and chocolate shavings, if desired!

STORE IT: Let it cool and refrigerate in a sealed glass jar or container for up to 5 days.
REHEAT IT: Reheat in the microwave or a saucepan over medium-low heat until warm.

TART RASPBERRY-HONEY LEMONADE

Gluten-free, dairy-free, vegetarian, nut-free

This lemonade is basically summer in a glass—perfect for sipping on the patio... or, you know, just pretending you have one. With only four simple plant-based ingredients, it's an easy way to turn almost-forgotten berries into something *way* more exciting (because we all have that bag of frozen fruit hanging hanging out in the freezer!). Feel free to mix things up with strawberries, blueberries, or a combo of both—just be ready to tweak the honey to get that perfect balance. And for the ultimate summer pairing? A glass of this lemonade with some Slow Cooker Carnitas Tacos with Pineapple Salsa (page 209). Absolute *chef's kiss*.

MAKES FOUR 10-OUNCE LEMONADES

Prep time: 10 minutes
Cook time: 15 minutes

GOOOD TO KNOW: Save the leftover drained raspberries and add them to your overnight oats, chia pudding, or pancakes.

1 cup frozen raspberries
½ cup raw honey
¼ teaspoon kosher salt
⅔ cup fresh lemon juice (from 3 to 4 lemons)
Ice

1. Cook the raspberries in a medium saucepan over medium heat, stirring occasionally, until the berries soften and the juices are bubbling, 5 to 7 minutes. Stir in the honey and salt and continue to simmer until no whole raspberry pieces remain, 6 to 8 minutes. (There will be seeds and that's okay.)

2. Remove from the heat and stir in 3½ cups cold water. Strain the liquid through a fine-mesh sieve set over a pitcher to separate the seeds from the liquid. (See Goood to Know for how to repurpose those raspberries!) Stir the lemon juice into the raspberry liquid.

3. Fill four 12-ounce glasses with ice and pour in the lemonade.

STORE IT: Refrigerate in a sealed container (without the ice) for up to 7 days. Serve in ice-filled glasses.

SLEEPYTIME CHERRY TONIC

Gluten-free, dairy-free, vegetarian, vegan, nut-free

Ah, deep sleep—the ultimate prize that somehow feels harder to win these days. When I started adding magnesium to my nighttime routine, it was a total reset. And since I'm all about making things *delicious*, I found a way to turn it into a cozy little bedtime ritual with this sleepytime drink. Tart cherry juice isn't just here for flavor—it's actually been studied to support better sleep (bonus points!). Apple cider vinegar brings its own perks, believed to help regulate blood sugar and cholesterol. The result? A nighttime mocktail that's as tasty as it is functional. Sip, relax, and let the zzz's come rolling in.

MAKES ONE 12-OUNCE SERVING

Prep time: 5 minutes
Cook time: none

GOOOD TO KNOW: When choosing a magnesium powder, look for magnesium glycinate in the ingredient list as that's the type most studied to support better sleep.

¼ cup tart cherry juice
1 scoop (about a heaping ¾ teaspoon) unflavored magnesium powder
1 tablespoon apple cider vinegar
1 teaspoon pure maple syrup
Ice
1 cup unflavored or cherry sparkling water
Lime wedge (optional)

In a 16-ounce glass, whisk together the cherry juice, magnesium powder, vinegar, and maple syrup until the powder is dissolved. Fill the glass with ice and pour in the sparkling water. Add a squeeze of lime (if using).

STORE IT: Refrigerate without sparkling water in a sealed container for up to 4 days, then pour over ice and add the sparkling water when serving.

SWEET TREATS

If you're the type who *always* saves room for dessert, you're in the right place. But don't expect the usual suspects—these sweets follow the same vibe as the rest of the book, meaning plants get a starring role in fun, unexpected ways. The goal? Keep things *delicious* without making them feel like a "healthier" swap—because dessert should always feel like a treat.

These recipes are simple enough for anyone to whip up and perfect for any occasion—holidays, dinner parties, a company lunch, or even just for yourself on a Tuesday night. Whether you're in the mood for something fruity, chocolatey, nutty, or citrusy, you'll find something here to satisfy that sweet tooth!

Salty Peanut Butter Pretzel Energy Balls 318

Orange-Cardamom Olive Oil Cake 321

Mocha Brownie Cream Pie Sandwiches 323

Tahini Chocolate Chip Cookie Bars 327

Pistachio-Berry Crisp 328

Fudgy Sweet Potato Brownies 330

Chocolate-Cashew Freezer Fudge 333

Grammy's Pumpkin Bread 334

SALTY PEANUT BUTTER PRETZEL ENERGY BALLS

Gluten-free, dairy-free, vegetarian, vegan

If you're dashing out the door, powering up for a workout, or just need a midafternoon pick-me-up, these crunchy-salty-sweet bites have *got your back*. They come together in no time and are basically snack gold. Add them to your meal-prep lineup, stash a few in your bag for travel, or whip up a batch for a friend who's juggling *all the things*. Because pretzels and peanut butter were *meant* to be together, and these energy balls prove it.

MAKES 24 BALLS

Prep time: 15 minutes, plus 45 minutes chilling

GOOOD TO KNOW:
Be sure to use a natural peanut butter (with only peanuts and salt listed in the ingredients); this will yield the right amount of stickiness for the balls to stay together.

Not all peanut butters have the same texture or oil content. The extra bit of coconut oil will give you the right texture.

Don't skip the chill time, which makes shaping them easier.

3 ounces salted gluten-free pretzels (about 1½ cups)
1 cup gluten-free rolled oats
⅓ cup dairy-free mini chocolate chips
¼ cup chia seeds (2 ounces)
½ teaspoon kosher salt
1 cup creamy natural peanut butter (see Goood to Know)
⅓ cup pure maple syrup
1 teaspoon pure vanilla extract
1 tablespoon melted coconut oil, plus more as needed (see Goood to Know)

1. In a food processor, pulse the pretzels until ground into pieces mostly no bigger than ⅓ inch, eight to ten pulses. (Alternatively, place the pretzels in a sealed bag and crush them with a heavy object, like a rolling pin or can of beans.)

2. Pour the crushed pretzels into a large bowl and add the oats, chocolate chips, chia seeds, and salt. Mix in the peanut butter, maple syrup, vanilla, and coconut oil using a rubber spatula until no dry streaks remain and the mixture holds its shape when formed into balls. Add more coconut oil as needed if the mixture is a bit dry. Cover the bowl with a lid or plastic wrap and refrigerate until fully chilled and firm, at least 45 minutes or up to 2 hours.

3. Using a lightly oiled tablespoon or a 1-tablespoon cookie scoop, divide the mixture into twenty-four 1½-inch balls (about the size of a golf ball). Roll each scoop between your clean hands to shape it into a smooth ball. Place the balls on a large plate, and serve immediately or store.

STORE IT: Keep in a sealed container in a cool, dry place for up to 3 days. After the third day, they are still delicious but a bit less crunchy. I also enjoy these chilled!

ORANGE-CARDAMOM OLIVE OIL CAKE

Gluten-free, dairy-free, vegetarian, vegan option

If there's olive oil cake on a dessert menu, I *already* know how my meal is going to end—it's my all-time favorite. This version keeps things naturally sweet with maple syrup, coconut sugar, and fresh orange juice, making it perfect for those times when you want a treat but also want to feel good about what you're eating.

The orange-cardamom combo is a total match made in dessert heaven, especially alongside a warm mug of tea. And while the coconut cardamom whip is *technically* optional, I highly recommend it—it takes this humble cake from simple to *special*. Just don't forget to chill your coconut cream the night before so it's ready to whip when you are!

SERVES 8

Prep time: 20 minutes, plus 15 minutes resting

Cook time: 30 minutes

To make this vegan: Add an extra ½ teaspoon baking powder and swap in ¾ cup applesauce for the eggs. The cake will be a bit darker and stickier but still delicious.

FOR THE OLIVE OIL CAKE

Neutral oil spray
2 cups blanched almond flour
⅔ cup tapioca flour or arrowroot starch (or substitute cornstarch)
2 teaspoons baking powder
1 teaspoon ground cardamom
½ teaspoon kosher salt
⅓ cup coconut sugar or granulated sugar
⅓ cup olive oil
Zest of 1 orange (about 3 tablespoons)
3 large eggs
¼ cup pure maple syrup
¼ cup fresh orange juice (from 1 orange)
1 teaspoon almond extract
1 teaspoon pure vanilla extract

FOR THE CARDAMOM COCONUT WHIP (OPTIONAL):

One 13.5-ounce can coconut cream, refrigerated for at least 5 hours or up to overnight, unshaken
3 tablespoons pure maple syrup
1 teaspoon pure vanilla extract
½ teaspoon ground cardamom
¼ teaspoon kosher salt
Orange zest, for garnish (optional)

1. Preheat the oven to 325°F. Spray a 9-inch round cake pan with neutral oil spray and line it with enough parchment paper to overhang the rim of the cake pan for easy removal.

(continues)

SWEET TREATS

GOOOD TO KNOW:

This almond and tapioca flour ratio is the key to the perfect cake. Don't skip the tapioca flour! It's essential for the airy texture.

Add the leftover coconut water to your next smoothie to avoid food waste.

I highly recommend using a stand mixer for the cardamom whip as the coconut cream needs to be beaten aggressively to turn to stiff peaks.

2. In a medium bowl, whisk together the almond flour, tapioca flour, baking powder, cardamom, and salt. Set aside.

3. In a large bowl, whisk together the coconut sugar, olive oil, and orange zest until a sand-like texture forms. Add the eggs one at a time, whisking after each one to fully incorporate it. Add the maple syrup, orange juice, almond extract, and vanilla and mix well. Fold in the flour mixture with a rubber spatula until no white streaks remain. Transfer the batter to the prepared cake pan.

4. Bake until the top is golden brown and a toothpick inserted in the center comes out clean, 25 to 30 minutes. If the cake gets too brown before it finishes baking, cover it with a dome of aluminum foil.

5. Let the cake cool in the pan on a wire rack for 15 minutes.

6. **Meanwhile, if making the cardamom whip:** Open the chilled coconut cream can and carefully scoop out only the hardened white cream settled on the top. (Reserve the remaining coconut water in the can; see Goood to Know.) In the bowl of a stand mixer fitted with the whisk attachment (or in a large bowl using a hand mixer), whip the cream on high until stiff peaks begin to form, 2 to 3 minutes. Add the maple syrup, vanilla, cardamom, and salt and continue whipping until incorporated, about 20 seconds. Cover and refrigerate until ready to serve.

7. Lift the parchment paper edges to remove the cake from the pan. Place it on a large plate or cake stand. Slice the cake into 8 even wedges. If desired, serve with a dollop of cardamom whip on top and garnish with orange zest.

STORE IT: Keep the cake, covered or in a large sealed container, in a cool, dry place for up to 3 days. Refrigerate the cardamom whip in a sealed container for up to 5 days–you'll likely have extra!

REHEAT IT: If you'd like to warm up the cake before topping with the whip, optionally microwave it for 15 to 30 seconds to warm.

MOCHA BROWNIE CREAM PIE SANDWICHES

Gluten-free, dairy-free, vegetarian, nut-free

Most of the recipes in this book have a *purpose*—fueling you with protein, keeping you energized, or getting a veggie-packed meal on the table fast. But this one? This one is all about *pure joy*. Think of it as a brownie-cookie sandwich mash-up, inspired by the Little Debbie oatmeal cream pies I was *obsessed* with as a kid. These cookies are rich, sweet, and ridiculously fun to make. When they cool, they get those soft, crinkly tops—just like brownies—and are honestly *amazing* on their own. But add the fluffy mocha filling? Game over.

MAKES 8 SANDWICHES

Prep time: 30 minutes, plus 20 minutes cooling
Cook time: 10 minutes

GOOOD TO KNOW: The chocolate cookies shine on their own, so if you don't have time to make the filling, just make the cookies! Fold some chocolate chips into the batter for an added element.

Feel free to use regular chocolate, all-purpose flour, and unsalted butter, if desired.

FOR THE BROWNIE COOKIES

1 cup chopped dairy-free chocolate
4 tablespoons (½ stick) unsalted vegan butter
Gluten-free 1:1 baking flour
¼ cup cacao powder or unsweetened cocoa powder
2 teaspoons espresso powder
1 teaspoon baking powder
½ teaspoon kosher salt
3 large eggs
1 cup coconut sugar or granulated sugar
1 teaspoon pure vanilla extract
Flaky salt (optional)

FOR THE MOCHA FILLING

2 tablespoons milk of your choice (I prefer oat)
1 teaspoon espresso powder
1 cup confectioners' sugar
⅓ cup (⅔ stick) unsalted vegan butter, at room temperature
2 tablespoons cacao powder or unsweetened cocoa powder
1 teaspoon pure vanilla extract
Pinch of kosher salt

1. Position one oven rack in the lower third of the oven. Position a second rack about 3 inches below the broiler. Preheat the oven to 350°F. Line two sheet pans with parchment paper and set aside.

2. Microwave the chocolate in a small glass or microwave-safe bowl in 30-second increments until melted, stirring in between, about 2 minutes total.

(continues)

SWEET TREATS

STORE IT: Refrigerate assembled cookie sandwiches in a sealed container for up to 4 days.

REHEAT IT: Let the cookies rest on the counter at room temperature for at least 10 minutes to let the filling soften.

Immediately stir in the butter until thoroughly combined. Set aside for at least 5 minutes to cool, to prevent the hot chocolate from scrambling the eggs when added.

3. In a small bowl, whisk together the flour, cacao powder, espresso powder, baking powder, and salt. Set aside.

4. In a medium bowl, whisk the eggs until no streaks remain. Add the coconut sugar and continue whisking until the sugar dissolves. Whisk in the vanilla and the cooled chocolate until no egg streaks remain. Mix the dry ingredients into the wet ingredients until no dry streaks remain. The batter will be thinner than a typical cookie dough, with a sticky but runny consistency, like brownie batter.

5. Using a 2-tablespoon cookie scoop or a large spoon, scoop the batter onto the prepared sheet pans, leaving even space between the cookies to give them room to spread. Arrange for 8 cookies on each pan, for a total of 16 cookies.

6. Bake for 8 to 10 minutes, until the tops of the cookies are no longer sticky to the touch and the bottoms are crisp, switching the pan racks and rotating the sheet pans from front to back halfway through to ensure even baking.

7. Remove from the oven and sprinkle the hot cookies with flaky salt (if using). Let the cookies cool completely on the sheet pans for at least 20 minutes.

8. **Meanwhile, make the mocha filling:** In a small bowl, combine the milk and espresso powder in a small bowl and set aside.

9. In the bowl of a stand mixer fitted with the whisk attachment (or in a large bowl using a hand mixer), combine ½ cup of the confectioners' sugar and the butter and beat on low (to keep the sugar from flying out of the bowl) for about 10 seconds. Increase the speed to medium-high and beat until smooth and no dry streaks remain, about 30 seconds. Add the remaining ½ cup confectioners' sugar and continue to beat until completely smooth, about 45 seconds. Add the reserved espresso-milk mixture, the cacao powder, vanilla, and salt and beat until light and airy, about 1 minute.

10. Flip eight of the cookies upside down so that their bottoms face up and spread or pipe about 1 heaping tablespoon of the mocha filling on top, distributing all the filling evenly among the cookies. Top with the remaining cookies to create sandwiches and serve or store.

TAHINI CHOCOLATE CHIP COOKIE BARS

Gluten-free, dairy-free, vegetarian, vegan, nut-free

This is *the* dessert I pick for my birthday every year—and honestly, I crave it all the time. Luckily, these tahini bars are ridiculously easy to make, so satisfying that craving is never a problem. While testing this recipe, I cracked the code on how to get perfectly chewy, cookie-cake-like bars *whenever* I want, and bonus—they're vegan, dairy-free, and gluten-free! The tahini gives them a rich, nutty twist, but feel free to swap in peanut butter, cashew butter, or almond butter—whatever you've got. And don't skip the flaky salt on top—it adds just the right contrast to make these bars completely irresistible.

MAKES 12 BARS

Prep time: 10 minutes, plus 30 minutes cooling
Cook time: 25 minutes

GOOOD TO KNOW: This recipe is vegan, since the egg is replaced by applesauce, but you can swap in 1 whisked egg for the ¼ cup applesauce.

STORE IT: Keep in a sealed container in a cool, dry place for up to 4 days or freeze for up to 3 months.

REHEAT IT: From the freezer, microwave individual bars in 30-second increments until warm. Alternatively, thaw in the refrigerator overnight and microwave in 10-second increments to warm.

⅔ cup tahini
¼ cup unsweetened applesauce (see Goood to Know)
¼ cup pure maple syrup
2 tablespoons coconut sugar or light brown sugar
1 teaspoon pure vanilla extract
1¾ cups blanched almond flour
1¼ teaspoons baking soda
½ teaspoon kosher salt
½ cup chopped dairy-free chocolate or chocolate chips
Flaky salt (optional)

1. Preheat the oven to 350°F. Line a 9 × 9-inch baking dish with enough parchment paper to overhang all four sides for easy removal.

2. In a large bowl, whisk together the tahini, applesauce, maple syrup, coconut sugar, and vanilla until smooth. Stir in the almond flour, baking soda, and salt until just combined and no dry streaks remain. Gently fold in the chopped chocolate. Transfer the batter to the baking dish and spread it evenly with a rubber spatula.

3. Bake until the edges are golden brown and a toothpick inserted in the center comes out clean, 20 to 24 minutes.

4. Top with flaky salt (if using). Let the bars cool completely in the pan for at least 30 minutes. Lift the parchment paper edges to remove from the baking dish. Slice in a 3 × 4-inch grid to make 12 bars.

PISTACHIO-BERRY CRISP

Gluten-free, dairy-free option, vegetarian, vegan option

To make this dessert *as easy as possible*, I ditched the peeling, seeding, and chopping—because who has time for that? Instead, I went straight for a bag of frozen berries. Any mix works, but I usually go for a combo of raspberries, blueberries, and blackberries. Just dump them into a baking dish, whip up the crispy pistachio topping, and boom—dessert is practically done. This is the kind of crowd-friendly treat you can throw together anytime, year-round, with minimal effort but *maximum payoff*. Of course, don't forget a scoop of ice cream or a dollop of coconut whip.

SERVES 6 TO 8

Prep time: 10 minutes
Cook time: 45 minutes, plus 15 minutes cooling

To make this dairy-free and vegan: Use unsalted vegan butter.

GOOOD TO KNOW: Make this crisp your own! Swap out whatever berries you have on hand—all blueberries or strawberries or seasonal picks like black currants or gooseberries.

STORE IT: Refrigerate in a sealed container for up to 4 days or freeze for up to 3 months.

REHEAT IT: From the refrigerator, microwave individual servings until warm, 1 to 2 minutes, or return to a baking dish in a 350°F oven for 7 to 9 minutes to recrisp. From the freezer, thaw in the refrigerator for at least 8 hours, and reheat as above.

Avocado oil for the pan

FOR THE BERRY FILLING

32 ounces frozen mixed berries (about 6 cups)
¼ cup pure maple syrup
Juice of 1 lemon
2 tablespoons tapioca flour or arrowroot starch (can substitute cornstarch)
½ teaspoon ground cinnamon

FOR THE TOPPING

1¼ cups gluten-free rolled oats
⅔ cup blanched almond flour
½ cup salted roasted pistachios, chopped
⅓ cup coconut sugar or light brown sugar
½ teaspoon kosher salt
8 tablespoons (1 stick) unsalted butter, melted

1. Preheat the oven to 350°F. Lightly coat a 9 × 9-inch baking dish with oil.

2. **Make the berry filling:** In a large bowl, combine the berries, maple syrup, lemon juice, tapioca flour, and cinnamon and mix well. Transfer to the prepared baking dish and spread evenly.

3. **Make the topping:** In a medium bowl, whisk together the oats, almond flour, pistachios, coconut sugar, and salt. Stir in the melted butter and mix well. Evenly spoon the oat mixture on top of the berries, using clean hands to break up large clumps.

4. Bake until the filling is bubbling and the oat crisp is lightly golden on top, 40 to 45 minutes.

5. Let cool for 10 to 15 minutes on the counter before serving.

FUDGY SWEET POTATO BROWNIES

Gluten-free, dairy-free, vegetarian, vegan option, nut-free

This isn't a competition, but these dense, fudgy brownies might just take the crown. With a whole 1½ cups sweet potato puree "hidden" inside, beta-carotene has never tasted so good! These one-bowl wonders, topped with a thin layer of melted and cooled chocolate for that extra bite-meets-melt-in-your-mouth experience, are deeply chocolatey and ridiculously satisfying. The flaky salt on top is optional, but I *highly* recommend it.

MAKES 16 BROWNIES

Prep time: 10 minutes, plus 1 hour cooling and chilling

Cook time: 25 minutes

To make this vegan: Swap out the eggs for ½ cup applesauce.

GOOOD TO KNOW: To make the 1½ cups puree needed, roast 2 medium sweet potatoes in a 375°F oven for 40 to 50 minutes or until fork-tender. Peel and mash the potatoes very well.

STORE IT: Refrigerate in a sealed container for up to 4 days or individually wrap in plastic wrap inside a sealed bag and freeze for up to 3 months.

REHEAT IT: From the freezer, thaw on the counter for 20 to 30 minutes.

FOR THE BROWNIES

1 cup oat flour
½ cup cacao powder or unsweetened cocoa powder
½ teaspoon baking soda
½ teaspoon kosher salt
½ cup coconut sugar or light brown sugar
⅓ cup coconut oil, melted
2 large eggs, at room temperature, whisked
1 teaspoon pure vanilla extract
One 15-ounce can sweet potato puree (see Goood to Know for using fresh)

FOR THE CHOCOLATE TOPPING

½ cup roughly chopped dairy-free chocolate or chocolate chips
1 tablespoon coconut oil
Flaky salt (optional)

1. **Make the brownies:** Preheat the oven to 350°F. Line a 9 × 9-inch baking dish with parchment paper to overhang all four sides for easy removal.

2. In a medium bowl, whisk the oat flour, cacao powder, baking soda, and salt.

3. In a large bowl, whisk the coconut sugar and coconut oil until a sand-like texture. Whisk in the eggs and vanilla and add the puree and mix well. Fold in the dry ingredients until the batter is smooth and no dry streaks remain. Transfer to the prepared dish and smooth.

4. Bake until a toothpick inserted into the center comes out clean, 20 to 25 minutes. Let cool in the pan on a wire rack for at least 30 minutes.

5. **Meanwhile, make the chocolate topping:** Microwave the chocolate and coconut oil in a small microwave-safe bowl in 15-second increments, mixing well after each, until completely melted, about 1 minute. Pour over the cooled brownies and spread it into a smooth layer. Top with flaky salt (if using). Refrigerate, uncovered, until the chocolate has hardened, 30 to 40 minutes.

6. Lift the parchment edges to remove the brownies. Slice in a 4 × 4-inch grid.

CHOCOLATE-CASHEW FREEZER FUDGE

Gluten-free, dairy-free, vegetarian, vegan

This better-for-you fudge is one of the easiest no-bake desserts out there—and who *doesn't* love fudge? These little squares of chocolaty goodness come together in no time and are perfect for stashing in the freezer, ready to satisfy your sweet tooth *whenever* the craving strikes. I love making a batch during my weekly meal prep so I always have a quick, feel-good treat on hand. And if you're a peanut butter fan? Swap out the almond butter—you *won't* be disappointed.

MAKES 12 BARS

Prep time: 15 minutes, plus 2 hours freezing

GOOOD TO KNOW: Use this freezer fudge recipe as a base and make it your own! Swap the almond butter for other nut or seed butters, change up the type of nuts (or omit them completely), or mix in elements like freeze-dried fruit, coconut flakes, or your favorite candies.

1 cup creamy almond butter
⅓ cup melted coconut oil
¼ cup pure maple syrup
¼ cup cacao powder or unsweetened cocoa powder
¾ cup whole unsalted raw cashews
¾ cup chopped dairy-free chocolate or chocolate chips
Flaky salt (optional)

1. Line a 9 × 9-inch baking dish with enough parchment paper to overhang all four sides for easy removal.

2. In a large bowl, combine the almond butter, coconut oil, and maple syrup and mix well with a wooden or large metal spoon. Add the cacao powder and mix until combined. Fold in the cashews and chopped chocolate with a rubber spatula, making sure that all the cashews and chocolate pieces are fully coated in the fudge batter.

3. Pour the batter into the baking dish, spreading it evenly to all four corners using an offset or rubber spatula. Sprinkle flaky salt over the top (if using). Freeze until hardened, 1 to 2 hours.

4. Lift the parchment paper edges to remove the fudge from the baking dish. Cut in a 4 × 3-inch grid to make 12 bars.

STORE IT: Freeze in a sealed container with parchment between the fudge layers for up to 3 months.

REHEAT IT: Thaw on the counter for 10 to 15 minutes to soften slightly before enjoying.

GRAMMY'S PUMPKIN BREAD

Gluten-free, dairy-free, vegetarian, nut-free

This recipe is *extra* special to my family, and for the first time ever, I'm sharing it here. My grammy passed it down to my mom, who bakes it every single year without fail, and when I was a kid obsessed with baking, she passed it down to me. Some of my favorite memories are of the two of us in the kitchen the night before Thanksgiving, whipping up batch after batch—along with a *legendary* mess. This version of our beloved pumpkin bread has a few simple swaps, but if you want to stick with the original, then granulated sugar and all-purpose flour will do the trick. And just so you know—my grammy gave *both* versions her stamp of approval—and I'm honored to share it with you!

MAKES 8 SLICES

Prep time: 15 minutes
Cook time: 1 hour

GOOOD TO KNOW: Feel free to use all-purpose flour, if desired.

When enjoying leftovers, toast the slices in the air fryer or oven for a few minutes or microwave for about 30 seconds to warm it up. A little butter and cinnamon on top make this the best fall dessert!

STORE IT: Keep in a sealed container in a cool, dry place for up to 4 days.

REHEAT IT: You can toast leftover slices in the air fryer or oven for a few minutes or microwave for 30 seconds to warm.

½ cup avocado oil, plus more for the pan
1½ cups coconut sugar or granulated sugar
2 large eggs
¾ cup canned pumpkin puree
1¾ cups gluten-free 1:1 baking flour (see Goood to Know)
1 teaspoon baking soda
½ teaspoon baking powder
½ teaspoon ground cinnamon
½ teaspoon ground cloves
½ teaspoon ground nutmeg
½ teaspoon kosher salt

1. Preheat the oven to 325°F. Lightly coat a 9 × 5-inch loaf pan with oil and line with enough parchment paper to overhang all four sides for easy removal.

2. In a large bowl, whisk together the coconut sugar and the ½ cup avocado oil until a sand-like texture forms. Add the eggs and continue to whisk until thoroughly combined. Stir in the pumpkin puree.

3. In a medium bowl, whisk together the flour, baking soda, baking powder, cinnamon, cloves, nutmeg, and salt. Add the dry ingredients to the wet ingredients and stir until just combined. Add ⅓ cup water and continue stirring until the batter is completely smooth and evenly mixed. Transfer the batter to the loaf pan and spread it out evenly with a rubber spatula.

4. Bake until the edges are crisp, the top is golden, and a toothpick inserted into the center comes out clean, about 1 hour. Let the bread cool completely in the pan. Lift the parchment paper edges to remove the bread from the pan. Cut into 8 slices and serve.

EVERY INGREDIENT YOU'LL NEED

To make things easier, I've created a master list of all the ingredients used in every recipe. Of course you don't have to buy everything here, but this list is an easy way to get an idea of the ingredients used throughout the book. Moving, looking to stock up, or don't know what's good to have on hand? You can also use this list as a reference for keeping basics in your pantry, fridge, and freezer.

OILS & VINEGARS
Apple cider vinegar
Avocado oil
Balsamic vinegar
Coconut oil
Olive oil
Red wine vinegar
Rice vinegar
Toasted sesame oil

SWEETENERS, SAUCES & MORE
Baking powder
Baking soda
Buffalo sauce
Chipotle peppers in adobo
Coconut aminos
Coconut sugar
Confectioners' sugar
Dijon mustard
Nutritional yeast
Pure maple syrup
Raw honey
Sriracha
Thai red curry paste
White miso paste

CANNED GOODS, BROTHS & BEANS
Artichokes (water-packed)
Black beans
Butter beans
Cannellini or navy beans
Capers
Chickpeas
Coconut cream
Crushed tomatoes
Full-fat coconut milk
Kidney beans
Light coconut milk
Low-sodium beef broth
Low-sodium chicken broth
Low-sodium vegetable broth
Marinara sauce
Pinto beans
Pitted Kalamata olives
Roasted red peppers (water-packed)
Sun-dried tomatoes (oil-packed)
Tomato paste

SPREADS, BUTTERS, NUTS & SEEDS
Almond butter (creamy)
Cashew butter
Chia seeds
Peanut butter (creamy)
Sunflower butter
Tahini
Unsalted raw almonds
Unsalted raw cashews
Unsalted raw walnuts

GRAINS & FLOURS
Arborio rice
Blanched almond flour
Brown rice
Coconut flour
Gluten-free 1:1 baking flour
Gluten-free panko bread crumbs
Gluten-free rolled oats
Jasmine rice
Oat flour
Pasta (brown rice, corn-and-rice-based, or regular)
Quinoa (white or tricolor)
Stone-ground instant yellow-corn polenta
Tapioca flour or arrowroot starch (can substitute cornstarch)
Tortillas (corn, almond flour, chickpea flour)
Wild rice blend or wild rice

FRUIT
Apples
Avocados
Bananas
Blueberries (fresh or frozen)
Cranberries (dried)
Dates
Lemons
Limes
Mangoes
Oranges
Pineapple
Raspberries (fresh or frozen)
Strawberries (frozen)

VEGETABLES
Acorn squash
Arugula
Asparagus
Baby spinach
Beets
Broccoli
Brussels sprouts
Butternut squash
Cabbage
Carrots (whole and shredded)
Cauliflower
Celery
Cherry tomatoes
Corn (frozen, canned, or fresh)
Cucumbers
Eggplant
Fennel
Garlic
Ginger
Green and red bell peppers
Green beans
Green onion
Green peas (fresh or frozen)
Jalapeño peppers
Japanese sweet potatoes
Leeks
Lettuce (romaine or butter lettuce)
Mushrooms (white, Baby Bella, oyster, wild, etc.)
Parsnips
Poblano peppers
Red onions
Roma tomatoes
Russet potatoes
Shallots
Shredded curly kale
Spaghetti squash
Summer squash
Sweet potatoes
Yellow onions
Yukon Gold potatoes
Zucchini

FRESH HERBS
Basil
Chives
Cilantro
Dill
Mint
Parsley
Rosemary
Sage
Thyme

MEAT
Beef short ribs (bone-in)
Chicken (whole)
Chicken breasts (boneless, skinless)
Chicken thighs (boneless, skinless)
Flank steak or skirt steak
Ground beef (85% lean)
Ground chicken (90% lean)
Ground lamb (85% lean)
Ground pork (90% lean)
Ground sausage (spicy or sweet Italian, removed from links and casings discarded, if necessary)
Ground turkey (93/7)
Italian-style chicken sausage (fully cooked)
Pork chops (boneless)
Pork shoulder or pork butt
Pork tenderloin
Prosciutto
Shaved Angus steak
Uncured bacon
Uncured pork and beef pepperoni

FISH & SHELLFISH
Medium peeled and deveined raw shrimp
Salmon fillets (skinless)
Swordfish steaks

PLANT-BASED PROTEIN
Firm or high-protein super-firm tofu
Lentils
Shelled edamame (fresh or frozen)
Tempeh

DAIRY, DAIRY SUBSTITUTES & EGGS
Butter (unsalted dairy or unsalted vegan butter)
Cheddar cheese
Eggs
Feta cheese (block and crumbled)
Goat cheese (soft)
Gruyère cheese
Milk (whole, soy, nut, coconut, or oat)
Mozzarella cheese
Parmesan
Part-skim ricotta cheese
Plain whole-milk or low-fat Greek yogurt or dairy-free yogurt
Shredded dairy-free cheese
4% milkfat small-curd cottage cheese

SPICES
Cayenne pepper
Chili powder
Dried basil
Dried oregano
Dried rosemary
Dried thyme
Garlic powder
Ground allspice
Ground black pepper
Ground cardamom
Ground cinnamon
Ground cloves
Ground cumin
Ground ginger
Ground nutmeg
Ground sage
Ground turmeric
Kosher salt
Onion powder
Red pepper flakes
Sesame seeds
Smoked paprika

SWEETS & EXTRAS
Almond extract
Cacao powder
Chocolate chips
Ground flaxseed
Pumpkin puree
Pure vanilla extract
Unsweetened shredded coconut
Vegetarian vanilla protein powder

EVERY INGREDIENT YOU'LL NEED

SEASONAL PRODUCE LIST

I've talked about the benefits of eating seasonally for taste, nutrients, accessibility, and affordability. Here's a quick guide to common seasonal produce during each season. If you shop at a farmers' market or take advantage of Community Supported Agriculture (CSA), you'll likely find some combination of the following in each season.

WINTER
Acorn squash
Beets
Broccoli
Brussels sprouts
Butternut squash
Cabbage
Carrots
Curly kale
Leeks
Lemons
Limes
Onions
Oranges
Parsnips
Pomegranates
Potatoes
Pumpkin
Spaghetti squash
Sweet potatoes
Turnips

SPRING
Artichokes
Asparagus
Broccoli
Cabbage
Carrots
Collard greens
Garlic
Kale
Lemons
Lettuce (arugula, butter, and romaine)
Limes
Mushrooms
Onions
Peas
Rhubarb
Spinach
Strawberries
Turnips

SUMMER
Beets
Bell peppers
Blackberries
Blueberries
Corn
Cucumbers
Eggplant
Garlic
Green beans
Lemons
Limes
Mangoes
Raspberries
Strawberries
Summer squash
Tomatoes
Zucchini

FALL
Acorn squash
Apples
Beets
Bell peppers
Broccoli
Brussels sprouts
Butternut squash
Cabbage
Carrots
Cauliflower
Celery
Collard greens
Cranberries
Garlic
Ginger
Green beans
Kale
Lemons
Lettuce (butter and romaine)
Limes
Mushrooms
Onions
Parsnips
Pomegranates
Potatoes
Pumpkin
Radishes
Spaghetti squash
Spinach
Sweet potatoes
Turnips

SUBSTITUTION GUIDES

Making the recipes in this book meet the needs of as many people as possible was a primary focus of mine. While I've sprinkled my tips for swaps and substitutions throughout, below are guides for my top suggestions. Remember that each recipe was tested to work best with the ingredients listed, so I can't guarantee perfect results when swaps are made, but I want you to feel empowered to make substitutions as needed and adjust accordingly.

PLANT-BASED SUBSTITUTIONS

While plant-based recipes are shared throughout this book (including in the Plant-Powered chapter, page 220), almost every recipe can be modified to meet a plant-based diet. My suggested swaps below are for plant-based folks, or those who just want to include more plant-based options in their diet. Many of these suggestions are detailed in the headnotes or Goood to Know tip for each recipe. When it comes to dairy, especially cheese, if the suggested swap doesn't sound good to you, you can typically just omit it.

INGREDIENT	SUBSTITUTION OPTIONS
Eggs	In savory dishes: egg substitute (mung bean– or chickpea-based); in baking: applesauce, flax eggs, chia eggs (results can vary)
Boneless, skinless chicken breast or thighs	Firm or high-protein super-firm tofu, tempeh, seitan*, roasted chickpeas, sautéed cannellini or navy beans, Great Northern beans, roasted or sautéed mushrooms
Ground chicken, turkey, lamb, pork, beef, or sausage	Plant-based crumbles, plant-based veggie meatballs, plant-based veggie sausage, crumbled firm or high-protein super-firm tofu, roasted chickpeas, sautéed beans of choice, jackfruit, lentils
Precooked sausage (pork or chicken)	Plant-based veggie sausage, roasted chickpeas, roasted or sautéed mushrooms, edamame, roasted cauliflower florets
Shaved or whole steak	Roasted or sautéed mushrooms
Pork chops or tenderloin	Firm tofu, roasted cauliflower steaks
Pork shoulder (shredded)	Jackfruit, roasted or sautéed mushrooms, roasted cabbage
Salmon or swordfish	Roasted chickpeas, firm or high-protein super-firm tofu, jackfruit
Shrimp	Roasted chickpeas, heart of palm, roasted cauliflower florets, edamame
Cheddar, mozzarella, or Gruyère cheese	Dairy-free shredded cheese (coconut oil, cashew, or soy based), nutritional yeast, soaked and blended cashews
Feta or goat cheese	Dairy-free feta cheese
Parmesan	Nutritional yeast, finely processed cashews
Ricotta cheese	Dairy-free ricotta cheese
Whole milk	Soy milk, unflavored almond milk, oat milk
Unsalted butter	Unsalted vegan butter, coconut oil
Greek yogurt	Cashew or coconut-based dairy-free yogurt
Cottage cheese	Dairy-free ricotta cheese, silken tofu (blended)

*Contains gluten

PROTEIN SUBSTITUTIONS

INGREDIENT	SUBSTITUTION OPTIONS
Boneless, skinless chicken breast	Boneless, skinless turkey breast; boneless, skinless chicken thighs
Boneless, skinless chicken thighs	Boneless, skinless chicken breast; bone-in, skin-on chicken thighs
Ground chicken	Ground turkey, ground pork, ground beef
Ground turkey	Ground chicken, ground pork, ground beef
Ground lamb	Ground beef, ground pork, ground chicken
Ground pork	Ground sausage (pork or chicken), ground beef, ground chicken
Ground sausage (pork or chicken)	Ground pork, ground chicken, ground beef
Fully cooked chicken sausage	Fully cooked pork sausage, boneless chicken breast (cooked), ground chicken (cooked)
Ground beef	Ground turkey, ground lamb, shaved steak
Shaved Angus steak	Ground beef
Pork chops	Bone-in, skin-on chicken thighs
Uncured bacon	Turkey bacon, precooked pork sausage, precooked chicken sausage
Salmon	Cod; haddock; halibut; pollock; shrimp; canned salmon; boneless, skinless chicken breast; boneless, skinless chicken thighs
Shrimp	Scallops; salmon; cod; haddock; pollock; boneless, skinless chicken breast; boneless, skinless chicken thighs
Firm tofu	High-protein super-firm tofu; tempeh; seitan*; mushrooms; jackfruit; salmon; boneless, skinless chicken breast; boneless, skinless chicken thighs
Tempeh	Firm or high-protein super-firm tofu; seitan*; mushrooms; jackfruit; salmon; boneless, skinless chicken breast; boneless, skinless chicken thighs
Black beans	Pinto beans, kidney beans, cannellini or navy beans, chickpeas, lentils
Butter beans	Cannellini or navy beans, Great Northern beans, fava beans, chickpeas, edamame
Cannellini or navy beans	Great Northern beans, butter beans, chickpeas, pinto beans
Chickpeas	Cannellini or navy beans, pinto beans, butter beans, fava beans, lentils, edamame
Kidney beans	Black beans, pinto beans, cannellini or navy beans
Pinto beans	Kidney beans, black beans, cannellini or navy beans
Edamame	Sugar snap peas, green peas, fava beans, black-eyed peas, butter beans
Almonds	Cashews, sunflower seeds, macadamia nuts, walnuts, pumpkin seeds
Cashews	Almonds, sunflower seeds, macadamia nuts, walnuts
Walnuts	Pine nuts, pumpkin seeds, cashews, pecans
Eggs	In savory dishes: egg substitute (mung bean– or chickpea-based); in baking: applesauce, flax eggs, chia eggs (results can vary)

*Contains gluten.

STAPLES, CANNED & PACKAGED SUBSTITUTIONS

INGREDIENT	SUBSTITUTION OPTIONS
Avocado oil	Olive oil or any neutral oil
Olive oil	Avocado oil or any neutral oil
Toasted sesame oil	Untoasted sesame oil, peanut oil, walnut oil, avocado oil
Apple cider vinegar	White wine vinegar, champagne vinegar, rice vinegar
Balsamic vinegar	Red wine vinegar, coconut aminos, reduced-sodium tamari, gluten-free reduced-sodium soy sauce, reduced-sodium soy sauce*
Rice vinegar	Apple cider vinegar, white wine vinegar, champagne vinegar, sherry vinegar
Red wine vinegar	Balsamic vinegar, sherry vinegar, white wine vinegar
Pure maple syrup	Honey, date syrup, agave nectar
Honey	Pure maple syrup, date syrup, agave nectar
Coconut aminos	Reduced-sodium tamari, gluten-free reduced-sodium soy sauce, reduced-sodium soy sauce*
Sriracha	Chili garlic sauce, red pepper flakes, gochujang*
Tapioca flour	Arrowroot starch, cornstarch
Chicken broth (low-sodium)	Chicken bone broth, vegetable broth, bouillon powder (mixed with water), (all low-sodium)
Vegetable broth (low-sodium)	Chicken broth, chicken bone broth, bouillon powder (mixed with water) (all low-sodium)
Beef broth (low-sodium)	Beef bone broth, mushroom broth, chicken broth (all low-sodium)
Full-fat coconut milk	Light cream, whole milk, or whole-milk or low-fat Greek yogurt thinned with water
Coconut cream	Heavy cream, full-fat coconut milk
Rice	Quinoa, cauliflower rice, broccoli rice, orzo, couscous*, farro* (when cooked separately)
Quinoa	Rice, orzo, couscous*, farro*, cauliflower rice, broccoli rice (when cooked separately)
Pasta	Heart of palm pasta, spaghetti squash, zucchini noodles, shirataki noodles
Chipotle peppers in adobo	Smoked paprika, ground chipotle powder, chipotle hot sauce
Miso paste	Tahini, coconut aminos, reduced-sodium tamari, gluten-free reduced-sodium soy sauce, reduced-sodium soy sauce*, fish sauce
Tahini	Sunflower butter, almond butter, cashew butter, whole-milk or low-fat Greek yogurt
Peanut butter	Almond butter, sunflower butter, cashew butter, tahini
Almond butter	Cashew butter, peanut butter, sunflower butter, tahini
Cashew butter	Almond butter, sunflower butter, tahini, peanut butter
Buffalo sauce	Cayenne pepper hot sauce and melted butter (4:1 ratio)
Gluten-free all-purpose flour	All-purpose flour*
Nutritional yeast	Parmesan, miso paste, brewer's yeast*

*Contains gluten

SUBSTITUTION GUIDES

ACKNOWLEDGMENTS

There are so many people who made this book possible, but it all started with my amazing followers—thank you for giving me your time, attention, and trust daily. To my incredible social media community, newsletter subscribers, and beyond: Thank you for making my dreams a reality. Your support gave me the confidence to write this book. You cooked along with me, followed my meal plans, used my strategies, and shared them with your friends, family, coworkers, and more. Every single tag, mention, message, and comment has made a difference and directly inspired the contents of this book. I hope it serves as a small token of my appreciation.

To my husband, Brian: From day one you've supported my dream and never doubted I would achieve it—even when I felt like giving up. When I decided I wanted to write a cookbook, you showed up for me in every way, just like you always do. From testing recipes all day long for the proposal to celebrating with me when I turned in my final manuscript, you've been by my side every step of the way. You're my rock, the most selfless person I know, and my why. I'm so lucky to have you in my corner.

To my parents, siblings, and entire family: I couldn't ask for a better support system—both in life and navigating this process. So many of the recipes in the book are inspired by you, because cooking for you all is what started my journey years ago and will forever be my favorite thing to do. Thank you for being so understanding over the past two years as I poured myself into writing, and for checking in after late nights and long testing days. I'm so excited to finally share this with you.

To my literary agent, Andrea Barzvi: When we first met, I felt like someone finally "got" me and understood what I was capable of. You've not only made it your priority to make the book as perfect as possible, but you've also made me a more confident business owner, writer, and person. Thank you for believing in me from the beginning and shaping the book into what it is today. Your thoughtfulness on every single detail means the world to me and cannot be overstated.

To my collaborator, Lauren Deen: Being a first-time author is scary, but every step of the way you made me feel comfortable, confident, and supported. This book would not be the beautiful, information-packed resource it is without your incredible intentionality and hard work. I couldn't have asked for a better partner in this process, and I'll always treasure our long Zoom calls and late-night email notes. Here's to successfully weighing our halved cherry tomatoes and measuring our diced onion—even when it gave us both headaches.

A very special thanks to Sarah Zorn for the hours of recipe testing and suggestions and support—125+ recipes in a short stretch was a challenge, and you rose to it!

To my manager, Deanna Ritter: From the first spark of an idea to the final stretch, you've been there for me in every way. Thank you for being my biggest advocate, sounding board, and champion of every idea (yes, all of them). I'm lucky to have someone who believes in this mission as much as I do on my side, and I can't wait to see what else we create together.

To my incredible team member Kate Klein: Joining mid-project as a new member of my team was overwhelming and confusing, but you took on every task perfectly and handled everything with grace and precision. Thank you for treating my recipes with such care, helping shape wild ideas into reality, and doing whatever was needed to bring this book to life. I'll forever be grateful to you for your dedication to this project and willingness to do anything needed to make it happen.

To my photography team—Ashleigh Amoroso, Ashley Holt, Yvette Dizon Hunter, Audrey Davis, Ish Holmes, and Liese Rose: I came into our shoot knowing I wanted the photos to be unlike any other cookbook out there, and you all delivered beyond my wildest dreams. You made my goal of making nutrient-dense, veggie-packed food exciting and bold a reality and made it look so easy (although I know it wasn't). Not only did the photos completely elevate the book, but you also made the process so much fun. Preparing, styling, and shooting more than 125 recipes in two weeks is no small feat, but you made it feel joyful and I'm so amazed by all of you. It will always be one of my favorite parts of creating the book and a memory I'll cherish forever.

To my illustrator, Cassidy Hart: Your illustrations beautifully captured the spirit of the book and brought personality and clarity to its pages. (And thank you for doing it on such a tight deadline!)

To my editor, Cassie Jones: From the beginning, even as a first-time author, you trusted me and gave me the creative freedom to make this book my own. Thank you for believing in me, supporting all my choices, paying attention to every detail, and answering all my questions along the way and providing feedback that made the book stronger. I'm so proud of how the book has evolved since we first discussed it—your perspective has been so valuable through every stage. It has been such an honor to work with you and the entire HarperCollins team, and a special thanks to Nicole Braun, Shelby Peak, Alison Bloomer, Julianna Lee, Anna Brower, Tess Day, and Melissa Esner for each of your important contributions.

Copley and Cashew: I know you can't read, but having you two at my side each day kept me sane. Thanks for doing the heavy lifting on this one and always cleaning up the scraps.

UNIVERSAL CONVERSION CHART

OVEN TEMPERATURE EQUIVALENTS

250°F = 120°C
275°F = 135°C
300°F = 150°C
325°F = 160°C
350°F = 180°C
375°F = 190°C
400°F = 200°C
425°F = 220°C
450°F = 230°C
475°F = 240°C
500°F = 260°C

MEASUREMENT EQUIVALENTS

Measurements should always be level unless directed otherwise.

⅛ teaspoon = 0.5 mL
¼ teaspoon = 1 mL
½ teaspoon = 2 mL
1 teaspoon = 5 mL
1 tablespoon = 3 teaspoons = ½ fluid ounce = 15 mL
2 tablespoons = ⅛ cup = 1 fluid ounce = 30 mL
4 tablespoons = ¼ cup = 2 fluid ounces = 60 mL
5⅓ tablespoons = ⅓ cup = 3 fluid ounces = 80 mL
8 tablespoons = ½ cup = 4 fluid ounces = 120 mL
10⅔ tablespoons = ⅔ cup = 5 fluid ounces = 160 mL
12 tablespoons = ¾ cup = 6 fluid ounces = 180 mL
16 tablespoons = 1 cup = 8 fluid ounces = 240 mL

INDEX

Note: Page references in *italics* indicate photographs.

A

Almond-Vanilla Chia Pudding, *66*, 69
Apple Fennel Pan Sauce, Seared Pork Chops with, 262–63, *263*
Artichoke(s)
    Mediterranean-Inspired Chickpea Chopped Salad, *94*, 95
    and Spinach Dip, Dairy-Free, 130–31, *131*
Asparagus
    Lemon-Caper Shrimp and Linguine, 266–67, *267*
    and Prosciutto, Sheet Pan Pesto Pizza with, 201–2, *203*
Avocado(s)
    Chickpea Guacamole, *127*, 128
    Corn, and Black Bean Dip, *132*, 133
    Slaw, Spiced Sweet Potato Tacos with, 235–37, *236*
    Toast, Hidden Protein Smashed, 88, *89*

B

Bacon and Chive Egg Muffins, *76*, 77–78
Banana(s)
    -Chai Smoothie, 63, *64*
    Green Smoothies, Four Ways, 63, *64–65*
    Orange Cream Smoothie, 63, *64*
    and Peanut Butter Smoothie, 63, *65*
Barbecue Sauce, Tangy Maple, *297*, 298
Basil
    Dairy-Free Walnut Pesto, *300*, 301
    Marry Me Turkey Meatballs, 182–83, *183*
    -Strawberry Smoothie, 63, *65*
    -Tomato Butter Bean Skillet, *242*, 243
Bean(s). *See also* Chickpea(s); Edamame
    Barbecue Chicken Chopped Salad, *116*, 117
    and Beef Taco Skillet, Stovetop, 144–45, *145*
    Black, and Poblano Tacos, Baked, *214*, 215–16
    Black, and Sweet Potato Bowls, Chipotle, 113–14, *115*
    Black, Avocado, and Corn Dip, *132*, 133
    Black, Breakfast Burritos, Sheet Pan, 79–80, *81*
    Black, Soup, Pantry Staples, 226–27, *227*
    Butter, Tomato-Basil Skillet, Saucy, *242*, 243
    Hidden Protein Smashed Avocado Toast, 88, *89*
    Mom's Game-Day Chili with Sweet Honey Bread, 206–8, *207*
    Not-Your-Average Burrito Bowls with Sheet Pan Salsa, 193–94, *195*
    types of, 21
    Weeknight Honey-Garlic Turkey Skillet, *154*, 155
    White, Spicy Sausage, and Kale Soup, 172–73, *173*
Beef
    and Bean Taco Skillet, Stovetop, 144–45, *145*
    and Broccoli, Saucy, 180, *181*
    Caramelized Onion, Steak, and Cheese Skillet, 152, *153*
    French Onion Meatball Skillet, *198*, 199–200
    Mom's Game-Day Chili with Sweet Honey Bread, 206–8, *207*
    Skirt Steak with Chimichurri, *258*, 259
    Slow Cooker Short Ribs, 253–54, *255*
Beet
    Roasted Brussels Sprouts, and Sweet Potato Salad, 92–93, *93*
    and Whipped Feta Dip, 126, *127*
Berry(ies)
    Dark Chocolate and Raspberry Chia Pudding, *66*, 68
    Dreamy Blueberry Matcha Latte, *305*, 309
    Lemon-Blueberry Overnight Oats, *60*, 62
    -Pistachio Crisp, 328, *329*
    Strawberry-Basil Smoothie, 63, *65*
    Tart Raspberry-Honey Lemonade, *312*, 313
Biscuits, High-Protein Breakfast, Two Ways, *72*, 73–75
Blueberry
    -Lemon Overnight Oats, *60*, 62
    Matcha Latte, Dreamy, *305*, 309

Bread
    Hidden Protein Smashed Avocado Toast, 88, *89*
    Pumpkin, Grammy's, 334, *342*
    Sweet Honey, *207*, 208
Broccoli
    and Beef, Saucy, 180, *181*
    Cheddar, and Chicken Breakfast Biscuits, 74–75, *75*
    Jenn's Viral Baked Feta, Chicken, Quinoa, and Veggies, *186*, 187
    Roasted Lemon, with Feta, 287, *289*
Broccolini and Tofu, Sweet and Spicy, 168–69, *169*
Broth, 21
Brownies, Fudgy Sweet Potato, 330–31, *331*
Brussels Sprouts
    Roasted, Sweet Potato, and Beet Salad, 92–93, *93*
    Sesame-Crisped, *284*, 285
Buffalo Chickpea Stuffed Sweet Potatoes, *150*, 151
Buffalo Tempeh Strips, Crusted, 246–47, *247*
Burrito Bowls, Not-Your-Average, with Sheet Pan Salsa, 193–94, *195*
Burritos, Sheet Pan Black Bean Breakfast, 79–80, *81*

C

Cabbage
    Barbecue Chicken Chopped Salad, *116*, 117
    Chipotle Sweet Potato and Black Bean Bowls, 113–14, *115*
    Pineapple-Shrimp Lettuce Wraps, 106–7, *107*
    Spiced Sweet Potato Tacos with Avocado Slaw, 235–37, *236*
Cake, Orange-Cardamom Olive Oil, *320*, 321–22
Canned goods, 21
Carrot Slaw, Crunchy Pork Lettuce Wraps with, 108–9, *109*
Cashew(s)
    -Chocolate Freezer Fudge, *332*, 333
    Dairy-Free Spinach and Artichoke Dip, 130–31, *131*
    Sheet Pan Butternut Squash Mac and "Cheese," *232*, 233–34
    Sun-Dried Tomato Cream, Sheet Pan Gnocchi with, 230–31, *231*
Cauliflower
    Banana-Chai Smoothie, 63, *64*
    and Chickpea Bowls, Herby, with Lemon-Dill Sauce, 174–75, *175*
    Orange Cream Smoothie, 63, *64*
    and Parsnip Puree, 288, *289*
    Pizza Skillet, 204–5, *205*
Cheese
    Bacon and Chive Egg Muffins, *76*, 77–78
    Baked Black Bean and Poblano Tacos, *214*, 215–16
    Caramelized Onion, and Steak Skillet, 152, *153*
    Cauliflower Pizza Skillet, 204–5, *205*
    Creamy Spinach Chicken, 196–97, *197*
    Deconstructed Turkey Lasagna Skillet, 188–89, *189*
    Dump-and-Bake Hidden Protein Pasta, *158*, 159
    French Onion Meatball Skillet, *198*, 199–200
    Garlicky Mushroom and Sage Risotto, 256–57, *257*
    Goat, and Kale Egg Muffins, *76*, 77–78
    Goat, Leek, and Potato Frittata, 86–87, *87*
    Goat, Spinach, and Sun-Dried Tomato Stuffed Chicken, 140–41, *141*
    Grain-Free Chicken Parmesan, 275–76, *277*
    Greek-Style Crispy Chickpea Bowls, 118–19, *119*
    High-Protein Breakfast Biscuits, Two Ways, *72*, 73–75
    High-Protein Egg Muffins, Two Ways, *76*, 77–78
    Jenn's Viral Baked Feta, Chicken, Quinoa, and Veggies, *186*, 187
    Mashed Chipotle Chickpea Quesadillas, 244–45, *245*
    Mediterranean-Inspired Chickpea Chopped Salad, *94*, 95
    Mediterranean-Inspired Salmon and Orzo Bake, *146*, 147
    Mediterranean-Inspired Smashed Tacos, 264–65, *265*
    One-Pot Quinoa Bake with Butternut Squash, Kale, and Feta, 156, *157*
    Roasted Lemon Broccoli with Feta, 287, *289*
    Sheet Pan Pesto Pizza with Asparagus and Prosciutto, 201–2, *203*
    Spiced Lamb Meatballs with Tomato-Cucumber Salad, 164–65, *165*
    Stovetop Beef and Bean Taco Skillet, 144–45, *145*
    Street-Corn-Inspired Shrimp Skillet, 166–67, *167*
    Whipped Feta and Beet Dip, 126, *127*
Cherry Tonic, Sleepytime, 314, *315*
Chia (seeds), 22
    Green Smoothies, Four Ways, 63, *64–65*
    Overnight Oats, Two Ways, *60*, 61–62

Pudding, Three Ways, *66,* 67–69
Salty Peanut Butter Pretzel Energy Balls, 318, *319*

Chicken
  Barbecue, and Pineapple Lettuce Cups, Sheet Pan, *178,* 179
  Barbecue, Chopped Salad, *116,* 117
  Broccoli, and Cheddar Breakfast Biscuits, 74–75, *75*
  Cilantro-Lime Pasta Salad, 101–2, *103*
  Creamy Spinach, 196–97, *197*
  cutting into serving pieces, 252
  Feta, Quinoa, and Veggies, Jenn's Viral Baked, *186,* 187
  Garlic and Herb Spatchcock, *250,* 251–52
  Hidden Veggie Spaghetti with Crispy Kale and Sausage, *272,* 273–74
  No-Fail Baked, 102
  Parmesan, Grain-Free, 275–76, *277*
  Pot Pie Soup, 138, *139*
  Spinach, Goat Cheese, and Sun-Dried Tomato Stuffed, 140–41, *141*
  Thighs, Lemony, and Rice, 136–37, *137*
  and Vegetable Skewers, Greek-Style, *190,* 191–92

Chicken Sausage
  Spicy Sausage, White Bean, and Kale Soup, 172–73, *173*
  Spinach, and Rice, One-Pot, *170,* 171

Chickpea(s)
  Bowls, Greek-Style Crispy, 118–19, *119*
  Buffalo, Stuffed Sweet Potatoes, *150,* 151
  and Cauliflower Bowls, Herby, with Lemon-Dill Sauce, 174–75, *175*
  Chopped Salad, Mediterranean-Inspired, *94,* 95
  Garlicky Hummus, *127,* 129
  Golden Turmeric Herby Quinoa Salad, *98,* 99–100
  Guacamole, *127,* 128
  Quesadillas, Mashed Chipotle, 244–45, *245*
  Snack Mix, Crispy Ranch, 122, *123*

Chili, Mom's Game-Day, with Sweet Honey Bread, 206–8, *207*

Chocolate
  -Cashew Freezer Fudge, *332,* 333
  Chip Tahini Cookie Bars, *326,* 327
  Cookie Dough Overnight Oats, *60,* 61
  Dark, and Raspberry Chia Pudding, *66,* 68
  Fudgy Sweet Potato Brownies, 330–31, *331*
  Hot, Rich and Creamy Vegan, 310, *311*
  Mocha Brownie Cream Pie Sandwiches, 323–24, *325*
  Salty Peanut Butter Pretzel Energy Balls, 318, *319*

Cilantro
  -Edamame Dip, High-Protein, 125, *127*
  -Lime Pasta Salad, 101–2, *103*
  Sauce, Creamy, 294, *297*

Coconut. *See also* Coconut milk
  -Mango Chia Pudding, *66,* 67

Coconut aminos, 20

Coconut milk, 21
  Coconut Curry Soup with Tofu and Rice Noodles, 224–25, *225*
  Coconut-Mango Chia Pudding, *66,* 67
  Coconut Rice, *218,* 219
  Rich and Creamy Vegan Hot Chocolate, 310, *311*

Cookie(s)
  Bars, Tahini Chocolate Chip, *326,* 327
  Mocha Brownie Cream Pie Sandwiches, 323–24, *325*

Corn
  Avocado, and Black Bean Dip, *132,* 133
  Barbecue Chicken Chopped Salad, *116,* 117
  Cilantro-Lime Pasta Salad, 101–2, *103*
  Street-, -Inspired Shrimp Skillet, 166–67, *167*

Crackers, Baked Sweet Potato, *123,* 124

Cucumber(s)
  Garlicky Sauce, 299, *300*
  Salad, Chilled, *218,* 219
  -Tomato Salad, Spiced Lamb Meatballs with, 164–65, *165*

D

Dips
  Avocado, Corn, and Black Bean, *132,* 133
  Chickpea Guacamole, *127,* 128
  Garlicky Hummus, *127,* 129
  High-Protein Cilantro-Edamame, 125, *127*
  Spinach and Artichoke, Dairy-Free, 130–31, *131*
  Whipped Feta and Beet, 126, *127*

Dressings
  Herby Yogurt Ranch, *300,* 302
  Lemony Red Wine Vinaigrette, 303
  Maple-Tahini, 93

E

Edamame
  -Cilantro Dip, High-Protein, 125, *127*
  Crispy Quinoa, and Peanut Salad, *104,* 105

Eggplant
    Sheet Pan Gnocchi with Sun-Dried Tomato Cashew Cream, 230–31, *231*
Egg(s)
    Casserole, Pesto and Roasted Red Pepper, *82*, 83
    Chipotle Sweet Potato Breakfast Hash, 84–85, *85*
    High-Protein Breakfast Biscuits, Two Ways, *72*, 73–75
    Leek, Potato, and Goat Cheese Frittata, 86–87, *87*
    Muffins, High-Protein, Two Ways, *76*, 77–78
    Sheet Pan Black Bean Breakfast Burritos, 79–80, *81*
Energy Balls, Salty Peanut Butter Pretzel, 318, *319*
Equipment, 40
Espresso
    Mocha Brownie Cream Pie Sandwiches, 323–24, *325*
    Salted Tahini-Maple Latte, *304*, 307

F

Fish. *See* Salmon; Swordfish
Flours, 22
Food safety guidelines, 30–31
Freezing food, 35
Frittata, Leek, Potato, and Goat Cheese, 86–87, *87*
Fruits. *See also specific fruits*
    seasonal produce list, 338
Fudge, Chocolate-Cashew Freezer, *332*, 333

G

Garlic
    Garlicky Hummus, *127*, 129
    Garlicky Mushroom and Sage Risotto, 256–57, *257*
    and Herb Spatchcock Chicken, *250*, 251–52
    Roasted, Mashed Potatoes, 280, *281*
Gnocchi, Sheet Pan, with Sun-Dried Tomato Cashew Cream, 230–31, *231*
Grains, 22
Greens. *See also specific greens*
    Green Smoothies, Four Ways, 63, *64–65*
Guacamole, Chickpea, *127*, 128

H

Herb(s). *See also specific herbs*
    dried, 23
    and Garlic Spatchcock Chicken, *250*, 251–52
    Golden Turmeric Herby Quinoa, *98*, 99–100
    Herby Yogurt Ranch Dressing, *300*, 302
    Skirt Steak with Chimichurri, *258*, 259
Honey
    Bread, Sweet, *207*, 208
    -Raspberry Lemonade, Tart, *312*, 313
Hummus, Garlicky, *127*, 129

K

Kale
    Barbecue Chicken Chopped Salad, *116*, 117
    Butternut Squash, and Feta, One-Pot Quinoa Bake with, 156, *157*
    Crispy, and Sausage, Hidden Veggie Spaghetti with, *272*, 273–74
    and Goat Cheese Egg Muffins, *76*, 77–78
    Salad, Goes-with-Anything, 283, *284*
    Spicy Sausage, and White Bean Soup, 172–73, *173*
Knife skills, 39

L

Lamb
    Bolognese, Brian's Favorite, 260–61, *261*
    Meatballs, Spiced, with Tomato-Cucumber Salad, 164–65, *165*
    Mediterranean-Inspired Smashed Tacos, 264–65, *265*
Lemon
    -Blueberry Overnight Oats, *60*, 62
    Broccoli, Roasted, with Feta, 287, *289*
    -Dill Sauce, Herby Chickpea and Cauliflower Bowls with, 174–75, *175*
    Lemony Red Wine Vinaigrette, 303
    Tart Raspberry-Honey Lemonade, *312*, 313
Lentil Salad, Farmers' Market, 96, *97*
Lettuce Cups, Sheet Pan Barbecue Chicken and Pineapple, *178*, 179
Lettuce Wraps
    Crunchy Pork, with Carrot Slaw, 108–9, *109*
    Pineapple-Shrimp, 106–7, *107*

M

Mango
    -Coconut Chia Pudding, *66*, 67
    Salsa, Blackened Swordfish with, 268–69, *269*
Maple
    Barbecue Sauce, Tangy, *297*, 298
    -Dijon Pork Tenderloin, 212–13, *213*

-Tahini Dressing, 93
-Tahini Latte, Salted, *304,* 307
Matcha
    Blueberry Latte, Dreamy, *305,* 309
    Latte, My Everyday, *305,* 306
Meal planning, 11–26
    benefits of, 2
    fridge and freezer foods, 24–26
    grocery lists, 16–17
    grocery shopping, 28–29
    how to get it done, 10
    identifying your style, 9
    keys to success, 5
    meal storage, 34–35
    putting into practice, 14
    reheating food, 31, 35
    roadblocks to, 36–37
    stocking pantry for, 19–23
    storage equipment, 34
    things to consider, 13
    twelve weeks of plans and lists, 15
    weekly plan, 12
Meal prepping, 30–33
    benefits of, 2
    breakfast and lunch, 32
    knife skills, 39
    tips for, 33
Meatball(s)
    French Onion, Skillet, *198,* 199–200
    Marry Me Turkey, 182–83, *183*
    Spiced Lamb, with Tomato-Cucumber Salad, 164–65, *165*
Milk. *See also* Coconut milk
    Dreamy Blueberry Matcha Latte, *305,* 309
    Golden, Latte, *304,* 308
    My Everyday Matcha Latte, *305,* 306
    Salted Tahini-Maple Latte, *304,* 307
Miso Salmon with Acorn Squash, 270–71, *271*
Mocha Brownie Cream Pie Sandwiches, 323–24, *325*
Muffins, High-Protein Egg, Two Ways, *76,* 77–78
Mushroom(s)
    Caramelized Onion, Steak, and Cheese Skillet, 152, *153*
    Cauliflower Pizza Skillet, 204–5, *205*
    Not-Your-Average Burrito Bowls with Sheet Pan Salsa, 193–94, *195*
    Oyster, Spicy Balsamic, 176–77, *177*
    and Sage Risotto, Garlicky, 256–57, *257*
    and Wild Rice Soup, Creamy, 223–24, *224*

N

Noodles
    Red Curry, with Sautéed Green Onion and Pork, *162,* 163
    Rice, and Tofu, Coconut Curry Soup with, 224–25, *225*
    Sesame, Sweet and Spicy Tempeh with, 240–41, *241*
Nut butters, 22
Nutritional yeast
    "Cheesy" Polenta, 282, *284*
    Dairy-Free Walnut Pesto, *300,* 301
    Goes-with-Anything Kale Salad, 283, *284*
Nuts, 22. *See also specific nuts*

O

Oat(s), 22
    Bars, Hidden Veggie, 70–71, *71*
    Overnight, Two Ways, *60,* 61–62
    Pistachio-Berry Crisp, 328, *329*
    Salty Peanut Butter Pretzel Energy Balls, 318, *319*
Oils, 20
Onion(s)
    Caramelized, Steak, and Cheese Skillet, 152, *153*
    French, Meatball Skillet, *198,* 199–200
    Pickled, 114, *115*
Orange
    -Cardamom Olive Oil Cake, *320,* 321–22
    Cream Smoothie, 63, *64*

P

Parsnip and Cauliflower Puree, 288, *289*
Pasta, 22
    Brian's Favorite Lamb Bolognese, 260–61, *261*
    Creamy Lemon Pesto, with Walnut Crumbs, 228–29, *229*
    Deconstructed Turkey Lasagna Skillet, 188–89, *189*
    Dump-and-Bake Hidden Protein, *158,* 159
    Hidden Veggie Spaghetti with Crispy Kale and Sausage, *272,* 273–74
    Lemon-Caper Shrimp and Linguine, 266–67, *267*
    Mediterranean-Inspired Salmon and Orzo Bake, *146,* 147

Pasta (con't)
    Salad, Cilantro-Lime, 101–2, *103*
    Sheet Pan Butternut Squash Mac and "Cheese," *232*, 233–34
    Sheet Pan Gnocchi with Sun-Dried Tomato Cashew Cream, 230–31, *231*
    Sun-Dried Tomato, One-Pot Creamy, 148, *149*
Peanut Butter
    and Banana Smoothie, 63, *65*
    Crispy Quinoa, Peanut, and Edamame Salad, *104*, 105
    Lick-the-Bowl Peanut Sauce, 295, *297*
    Pretzel Energy Balls, Salty, 318, *319*
Pepper(s)
    Baked Black Bean and Poblano Tacos, *214*, 215–16
    Caramelized Onion, Steak, and Cheese Skillet, 152, *153*
    Farmers' Market Lentil Salad, 96, *97*
    Greek-Style Chicken and Vegetable Skewers, *190*, 191–92
    Mediterranean-Inspired Chickpea Chopped Salad, *94*, 95
    Pork, and Onion Breakfast Biscuits, *72*, 73–74
    Roasted Red, and Pesto Egg Casserole, *82*, 83
    Smoky Chipotle Sauce, 296, *297*
Pesto
    Pasta, Creamy Lemon, with Walnut Crumbs, 228–29, *229*
    Pizza, Sheet Pan, with Asparagus and Prosciutto, 201–2, *203*
    and Roasted Red Pepper Egg Casserole, *82*, 83
    Walnut, Dairy-Free, *300*, 301
Pickled Onions, 114, *115*
Pineapple
    and Barbecue Chicken Lettuce Cups, Sheet Pan, *178*, 179
    Salsa, Slow Cooker Carnitas Tacos with, 209–11, *210*
    -Shrimp Lettuce Wraps, 106–7, *107*
Pistachio-Berry Crisp, 328, *329*
Pizza, Sheet Pan Pesto, with Asparagus and Prosciutto, 201–2, *203*
Polenta, "Cheesy," 282, *284*
Pork
    Bacon and Chive Egg Muffins, *76*, 77–78
    Cauliflower Pizza Skillet, 204–5, *205*
    Chops, Seared, with Apple Fennel Pan Sauce, 262–63, *263*
    and Green Onion, Sautéed, Red Curry Noodles with, *162*, 163
    Hidden Veggie Spaghetti with Crispy Kale and Sausage, *272*, 273–74
    Lettuce Wraps, Crunchy, with Carrot Slaw, 108–9, *109*
    Pepper, and Onion Breakfast Biscuits, *72*, 73–74
    Sheet Pan Pesto Pizza with Asparagus and Prosciutto, 201–2, *203*
    Slow Cooker Carnitas Tacos with Pineapple Salsa, 209–11, *210*
    Spicy Sausage, White Bean, and Kale Soup, 172–73, *173*
    Tenderloin, Maple-Dijon, 212–13, *213*
Potato(es). *See also* Sweet Potato(es)
    Chicken Pot Pie Soup, 138, *139*
    Garlic and Herb Spatchcock Chicken, *250*, 251–52
    Leek, and Goat Cheese Frittata, 86–87, *87*
    Roasted Garlic Mashed, 280, *281*
Pretzel(s)
    Crispy Ranch Chickpea Snack Mix, 122, *123*
    Peanut Butter Energy Balls, Salty, 318, *319*
Prosciutto and Asparagus, Sheet Pan Pesto Pizza with, 201–2, *203*
Pudding, Chia, Three Ways, *66*, 67–69
Pumpkin
    Bread, Grammy's, 334, *342*
    Hidden Veggie Oat Bars, 70–71, *71*

Q

Quesadillas, Mashed Chipotle Chickpea, 244–45, *245*
Quinoa, 22
    Bake, One-Pot, with Butternut Squash, Kale, and Feta, 156, *157*
    Chipotle Sweet Potato and Black Bean Bowls, 113–14, *115*
    Crispy, Peanut, and Edamame Salad, *104*, 105
    Feta, Chicken, and Veggies, Jenn's Viral Baked, *186*, 187
    Fluffy Does-it-All, *289*, 291
    Greek-Style Crispy Chickpea Bowls, 118–19, *119*
    Salad, Golden Turmeric Herby, *98*, 99–100

R

Ranch Dressing, Herby Yogurt, *300,* 302
Raspberry
    and Dark Chocolate Chia Pudding, *66,* 68
    -Honey Lemonade, Tart, *312,* 313
Recipes and ingredients
    about the recipes, 6–7
    best practices, 39
    ingredients master list, 336–41
    ingredient substitutes, 26
    pantry ingredients, 19–23
    plant-based substitutes, 339
    protein substitutions, 340
    recipe dietary labels, 39
    staples, canned, and packaged substitutions, 341
    swap and save, 29
Rice, 22
    Chicken Sausage, and Spinach, One-Pot, *170,* 171
    Coconut, *218,* 219
    French Onion Meatball Skillet, *198,* 199–200
    Garlicky Mushroom and Sage Risotto, 256–57, *257*
    Herby Chickpea and Cauliflower Bowls with Lemon-Dill Sauce, 174–75, *175*
    and Lemony Chicken Thighs, 136–37, *137*
    Marry Me Turkey Meatballs, 182–83, *183*
    Not-Your-Average Burrito Bowls with Sheet Pan Salsa, 193–94, *195*
    Spicy Tofu Crunch Bowls, *110,* 111–12
    Steamed, Jenn's, *289,* 290
    Sticky Balsamic Oyster Mushrooms, 176–77, *177*
    Stovetop Beef and Bean Taco Skillet, 144–45, *145*
    Wild, and Mushroom Soup, Creamy, 223–24, *224*
Risotto, Garlicky Mushroom and Sage, 256–57, *257*

S

Sage and Mushroom Risotto, Garlicky, 256–57, *257*
Salads
    Barbecue Chicken Chopped, *116,* 117
    Chickpea Chopped, Mediterranean-Inspired, *94,* 95
    Cilantro-Lime Pasta, 101–2, *103*
    Crispy Quinoa, Peanut, and Edamame, *104,* 105
    Cucumber, Chilled, *218,* 219
    Golden Turmeric Herby Quinoa, *98,* 99–100
    Kale, Goes-with-Anything, 283, *284*
    Lentil, Farmers' Market, 96, *97*
    Roasted Brussels Sprouts, Sweet Potato, and Beet, 92–93, *93*
    Tomato-Cucumber, Spiced Lamb Meatballs with, 164–65, *165*
Salmon
    Bites with Coconut Rice and Chilled Cucumber Salad, 217–19, *218*
    Miso, with Acorn Squash, 270–71, *271*
    and Orzo Bake, Mediterranean-Inspired, *146,* 147
Salsa
    Mango, Blackened Swordfish with, 268–69, *269*
    Pineapple, Slow Cooker Carnitas Tacos with, 209–11, *210*
    Sheet Pan, Not-Your-Average Burrito Bowls with, 193–94, *195*
Salt, note on, 23
Sauces, 20
    Cilantro, Creamy, 294, *297*
    Cucumber Garlicky, 299, *300*
    Dairy-Free Walnut Pesto, *300,* 301
    Maple Barbecue, Tangy, *297,* 298
    Peanut, Lick-the-Bowl, 295, *297*
    Smoky Chipotle, 296, *297*
Sausage
    Chicken, Spinach, and Rice, One-Pot, *170,* 171
    and Crispy Kale, Hidden Veggie Spaghetti with, *272,* 273–74
    Spicy, White Bean, and Kale Soup, 172–73, *173*
Seed butters, 22
Sesame
    -Crisped Brussels Sprouts, *284,* 285
    Noodles, Sweet and Spicy Tempeh with, 240–41, *241*
    Tofu, Sticky, 238–39, *239*
Shrimp
    Garlic Butter, and Spaghetti Squash, 142–43, *143*
    and Linguine, Lemon-Caper, 266–67, *267*
    -Pineapple Lettuce Wraps, 106–7, *107*
    Skillet, Street-Corn-Inspired, 166–67, *167*
Smoothies, Green, Four Ways, 63, *64–65*
Soups
    Black Bean, Pantry Staples, 226–27, *227*
    Chicken Pot Pie, 138, *139*
    Coconut Curry, with Tofu and Rice Noodles, 224–25, *225*
    Spicy Sausage, White Bean, and Kale, 172–73, *173*
    Wild Rice and Mushroom, Creamy, 223–24, *224*
Spices, 23

Spinach
- and Artichoke Dip, Dairy-Free, 130-31, *131*
- Cauliflower Pizza Skillet, 204-5, *205*
- Chicken, Creamy, 196-97, *197*
- Chicken Sausage, and Rice, One-Pot, *170*, 171
- Goat Cheese, and Sun-Dried Tomato Stuffed Chicken, 140-41, *141*
- Pesto and Roasted Red Pepper Egg Casserole, *82*, 83

Squash. *See also* Zucchini
- Acorn, Miso Salmon with, 270-71, *271*
- Butternut, Kale, and Feta, One-Pot Quinoa Bake with, 156, *157*
- Butternut, Mac and "Cheese," Sheet Pan, *232*, 233-34
- Farmers' Market Lentil Salad, 96, *97*
- Grammy's Pumpkin Bread, 334, *342*
- Hidden Veggie Oat Bars, 70-71, *71*
- Spaghetti, and Garlic Butter Shrimp, 142-43, *143*

Strawberry-Basil Smoothie, 63, *65*
Sweeteners, 20
Sweet Potato(es)
- and Black Bean Bowls, Chipotle, 113-14, *115*
- Brownies, Fudgy, 330-31, *331*
- Buffalo Chickpea Stuffed, *150*, 151
- Chipotle Breakfast Hash, 84-85, *85*
- Crackers, Baked, *123*, 124
- Roasted Brussels Sprouts, and Beet Salad, 92-93, *93*
- Tacos, Spiced, with Avocado Slaw, 235-37, *236*
- Wedges, Japanese, *284*, 286

Swordfish, Blackened, with Mango Salsa, 268-69, *269*

T

Tacos
- Baked Black Bean and Poblano, *214*, 215-16
- Mediterranean-Inspired Smashed, 264-65, *265*
- Slow Cooker Carnitas, with Pineapple Salsa, 209-11, *210*
- Spiced Sweet Potato, with Avocado Slaw, 235-37, *236*

Tahini, 22
- Chocolate Chip Cookie Bars, *326*, 327
- Garlicky Hummus, *127*, 129
- -Maple Dressing, 93
- -Maple Latte, Salted, *304*, 307

Tempeh
- Strips, Crusted Buffalo, 246-47, *247*
- Sweet and Spicy Tempeh, Sesame Noodles, 240-41, *241*

Toast, Hidden Protein Smashed Avocado, 88, *89*
Tofu
- and Broccolini, Sweet and Spicy, 168-69, *169*
- and Rice Noodles, Coconut Curry Soup with, 224-25, *225*
- Spicy, Crunch Bowls, *110*, 111-12
- Sticky Sesame, 238-39, *239*

Tomato(es)
- -Basil Saucy Butter Bean Skillet, *242*, 243
- Brian's Favorite Lamb Bolognese, 260-61, *261*
- canned, 21
- -Cucumber Salad, Spiced Lamb Meatballs with, 164-65, *165*
- Hidden Veggie Spaghetti with Crispy Kale and Sausage, *272*, 273-74
- Marry Me Turkey Meatballs, 182-83, *183*
- Mediterranean-Inspired Smashed Tacos, 264-65, *265*
- Not-Your-Average Burrito Bowls with Sheet Pan Salsa, 193-94, *195*
- Sun-Dried, Cashew Cream, Sheet Pan Gnocchi with, 230-31, *231*
- Sun-Dried, Pasta, One-Pot Creamy, 148, *149*
- Sun-Dried, Spinach, and Goat Cheese Stuffed Chicken, 140-41, *141*

Tortillas. *See also* Tacos
- Mashed Chipotle Chickpea Quesadillas, 244-45, *245*
- Sheet Pan Black Bean Breakfast Burritos, 79-80, *81*

Turkey
- Lasagna Skillet, Deconstructed, 188-89, *189*
- Meatballs, Marry Me, 182-83, *183*
- Skillet, Garlic, *154*, 155

Turmeric
- Golden Milk Latte, *304*, 308
- Herby Quinoa Salad, Golden, *98*, 99-100

V

Vanilla-Almond Chia Pudding, *66*, 69
Vegetables. *See also specific vegetables*
- canned or jarred, 21
- seasonal produce list, 338

Vinaigrette, Lemony Red Wine, 303
Vinegars, 20

W

Walnut
- Crumbs, Creamy Lemon Pesto Pasta with, 228–29, *229*
- Pesto, Dairy-Free, *300,* 301

Wild Rice and Mushroom Soup, Creamy, 223–24, *224*

Wraps. *See* Lettuce Wraps

Y

Yogurt
- Coconut-Mango Chia Pudding, *66,* 67
- Creamy Cilantro Sauce, 294, *297*
- Cucumber Garlicky Sauce, 299, *300*
- Herby Chickpea and Cauliflower Bowls with Lemon-Dill Sauce, 174–75, *175*
- High-Protein Cilantro-Edamame Dip, 125, *127*
- Ranch Dressing, Herby, *300,* 302
- Vanilla-Almond Chia Pudding, *66,* 69

Z

Zucchini
- Farmers' Market Lentil Salad, 96, *97*
- Greek-Style Chicken and Vegetable Skewers, *190,* 191–92
- Hidden Veggie Oat Bars, 70–71, *71*

Without limiting the exclusive rights of any author, contributor or the publisher of this publication, any unauthorized use of this publication to train generative artificial intelligence (AI) technologies is expressly prohibited. HarperCollins also exercise their rights under Article 4(3) of the Digital Single Market Directive 2019/790 and expressly reserve this publication from the text and data mining exception.

The material on linked sites referenced in this book is the author's own. HarperCollins disclaims all liability that may result from the use of the material contained at those sites. All such material is supplemental and not part of the book. The author reserves the right to close the website in her sole discretion at any time.

DON'T THINK ABOUT DINNER. Copyright © 2026 by Jenneatsgoood LLC. All rights reserved. No part of this book may be used or reproduced in any manner whatsoever without written permission except in the case of brief quotations embodied in critical articles and reviews. For information, address HarperCollins Publishers, 195 Broadway, New York, NY 10007. In Europe, HarperCollins Publishers, Macken House, 39/40 Mayor Street Upper, Dublin 1, D01 C9W8, Ireland.

HarperCollins books may be purchased for educational, business, or sales promotional use. For information, please email the Special Markets Department at SPsales@harpercollins.com.

hc.com

FIRST EDITION

Photographs by Ashleigh Amoroso
Collaborator: Lauren Deen
Designed by Alison Bloomer
Illustrations by Cassidy Hart

Library of Congress Cataloging-in-Publication Data has been applied for.

ISBN 978-0-06-342579-8

Printed in Canada

26 27 28 29 30   TC   10 9 8 7 6 5 4 3 2 1